THROUGH VEILS OF WORDS

Verbal Duels and Word Play Series
Series Editor: Dr. Giulia Marchetti

Volumes in this series:
1) Through Veils of Words: Performing Politics, Gender and Identity
in the Tuscan *Contrasto*, by Valentina Pagliai

THROUGH VEILS OF WORDS

Performing Politics, Gender and Identity in the Tuscan *Contrasto*

Valentina Pagliai

HUDSON WRITERS

First published: August 2015

Cover design by PixelStudio & ArtisticWorld

Published by Hudson Writers
North Plainfield, NJ 07060
United States of America

ISBN: 1941997031
ISBN-13: 978-1-941997-03-1

To my grandmothers
Lina and Iole

CONTENTS

LIST OF ILLUSTRATIONS
AND SCHEMAS

Illustrations:

Schemas:

FOREWORD

On the 15th anniversary from the completion on this book, originally my PhD dissertation at the University of California Los Angeles, I am glad to finally be able to make its results public. The field of studies including verbal duels and other forms of word play is still a small one, and yet one that has been gaining attention in the past decade. For this reason I decided to make this work available to those who may be interested. I thank again my friends and colleagues who made this publication possible. A particular thanks to this series' editor, Giulia Marchetti, for her critiques and invaluable help.

ACKNOWLEDGMENTS

I would like to thank all of those people that, with their help and patience, made this work possible. In particular, I want to mention Melissa Pashigian, Jennifer F. Reynolds, Timothy Sundeen, Cynthia Strathmann, Eleanor Zucker, Livia Tonti, Bruna Logli, Fabrizio Ferroni, Gianni Frati, Ettore Del Bene, and Gianni Ciolli for their friendship as well as their important advice. A special thanks to my parents, Lelia Nesti and Raffaello Pagliai, for volunteering as research assistants. Thanks to Robert Garot for proofreading the manuscript. Thanks too, to the Professors who followed me during the course of my studies: Candy Goodwin, Marcyliena Morgan, Paul Kroskrity, Mariko Tamanoi and Edward Tuttle. Thanks to the Department of Anthropology at UCLA for helping and sustaining me during these years, and making this research possible. Finally, I want to thank Altamante Logli, Realdo Tonti, Gabriele Ara and all the *Poeti Bernescanti* for letting me videotape their performances.

1
INTRODUCTION

I. Preface.

There was a time when my grandmother Lina dreamed the Aeneid for many nights. One day she told me about it. She said those verses, long lost in her memories, were coming back at her, and she could recall everything perfectly. But then, as she awoke, they disappeared again. Finally, she made up her mind to catch those words, by forcing herself to wake up and write them down. Useless! They disappeared too fast. (I can imagine her now, with her trembling hand chaining one enormous, imperfectly round letter after another. I can see her in her bed sleeping. So many nights I have been there, sleeping at her side, listening to her heavy breathing.) Then one day she came to me triumphant, and repeated a few verses. I listened in disbelief: they were, indeed, from the Aeneid. Where did she learn them? My grandmother had finished only three years of school, and that was back during World War I. She explained to me with a smile, that once people would sit together at night, and the elders would tell the stories of the ancient heroes. She had listened to them. She had learned them for us. But then the world had changed. There were no more storysingers; none of them was left.

Well, my grandmother was wrong. And I set out to find the storysingers, and found them: they are the heroes and heroines of my research, the protagonists of the story I am going to tell you. Now I wake up in the middle of the night. I quickly open my notebook and start writing before the words slip away from me, before the shadows in the hour of the wolf, may freeze them in my throat.

What is the cultural and social significance of verbal art? Which social themes are expressed and become relevant in performance? These are the fundamental questions that gave shape to this dissertation. The study of verbal art has often followed models that looked principally for norms and functions,[1] and were principally interested in interpreting or discovering (referential) meaning. My work instead looks at how verbal art is socially significant, especially for the local population who produces it and constitutes its audience. This meant focusing on the politics of verbal art, looking at norms and functions not only to understand a genre by dissecting it into its elements, but also to show how the connection between art and the political sphere happens in several ways and through different channels. This in turn required an understanding of the relations of force that shape art, and a reconstruction of their historical development.

Several visions of the relationship between art and the political sphere have been proposed in the past. Each of these visions of art is culturally and historically bound, and they reflect the ideologies of those who proposed them. In the following chapters, I will consider art as political, using the term "political" in its original sense, which was in the Greek word, namely the affairs of the *polis*, the city and the society. I consider politics as inclusive of and concerning the relationships among people as part of a *polis*, not just as a science of governing or as the theory of government.

This dissertation is also a study of a particular verbal art genre, the Tuscan *Contrasto*, a genre that fascinated me immediately for its beauty, its complexity – that makes its performance almost miraculous in the eyes of the spectator – and the compelling meanings as well as performative strength. Before I could answer the question of its social meaning, I needed to understand the genre itself, its structure and its use of language. More than that, I felt a need to construct a narrative of it, to tell its story. I wanted to fill the gaps of its history and the mystery of its origins, lost in the darkness of the centuries. And I wanted to make it possible for my readers to appreciate this form of poetry. But I chose to study the genre of the *Contrasto* also because it is a form of verbal duel, and as such, as I will try to show, an ideal place to look at interrelationships.

---

[1] William Labov's articulated study of "sounding" is a good example (1972).

II. Verbal Duels and the *Contrasto*.

Verbal duels are based on conflict and as such they highlight conflicts inside the fabric of society. They present different and opposite points of view on a topic and therefore they are bound to present different views of reality, right and truth. Art as political becomes a field where discourses of identity, gender and ethnicity become visible in their multiple connections and cross-overs. As John Comaroff and Simon Roberts write: "it is in the context of confrontation – when persons negotiate their social universe and enter discourse about it – that the character of that system is revealed" (1981:249; quoted in Briggs, 1996:5). In the *Contrasto* the connections between gender, identity and politics is revealed.

Conflict is indeed fundamental in the construction of reality (Briggs, 1996). Charles Briggs writes: "conflict provides a central force for the constitution of social relations" (1996:5). This view is in tune with Michael Foucault's (1978) theory of discourse, and conflicting discourses, as shaping the organization of political and power relations in a society. Verbal duels present conflicting discourses, and unveil fractured images of reality.

In verbal duels, the meaning, namely the referential function, tends to be subordinated to the indexical function of establishing authority (see Briggs, 1996, 17; also Bloch, 1975). In the *Contrasto* meaning can become contested as part of the duel itself. As a consequence, the conflicting discourse present in verbal duels can also offer occasion to oppose hegemonic discourses upheld by the nation-state (see for example Michael Herzfeld's study of Cretan sheep raiding, 1996). According to Briggs, "subtle stylistic or generic subversions may disrupt dominant discourses and reveal ways that authority is naturalized" (1996:13). As I will show, much stylistic and linguistic subversion happens in the *Contrasto*.

The *Contrasto* (plural = *Contrasti*) is a type of improvised sung poetry, performed in the context of public festivals and events. Diffused today throughout the regions of Tuscany,[2] Lazio and

---

[2] My fieldwork focused in particular on the Tuscan Contrasto. Tuscany is a region in central Italy, containing about 3.5 million people. It is closed to the North and East by the Apennine Mountains, (here it shares borders with the regions of Liguria and Emilia-Romagna to the North, and Le Marche to the East) and by the Tirreno Sea to the West, while a series of hillsides and plains connects it to the Umbria and Lazio regions to the South. Tuscany includes ten

Abruzzo, in Italy, it is performed by pairs of artists, mostly males, called *Poeti Bernescanti*,[3] *Poeti a Braccio*,[4] or simply *poeti*, "poets." The *Contrasto* takes its name, "contrast," from the fact that two different figures, ideas, or things are depicted in them. Each is then, in turn, defended and attacked, in an attempt to demonstrate the general inferiority of the one and superiority of the other. Thus, the *Contrasto* is a dialogue with the tendency to become a "duel." Following Luisa Del Giudice's definition, the *Contrasti* are "poetic 'contests,' traditionally improvised, between two specific and stated adversaries... Although they are often musically lively and border on dance tune, *Contrasti* are also dramatic and heated debates" (Del Giudice, 1995:75-76).

The performances are public, usually done during local events, including feasts organized by the various district units of the parties, or by the parishes. The arguments treated in a *Contrasto*, namely the "themes," are chosen by the audience. They vary and are potentially limitless. Examples are *Contrasti* involving figures in the family (e.g. "*Contrasto* between husband and wife"), popular characters (e.g. "blonde and brunette," "hunter and jackrabbit") or abstract concepts ("science and nature"); social and political *Contrasti* (e.g. "peasant and urbanite," "Russia and America"); historical *Contrasti* and *Contrasti* between various Tuscan cities, etc.[5]

Forms of verbal duels have been studied or at least attested in several cultures. One familiar to Americans is "playing the dozens" (Labov, 1972), used especially by African American adolescents. Although this form does not use rhyming, Peter Farb notices that "when the dozens is played in the West Indies – where the original

---

provinces. These are the provinces of Florence (which is also the regional capital), Arezzo, Grosseto, Lucca, Livorno, Massa-Carrara, Pisa, Pistoia, Prato and Siena. The provinces of Florence, Pistoia and Prato, where my research focused, constitute the northeastern part of the region. Tuscany is a transitional region, where southern and northern cultural elements meet. This is evident both in the language, and in its genres of verbal art, like songs (Leydi, Mantovani & Pederiva, 1973) and folktales (Lapucci, 1984).

[3] Literally "poets in Berni's style," after F. Berni, a Tuscan writer of the 16th century. I will come back to this in chapter 3.

[4] Literally, 'poets at/by arms.' The meaning and origins of this second name is obscure.

[5] The topics are supposed to be sung by two poets. When three poets are present, themes can be proposed that require the expression of three different points of view and thus three participants.

calypso was a somewhat similar insult contest – rhyme must be used" (Farb, 1974:108). William Labov distinguishes an older style of "playing the dozens", which was done in rhyme, from more contemporary African American verbal dueling forms, like "sounding" in which the rhyme is no more used (Labov, 1972:307). Another form of verbal duel recorded by Dundes, Leach, et al. (1970) is commonly used in Turkey by teen-agers (see also Farb, 1974:109). In this case most of the attacks revolve around masculinity, and have to be done in rhyme. In other parts of the world, highly complex forms of verbal duel are used by the Eskimos (Balikci, 1970) and by the Chamulas Mayan of Mexico (Gossen, 1976).

III. Performance.

I understood rather early in this study, that performance had to be the center, around which to spin the threads of my thoughts. In performance, everything would come together: ideas of gender, dialogical identities, political actions and finally invocations of Art. In performance, I saw resistance, representations, negotiations and proposals of alternative understandings of "given things." With time, I understood that the emergence of a coherent discourse from the flux of my thinking required a second fulcrum, like an anchor. I found it in ideology, in particular, in linguistic ideology. I will discuss performance in this section, and linguistic ideologies in the following ones.

According to Dell Hymes, performing always implies the assumption of a responsibility toward an audience, for what is performed and how (1981:132). The classic definition, given by Richard Bauman, is: "Performance as a mode of spoken verbal communication consists in the assumption of responsibility to an audience for a display of communicative competence" (1977:11). Both Hymes and Bauman are referring to an "aesthetic" responsibility, but the "moral" and "political" meanings are in the background. This can be better demonstrated if we compare the preceding definition to the words of theater director Eugenio Barba, who asks: "Do those who act through the theater also have a responsibility toward the 'spectators' who will never see them? Is their professional identity, created and lived in the present, part of a legacy?" (1995:36). This is what Barba calls the "responsibility" of the artists toward their "heirs." This responsibility toward our "heirs" should be taken not only in an artistic sense, but also in a political sense. The idea of responsibility gives back to art its agency in society, and allows us to look at a particular form of verbal art, like poetry, as a form of social action.

Steven Caton argues that poetics and politics are inseparable. In his work on Yemenite poetic performances, Caton is interested in the social context of the performances, and especially in their political context (1990:106-107). By being situated in a specific context, he argues, the poems become in turn politically meaningful, and they can move people to action. The Yemenite artists use their poetry to indicate possible courses of political action (1990:182). In this way, the artist mediates change and power, not just for her/himself, but also for the community as a whole (1990: 111).

Bauman (1986) has further argued that a narrated event really exists only in the moment of its performance. Namely, he considers events themselves to be "abstractions from narratives" (1986:5). This gives a very dynamic potential to verbal art performances. Performance becomes a way of creating, not just representing, the past and social reality itself. Social structure itself can be said to become emergent in performance (Bauman, 1977:42). Dennis Tedlock affirms that through performance the artist can create "verisimilitude" for his/her stories. This implies that the narrator constructs reality by using a particular narrative style (1983: 166). Thus not only social structure, but also a certain "reality" can be seen as "emergent" in performance. This conceptualization of performance leads to further implications. If social realities are "emergent" in performance, then performance can also "destabilize" accepted views of reality and truth, by constructing/representing alternative visions. Performance creates a space where different views of reality can be expressed and articulated.

Art as a political instrument, can legitimize, or de-legitimize, established norms and rules.[6] To understand how verbal art can

---

[6] Gainor, discussing theater, affirms that it can be a hegemonic tool or a tool for resistance (1995:XIV). Gainor writes that "theater has always been a locus of political force" (1995:XIV), and Livingston adds that it is "a site for the active transformation of culture" (1995:182). The performance could help establish a hegemonic view inside a society while at the same time being an instrument of resistance against an external entity, like a colonizer. This is true, for example, for the ritual speech of the Weyewa (1990:167), studied by Kuipers. Here, by using textual structures, the performer: "creates the conviction he is not speaking on his own, but on behalf of some distant person or spirit" (1990:6). These create an "authoritative" or "authentic" performance (1990:109). Kuipers recognizes them as a possibly hegemonic strategy (1990:171).

become an instrument of resistance against hegemonic culture, we must see how it represents, or "performs into existence," different views of "reality." As I will show in the following chapters, the performances of the *Contrasti* offer multiple views and interpretations of "reality." They complicate political stances, images of identity, and understandings of gender roles. They become a way of articulating different points of view, different visions of the world. These views, in turn, may be deeply opposed to "objective social realities" upheld by the Italian nation state and its institutions. In conclusion, the *Contrasto* introduces subaltern views of "reality" and "truth."

IV. Subalternities.

I use the term "subaltern" or "subalternities" to indicate not a social class (as Antonio Gramsci imagined it), but as ways to seeing reality which are alternative, and possibly opposed, to dominant or hegemonic ones. In my view, subalternity is a condition that cuts across social classes and other social categorizations.

For Gayatri Spivak (1987) what condemns the "subaltern" to its "subalternity," is the fact that subalternity itself, as a concept, as a category, is built by and with respect to a hegemonic thought. Since the intellectuals are part of the dominant class, any representation that they produce of the oppressed classes is a dominant representation, even when it opposes itself to the hegemony. The dominant thought, in a sense, represents and thus constructs its subalternity in a way that makes it inoffensive, or "masterable." One of these ways is by seeing the subaltern as "marginal" in society. For example, the representations that Italian intellectuals have done of the *Contrasto*, tend to preempt its importance as a genre. As I will show in the next chapters, the poets oppose their own views of "art" to the representations of it done by the intellectuals. This is a fundamental way of resistance, since representation creates *shared realities*.

I chose to identify the subaltern in what Mikhail Bakhtin saw as the centrifugal force, that in any society tends toward the creation of multiple possibilities. Bakhtin gave to these forces, as they are reflected in language, the name of *heteroglossia*, which represent "the co-existence of socio-ideological contradictions between the present and the past, between differing epochs of the past, between different socio-ideological groups in the present, between tendencies, schools, circles and so forth" (Bakhtin, 1981:291). As Susan Gal points out, the concept of heteroglossia is fundamental: it explains how even the representations and images proposed by the hegemony can be interpreted and used in counter-hegemonic ways (1989:359).

Bakhtin attributed creative power to any social interaction, thus theoretically distributing the creative potential to the whole society. The power for change that Gramsci attributed to the "great mind," the intellectual, Bakhtin found, on the contrary, in the elimination of the "great mind," or epic hero, from the scene (Dentith, 1995:50 and fol.). What is even more important, is that Bakhtin's vision leaves the door open to see hegemony no more as overpowering, but much more like struggling to survive as a mere orderly surface over a multiple, unstable, complex "organization of diversity." It is the difference between a society seen as panopticon (Foucault, 1980) in which every behavior and word is under the control of the overseeing power, and the realization of the opaqueness of the human soul, that makes such an overseeing impossible in the end. The study of the *Contrasto* allows me to show points of disaggregation where the tissue of hegemony had previously seemed most solid.

Bakhtin anticipated Michael Foucault's conceptualization of power. Foucault in fact wrote: "It seems to me that power must be understood in the first instance as the multiplicity of force relations ....; and lastly as the strategies in which they take effect, whose general design or institutional crystallization is embodied in the state apparatus, in the formulation of the law, in the various social hegemonies" (Foucault, 1978:92-93). For Foucault "the swarm of points of resistance traverses social stratification and individual unities. And it is doubtless the strategic codification of these points of resistance that makes a revolution possible," (Foucault, 1978:96). Similarly, I see subaltern realities as cutting across the social tissue, creating continuous "points of resistance."

V. Linguistic Ideologies.

To understand how the *Contrasto* introduces subaltern views of "reality" and "truth," we need to look at the characteristics of the genre, for example its structure and its language. We also need to consider the context in which the performances are done, as well as the historic development of the genre. We need to look at the texts that are produced by the artists. Finally, and most importantly, we need to look at the ideologies and linguistic ideologies that shape the genre and that are in turn upheld by it.

Linguistic ideologies have been defined as "a set of beliefs about language articulated by users as a rationalization or justification of perceived language structure and use" (Silverstein, 1979:193).

Following this definition, I will look at the linguistic ideologies shared by the poets, as they inform certain linguistic choices in art performances. These ideologies include definitions of what is "art" and what is not, and which are the discriminants between a successful and a "bad" performance.

By referring to linguistic ideologies, I mean to consider the systems of beliefs that both the audience and the artists have of the art form. Debates over the definition of linguistic ideologies can become debates over the definition of the community itself, its history, etc. (Morgan, 1994). These ideologies are a key to understanding the way the poets establish their authority as artists. I agree with Briggs (1992) then, that "finds social power achieved through the strategic use not just of particular discursive genres, but of talk about such genres and their appropriate use" (Woolard & Schieffelin, 1994: 60).

At the same time, I want to reflect on language ideology as "the cultural system of ideas about social and linguistic relationships, together with their loading of moral and political interest" (Irvine, 1989:346). The political aspect of language becomes evident in its linguistic ideologies. I will explore the ways in which these linguistic ideologies relate to "local political forces" (Kroskrity, 1992:308), mediating "between social structures and form of talk" (Woolard and Schieffelin, 1994:55).[7]

Any use of language originates in a political, value-charged context and influences/modifies the political relationship among speakers. In Leonid Voloshinov,[8] according to Simon Dentith, "the meanings carried by signs, take us into the world of values and are therefore ideological" (1995:23). He adds: "Meaning emerges in society and society is not an homogeneous mass but in itself divided by such factors as social class; signs do not therefore have fixed meanings but are always inflected in different ways to carry different values and attitudes" (Dentith, 1995:24). As there are no neutral uses of language, there are no neutral descriptions of it. Any description of language is political.

Both Gramsci and Voloshinov saw in the creation of standard rules and a standard language a way of enforcing or re-enforcing a particular authority (Dentith, 1995:26). At the same time, language can

---

[7] I consider language as "reflexive," namely as both "reflecting" and "shaping" social reality.

[8] The actual attribution of these writings to Bakhtin or Voloshinov is still debated.

be a way of expressing the individual creativity. Therefore, Dentith writes that Voloshinov "understands the creative activity of speakers to manifest itself in the various ways they use and transform the ideological meanings and values that confront them in their uses of language. In this way speakers are not the passive victims of language – are not merely subject to 'blind necessity', but are also agents in the continuing production of language" (1995:28). Thus the linguistic ideologies shared by the poets oppose themselves to another set of linguistic ideologies, which are part of dominant views of language (and art) in Italy.

Ideologies can be instruments of resistance or instruments of domination. Kathryn Woolard & Bambi Schieffelin write again that: "beliefs about what is or is not a real language ... enter into strategies of social domination. Such beliefs, and the related schemata for ranking languages as more or less evolved, have contributed to profound decisions about, for example, the civility or even the humanity of subjects of colonial domination" (1994:63).

Today, dominant linguistic ideologies in Italy are the result of the attempt, carried on by the Italian State over more than a hundred years, to constitute itself as a "nation-state."[9] As I will show in the next chapter, part of this attempt was the creation of a standard "national" Italian language and a "national art." These in turn were shaped by and reflected linguistic ideologies that had developed in Europe at the turn of the 17th century (see Bauman and Briggs, 2000), and which were deeply connected to nationalist ideologies – upheld by the emerging bourgeoisie. As Paul Kroskrity observes:

> *Language ideologies represent the perception of language and discourse that is constructed in the interest of a specific social or cultural group.* ... Nationalist programs of language standardization, for example, may appeal to a modern metric of communicative efficiency, but such language development efforts are pervasively underlain by political-economic considerations since the imposition of a state-supported hegemonic standard will always benefit some social groups over others (2000:8; italics in the original).

Kroskrity had previously advocated that "the 'pragmatic' sense of ideology – the strategies, practical symbols and systems of ideas used

---

[9] For a discussion of the difference between a "nation," a state, and a "nation-state," see Oommen, 1997:16 and fol.

for promoting, perpetuating or changing a social or cultural order – directs attention to the role of such local models of language structure and use as instruments of power and social control" (1992:307). Any study of nationalism and of the emergence of nations, thus, needs to consider linguistic ideologies.

The consideration of how linguistic ideologies mediate the construction of "nation" helps us to see nationalism as dynamic. While Benedict Anderson (1983) at the beginning of the eighties saw nations as "imagined communities," more recent studies have questioned the possibility to establish a model of national formation that may be valid across societies and historic periods (see Chatterjee, 1993). While looking at Italian nationalism, I soon realized that theories of national formation need to be contextualized. As Mariko Tamanoi notices, there are many "nationalisms" not just one (1998:10).

Tamanoi also warns against the danger of seeing "the nation-state as the only agency that is allowed to have its history" (1998:13). This would create an image of the nation-state as homogeneous, and imply that the people who are its "citizens" are acquiescent to its power and "buy" into its ideologies. Hegemonic views of language and identity never stand unopposed. Hegemony is never stable, but rather a fragile temporary attempt to maintain a certain social reality. As Michael Silverstein writes, nations are "a frequently fragile sociopolitical order, seething with contestation that emerges from actual plurilingualism, heteroglossia, and like indexes of at least potentially fundamental political economic conflict" (2000:128-129). Such an index is the *Contrasto*, with its construction and negotiation of alternative realities and alternative views of gender, social order, or belonging.

In any hegemonic enterprise, "reality" must rest unquestioned. There is a need to establish and maintain the boundary between "true" and "false." It is exactly this need that the *Contrasto* mimics and at the same time undermines, in a continuous play of opposite visions of truth and falsity. Thus, the *Contrasto* tends to show reality as more complex and "unstable."

VI. Performance, Gender and Identities.

Definitions of identity are also a highly ideological ground. As such, they have to be examined critically. As I wrote elsewhere: "boundaries of identity are created through history and expressed in language, or they are created through linguistic choices and come to be reflected into historic events" (Pagliai, 1995a:22). Joan Scott writes:

To historicize the question of identity - is to introduce an analysis of its production and thus an analysis of constructions of and conflicts about power; it is also, of course, to call into question the autonomy and stability of any particular identity as it claims to define and interpret a subject's existence (1992:16).

People renegotiate their identities in different social contexts. New social contexts will impose new identities (or make them relevant). Thus, identities are enacted situationally. Performances are an important means to create identifications. Verbal art can be at the base of the definition of a community. Thus, the study of the Tuscan *Contrasto* sheds light on definitions of ethnicity as well as ideologies of gender, group belonging, and art.

The linguistic ideologies connected to nationalism tend to reify "ethnic groups" and construct correspondences between "imagined" homogenous standard languages and "imagined" nationalities (see Kroskrity, 2000:26; Irvine and Gal, 2000:73; see also Anderson, 1990:125 and fol.). In the performance of *Contrasti*, as I will show, identities multiply and are connected to local "places." The poets, in their duels, construct and negotiate identities; they multiply them, and deconstruct "imaginations" of places and identities.

Gender studies as well are moving past dichotomies and bipolarities in gender identities, to cast their focus on class and power in society, and on gender relationships as part of them (Di Leonardo, 1991; Dubisch, 1986; Flax, 1987; Hall, Bucholtz & Moonwomon, 1992; Mascia-Lees, Sharpe & Ballerino Cohen, 1989). Kamala Visweswaran, for example, affirms that "understanding gender as a temporal construction underscores what it means to be 'at times a woman'" (1994:50; also Riley, 1988). As a consequence, definitions of gender and gender roles appear as necessarily multiple and ideological.

In the performance of the *Contrasto*, several images of "womanhood" are presented, and the dueling poets actively discuss images of gender roles. Performance does not just depict pre-existing genders and gender roles, but creates them, commenting on possibilities, and on possible forms of gender relationships. In performance, thus, gender relationships can be reproduced, contested and transformed.

VII. Methodology.

VII. a. Positioning the Anthropological Self.

Fieldwork presupposes theories and imposes choices. For me, some of the most important choices revolved around my positionality both as a native anthropologist and as a person concerned with the way my research could affect the future of the people and art forms I studied. I think some of these concerns surface in the following words I scribbled on my notebook (interestingly in English) while sitting in the living room of my parents' home in Tuscany:

Sometimes I wonder what I am really doing here. What kind of image am I building of Tuscany, by choosing to talk about the poets? And this ethnic identity I keep talking about, is it really something that exists, or a fruit of my desires and of my mind? I see the Knights of Orange passing through the Catholic streets of Ireland, I think of Europe crossed by silenced civil wars (wait, I cannot use that name, don't I know? we do not have civil wars here).[10] Yes, and I think of the Northern League,[11] I see the growing racism in these streets, and my paranoia tells me that we are not so far from stakes and lynchings. ...

And I, already a loser from the beginning, trying to find places with no names, hiding my name not to be called aloud; me with my woman label I cannot shed, no matter how fast I run, no matter what, no matter how. So feeble in my realities, that anybody can suck me into theirs. And then me again, waking up to the call of academia, ready to paint my portrait, ready to sell my own people (mine? since when?) to the vivisection of social sciences – until nothing may be left but ugliness.[12]

It was always easy to me, as a native anthropologist, to talk about the people I was studying as "my" people. After all, I could see my authority continuously reflected in the way other people thought that I readily "understood" what I was seeing and hearing. It is all too right, then, that I should spend a few words attempting a deconstruction of this authority.

I was born and raised in Pistoia, but I had been away for almost ten years. I have friendship and kinship relations there that made it

---

[10] When I wrote these fieldnotes, I was thinking in particular to the situation in Ireland and the Basque country. The Italian media often describe these civil wars as single acts of terrorism, while the larger issue of the presence of a war is carefully avoided.

[11] Of this Italian separatist party I will talk again later.

[12] From my fieldnotes, dated 7/7/98.

easier to have access to linguistic consultants for my research, but I knew very little about the *Contrasto*. Re-reading my fieldnotes, I feel strange seeing how this genre, that now appears to me so familiar and understandable, could once be so new and obscure. I remember feeling totally lost and fearing that I would never be able to understand.

My portrait of the *Contrasto* is a view from a particular prospective, not "the truth" about it. It cannot be taken to "stand for the experience of the whole group" (Scott, 1992:18), least we fall in a reductionist trap. Beware of the possibility that, as Scott writes,

> The fact of belonging to an identity group is taken as authority enough for one's speech: the direct experience of a group or culture - that is, membership in it - becomes the only test of true knowledge. ... The exclusionary implications of this are twofold: all those not of the group are denied even intellectual access to it, and those within the group whose experiences or interpretations do not conform to the established terms of identity must either suppress their views or drop out (1992:18).

My positionality must be taken into account. When I first encountered the poets, I had a set of pre-conceptions and more or less hidden agendas. As an anthropologist, my agenda was to shed light on linguistic ideologies and their connections to identity and politics. As a student, I needed the data to complete my Ph.D. dissertation. As a person, I had an even more hidden agenda, one that at times I tend to forget myself: I wanted (paraphrasing Dorinne Kondo) to write Tuscans into existence (Kondo, 1997:202).

I hoped to see the essence of "Tuscanness" emerge from my data (but it never did). As a foreigner living in the United States, I wanted to be able to point at an identity that I could call "mine," that would be different from the "American" and from the "Italian" ones. I have always particularly detested the images of Italy and Italians presented in the United States, as they are highly stereotypical and exoticizing. Part of my goals in writing this dissertation, was to deconstruct those images. Have I been successful? Or have I just constructed another exoticizing image? I am not sure.

I started this chapter as a story, an eternal story, as eternal as the need to tell, to narrate, about the complexities of being. Before the text there is the writer, a writer with memories, desires and emotions. As you read, I may at times disappear behind the "objectivity" of my words (the miracle of bestowed authority). To remind you about the "me" behind the authority of the "I" or the "we," I have left here and there in the chapters, reminders of the subjectivity of this "realistic" portrait (as any other attempts at systematization of knowledge). You (my readers) will see them; they are mostly in Italics – homage to Locke's dictate to keep rhetoric outside of "scientific language" (see Bauman and Briggs, 2000:154).

Finally, I consider this work as part of what Ana Zentella has called an "anthropolitical linguistics," that has the goal to "understand and facilitate a stigmatized group's attempts to construct a positive self within an economic and political context that relegates its members to static and disparaged ethnic, racial, and class identities, and that identifies them with static and disparaged linguistic codes" (Zentella, 1997:13). Although the poets are by no means a "stigmatized group," their art has been often excluded from dominant definitions of art, their language disparaged as nonsense (I will discuss this in chapter 7). It was my goal, then, to recognize the complex artistry of the *Contrasto*. I wanted to show its beauty, its multidimensionality, its historical depth, and its sociological as well as artistic importance. In sum, I wanted to show that the art form, as well as the personality of the artists, deserves appreciation and respect.

VII. b. Fieldwork.

When I started my fieldwork, I believed that the study of verbal art performances presupposed an ethnography of a culture. I was convinced that the understanding of any cultural phenomenon is connected to an understanding of the dynamics present in a culture as a whole. For this reason, I saw my research on the Tuscan *Contrasto* as one that needed to span from gender to linguistic ideology, from ethnic identity to politics. Only by understanding the interrelations between these apparently separate spheres of the Tuscan reality, I could hope to reconstruct the meaning of those art forms.

It was only after two seasons of pilot research (during July 1994 and from July to September 1995), and a few more months of "dead-end" pursuits, that I finally found the poets (in May 1997). Previously (and even later), I had been working on other genres of Tuscan verbal art, such as Community Theater, folk songs, and improvised (non-sung) poetry. It was with the help of my father, that I finally was able to contact the poet Realdo Tonti. At that time, Tonti was often performing with another poet, Altamante Logli. Around them was a group of "fans," most of them my age, who followed the poets in all of their performances and often contributed to organize them as well. In a few weeks, I became part of this group of "fans" and they more or less accepted me as a friend. For the next six months (from May to October 1997), I followed Logli and Tonti in all of their performances. Since they often performed with other poets, I met several Tuscan poets and recorded their performances. I went back to do more fieldwork in summer 1998, and again in September 1999.

During these three fieldwork seasons, I videotaped performances of 18 poets[13] (see schema #1). Moreover, out of the group of "fans" I joined in 1997, three "novices" poets emerged: Ettore Del Bene, Gabriele Ara and Gianni Ciolli. Thus, three generations of poets were included in my research. I videotaped a total of 24 performances.[14]

Schema #1: *Poeti Bernescanti*

Name	Performances Videotaped[15]	Comments
1) Gabriele Ara	3	Middle age, beginner, Prato
2) Elidio Benelli	2	Elder, Grosseto
3) Francesco Benelli	1	Elder, Grosseto
4) Lio Bianchi*	1	Elder, Siena
5) Nello Casati	4	Elder, Pistoia
6) Mauro Chechi	1	Middle age, Grosseto
7) Gianni Ciolli	9	Young, beginner, Prato
8) Ettore Del Bene	3	Young, disciple of Logli, Firenze
9) De Sanctis	1	Elder, (Viterbo?)
10) Altamante Logli	16	Elder, Firenze
11) Antonio Mariani*	1	Elder
12) Benito Mastacchini*	1	Elder
13) Pirazza	1	Elder, Bologna
14) Poet 2*	1	Elder, Arezzo
15) Poet 3*	1	Elder
16) Umberto Puntura	1	Elder, Maremma area

[13] An 19th poet, Pirazza, I had previously met and recorded in 1994.

[14] For a list of the performances recorded, including the titles of all the *Contrasti*, and the names of the poets who sang them, see Appendix B.

[15] Notice that, since the Poets perform in couples, the number of total performances videotaped does not correspond to the sum of the performances for each Poet.

17) Davide Riondino	2	Middle age, occasional poet, (Firenze?)
18) Liliana Tamberi	3	Young, disciple of EB, only woman, Grosseto?
19) Realdo Tonti	15	Middle age, Pistoia

* These poets were recorded as they performed at the annual meeting of Poeti Bernescanti in Ribolla (Grosseto), on April 19, 1998. My parents recorded the performance in my absence, so I never met them personally.

My fieldwork was not limited to videotaping the performances. Although I conducted only a few formal interviews with the poets (five total), I would take advantage of any occasion to spend time with them. Participant observation was a principal method for data gathering. I visited their homes, met their families, went with them to innumerable dinners, and I invited them to my home as well. Each of these occasions was like a "school lesson" in poetry, as the poets would continuously talk about their past performances, and about the essence of "good" art.

I had two very special research assistants, my parents Lelia Nesti and Raffaello Pagliai. They often accompanied me to the performances, and helped me with videotaping. We shared ideas, devised schedules, and discussed opinions. An important consequence of their presence was that the people I was studying had access to my personal life almost as much as I had access to theirs – although, of course, they were not interested in me as I was in them. I think this contributed to shape the view that the poets had of me, and made it easier for them to accept my sudden presence in their lives.

VII. c. Transcription.

Before closing this section, I need to write a final note about transcription. As Elinor Ochs has noticed (1979), transcription is already an interpretation. A transcription presupposes a theory of the data (see Duranti, 1994:40). As I wrote elsewhere, transcription can be considered as "a connecting ring between a theory, a methodology and a form of writing. ... As such, the transcribed text has at the same time an ideological, analytical and persuasive force. Transcription is a method for reflection from the moment of its construction, when it requires to operate choices" (Pagliai, 1997:65; original in Italian, my translation).

Hymes argues for the importance of keeping the original structure of a text, since otherwise much information will be lost, including "verbal organization" which is, in a sense, the context of the phrase. "Such structure," he writes, "is the matrix of the meaning and effect of the poem" (1981:42). In his works on Native American verbal art, Hymes gives particular importance to "metrics and poetics" and to the structure of the text itself (1981:61). These have revealed themselves particularly useful and meaningful in my analysis of the *Contrasto* as well.

For this reason, in my transcriptions, I have opted to follow the metric organization of the verses.[16] This allowed me to show the *Contrasto* as the poets themselves conceive it, namely as a series of stanzas. This simple transcription becomes more complex only in those instances in which my need to transcribe the answer of the audience necessitated a "break" in the compact unity of the stanzas.

VIII. Plan of the Chapters.

I wanted this dissertation to be an in-depth study of an art form. Therefore, I conceived of the chapters as a way to paint a portrait of the genre of the *Contrasto*. I started with a background (chapter 2), on which I then sketched the basic lines of the "figure" (chapter 3). Successively, I added shades and color by juxtaposing the elements of my composition: the political importance of the genre (chapter 4), the drawing of multiple images of places and identities (chapter 5), and the highlighting of gender hierarchies (chapter 6). Finally, I let the "figure" cast its multiple shades on the background itself (chapter 7).

From the point of view of theory, I decided to open and close my dissertation with a focus on linguistic ideologies. In chapter 2, these will be the linguistic ideologies connected to the creation of the Italian nation-state and to the standardization of the Italian language. In chapter 7, I will instead discuss ideologies about art from the point of view of Italian scholars and from the point of view of the *Poeti Bernescanti*.

Chapter 2 will be also dedicated to the discussion of the larger socio-historical and linguistic context in respect to which I situate the analysis of the *Contrasto*. After discussing the historical events that led to the formation of the Italian State, I will discuss how nationalist, local, and regional interest shaped the successive formation of the "nation," and influenced its present situation. I will then discuss at

---

[16] See Appendix A.

length the way in which an "Italian" language was "imagined" from a literate written tongue, to the standard language of the new state, and how successively it became transformed by its institutionalization and by its adoption as spoken language by the Italian citizens.

In chapter 3, I furnish the elements that define the genre of the *Contrasto*, and that are connected to its performance. I start, following the track already established for chapter 2, by discussing the history of the *Contrasto*, highlighting the successive convergence of its elements into the present form. I then discuss its metric and melodic structure, and its use of language. Finally, I discuss two elements that are necessary to an understanding of the *Contrasto* in its performance, namely context and audience. In discussing context, I argue first for the theoretical importance of this concept, and then pass to a description of the local contexts in which the performances are done. Similarly, in analyzing audience, I discuss the complexity of the definition of audience, as well as give an account of the various audiences that co-construct the performance of the *Contrasto*.

Chapters 4 through 7 rely more heavily on the data from my fieldwork. I discuss successively the *Contrasto* as political genre (chapter 4), the poets' construction and negotiation of place and identity (chapter 5), the representations of "women" in the *Contrasto* (chapter 6), and the poetic art shared by the poets (chapter 7). While the first three are based on the analysis of the poetry itself, the last one relies more on data from my field notes and from the interviews I conducted during fieldwork.

In chapter 4, I discuss the *Contrasto* of political argument, showing the construction of politics in the *Contrasto* and the political importance of the genre. After giving an analysis of its structure, I argue that this formal structure protects the poets and allows them to speak over "hot" political matters. On this base, I revisit Bloch's analysis of formal vs. informal languages.

In chapter 5, I discuss ethnic identity and place, arguing for the presence of a "repertoire of identities" which is represented, constructed, negotiated and deconstructed in the *Contrasto*. After reviewing theories on ethnicity which have been proposed in the past, including the concept of "repertoire of identities," I discuss how identities in Tuscany are connected to "places" and "place-names." I argue that – through the analysis of the "opening octets" of several *Contrasti* – a "repertoire" of ethnic identities becomes evident in the way the artists choose to represent themselves across contexts. Finally, I show how, in performance, the poets name and define, but also contest, definitions of places and the associated identities.

In chapter 6, after reviewing the recent debate in social sciences concerning definitions of gender and "womanhood," I analyze how the *Contrasti* represent existing power relationships among women. The poets represent power hierarchies involving women inside the family. Then, I discuss the role of ideologies in the way the poets construct images of womanhood.

In chapter 7, I compare views of "folk art" as they have been developed by Italian scholars over the course of the past two centuries. I then oppose to them the views of poetic art shared by the poets. In doing so, I discuss first the way the poets understand the origin and nature of art, and the reasons that led them to become poets. I then discuss their ethos, including moral and political views. Finally, I discuss their linguistic ideologies, as they constitute part of an aesthetic system regarding the art itself.

2
SITUATING THE *CONTRASTO*
IN THE POLITICAL-LINGUISTIC HISTORY OF
THE ITALIAN NATION

Language is not just a means of communication: it is first of all art, it is beauty, and that it is so even for the more humble social strata is seen in the smile aroused by the one who is not expressing himself well in a language or dialect which is usually foreign to him. ... The expression is never definitive, since the relationships of thought change continually, the ideal of beauty always changes, and only a spoken language can find in itself, or in other languages, the new shades of meaning, the new verbal links that are adequate to the new needs. (Gramsci, 1993:42)

I. Introduction.

Visions of art have historical and political roots. Indeed, there cannot be any way to distinguish what is "art" and what is not, outside of socio-cultural categories. To reach an understanding of the *Contrasto* as a verbal art genre, we need to start from an understanding of the forces that shaped the definition of verbal art for Italians. This includes understanding the formation of the "art realm" and of the "verbal realm," namely, how a language comes to be seen as a language, and thus how a certain form of language, comes to be seen as "artistic" or, in this case, "poetical."[17] In this chapter, therefore, I

---

[17] I realize that this is a very complex issue. An issue that in this chapter, and in this thesis, I can only start to put into focus, and not yet answer completely. Still,

will discuss the formation of the Italian language on the background of Tuscan and Italian history. I will then discuss the "ethnic formation" of the nation. Finally, I will provide an in-depth discussion of the "linguistic context," namely a discussion of the languages used in Italy and in Tuscany in particular, including an account of their historical formation.

Language is connected to hegemony, in the sense that each hegemony will impose its own language or, when possible, reconnect and appropriate the language of the preceding hegemony, to create an apparent (cultural and ideological) continuity. Gramsci already recognized that questions of "standard" language versus "dialects" are questions of power (1993:6-7). Seeing a connection between "linguistic unrest" and political unrest, he wrote: "Every time that the problem of the common language surfaces, it means that another series of problems is imposing itself: the formation and the enlargement of the leading class, the necessity to establish more intimate and secure relationships among the leading groups and the popular-national mass, namely to reorganize the cultural hegemony" (1993:9; my translation).

It was typical of the Nationalist movements of the nineteenth century to consider language and nation to be connected in "a relationship of correspondence and strict unity" (De Mauro, 1970:1).[18] These ideas reflected the influence of theorists and philosophers like Johann Gottfried Herder (1967), and characterized the period of Romanticism. In Herder's conceptualization "it is the possession of its own distinctive language that constitutes the touchstone of a people or *Volk*, the sine qua non of its national identity and spirit" (Bauman and Briggs, 2000:173; italics in the original). In such a language "dwell [a people's] whole world of tradition, history, religion and principles of life, its whole heart and soul" (Herder, 1967:58; quoted from Bauman and Briggs, 2000:174).

John Locke's proposal of a "scientific" language, to be the

---

it seems to me that from the beginning, it has to remain connected to my analysis, if only as background. The issue cannot be forgotten, or the risk is to flatten out the complex realities that are instantiated in the performances of *Contrasti*.

[18] This way of thinking was never completely abandoned in Europe and the West. It can be found today in various theorization of the "ethnic groups" as they are presented in the social sciences and in the political nationalistic and separatist movements. See also Blommaert and Vershueren, 1998.

necessary glue of society (or nation) (Bauman and Briggs, 2000:164), can also be seen as an ideological (*metadiscursive*, according to Bauman and Briggs, 2000) base of the language standardization and language planning effort in the new nations (2000:156). The national subject must be reflected in a "scientific" use of language. The scientific language offers the proof of the existence of the national subject.

Indeed, while positions such as those of Locke and Herder might on the surface appear contrastive, they are instead quite compatible if seen as ideological tenets on the background of nation state formation (Bauman and Briggs, 2000). The first found language to be isomorphic to one people, the second intended to make sure that language would become the base of the definition of an absolute truth, and it would as such be policed and imposed on the people. They both advocated linguistic homogeneity (Bauman and Briggs, 2000:199).

Thus, in the nineteenth century, identifying languages became a first step toward "identifying nations," or ethnic units (Irvine and Gal, 2000:50). In Italy, as I will show, this held true at the moment of the formation of the Italian nation state. A lot is at stake here. If Italy could not demonstrate to be a *Volk*, then it would not have had the authority as subject, to sit as sovereign nation among the other nations of Europe. Without an Italian language, there cannot be any Italian people. This is well exemplified in Johann Gottlieb Fichte's statement: "Wherever a separate language can be found, there is also a separate nation which has the right to manage its affairs and rule itself" ([1808] 1845-46:453; quoted in Irvine and Gal, 2000:63). The absence of such language, then, could mean that such a right was not going to be recognized.[19]

As I will show next, an Italian language emerged as the (historical) result of the tension between nationalist, regionalist, and local political goals. It emerged through negotiations and contrasts that lasted for centuries. Gramsci had already noticed that a common language "in any case is an effect and not a cause" of the forming of a nation-state (1975:2346; my translation). The creation of an Italian language was the result of the concurrent play of several political forces, each upholding different views of language (namely different linguistic ideologies). This in turn underlines the necessity to understand the specific context in which linguistic ideologies are formed and

---

[19] This is well exemplified by the fate of Macedonia, as discussed by Irvine and Gal (2000).

"practiced".

II. History and the Creation of the Italian Nation.

II. a. The Process of Unification.

Considering history is important not only to understand the macro-context of Tuscan verbal art performances, but also to understand the present political, ethnic and linguistic situation in Italy. At the beginning of the 1800, after the brief period of the Napoleonic conquest[20] and French domination, at the Restoration, the Italian peninsula was divided in several states, as shown in figure #1:

The Kingdom of Sardinia was ruled by the House of Savoy, and included parts of today's France. The northeast area was part of the Austrian-Hungarian Empire. The Duchies of Parma and Modena were independent states, connected to Austrian rule. In the south, the Kingdom of the Two Sicilies had been ruled for centuries by a Spanish dynasty, and was then under the Bourbons. The center of the peninsula was divided between the Papal state and the Tuscan State. The second had been under the authority of the house of Lorraine since 1737.

In 1861 the Italian Kingdom was created and the Tuscan nobility and the high class voted to join the new Italian state (1860). Florence was capital of Italy from 1864 to 1871, when Rome became the new capital.[21] As I wrote elsewhere:

Two competing parties had been behind the unification of Italy: the *monarchists* – championed by the Count of Cavour – were loyal to the House of Savoia, reigning on Piedmont and Sardinia; the *republicans*, represented by Mazzini, counted among them Giuseppe Garibaldi, who is honored today as the Italian national hero. The three 'wars of independence' fought to unify Italy were characterized by disagreements and even hostility between these two groups. This is well represented by the fact that Garibaldi, the 'maker of the nation,' died in confinement on the island of Caprera, rejected as dangerous by the new Italian kingdom. Neither the *monarchists* nor the *republicans* were representatives of the people, but only of a very restricted minority of nobles and wealthy

---

[20] Napoleon invaded Italy in 1796.

[21] For further readings on the period of the *Risorgimento*, see also Lepre, 1978.

intellectuals (Pagliai, 1995a:22 & fol.).[22]

Figure #1: The Italian peninsula in 1815.

Indeed Marriott notices, in regard to the *Carbonari* – the secret society that started the unrest in Italy that led to the wars of independence – that: "the members of that society were, however, recruited chiefly from the ranks of the nobles, the educated *bourgeoisie*, and the younger officers of the army" (1931:47). Considering this, the newly made Italian government had to do quite a bit of "face lifting"

---

[22] For a general discussion see D. M. Smith, 1969; King, 1967; Clough & Saladino, 1968.

to create an image of the *Risorgimento* as popular uprising.[23]

In the newly made Italian state, the Italian masses had no more voice than before the unification. Only an extreme minority had the right to vote, namely those who were males, at least 25 years old, literate (less that 2.5% of the population), and paying taxes for at least 40 liras a year: for a total of about 2% of the population (Hearder, 1983:245; Montroni, 1995:419). At the turn of the century, according to Giovanni Montroni, "the greatest part of the country remained extraneous, often hostile to the ruling class and to the new institutions" (1995:418). The intellectuals, busy at creating the new "nation," did not express the interest or views of the masses either. As I will show later, it was the *Poeti Bernescanti* (in central Italy) who expressed those voices.

The second part of the nineteenth century saw the beginning of a period of deep economic depression for Italy and Tuscany, that continued after the unification of the nation, leading at the end of 1800 to mass emigration. Thousands of people, in Tuscany like in the rest of Italy, were forced to emigrate to North and South America (United States and Argentina), Australia and North Africa (Bodnar, 1985:32-33).[24]

There were also strong economic imbalances among the various parts of Italy.[25] While northern Italy had already entered a period of industrialization, the southern regions were still massively rural. In the

---

[23] A notable example of this historical "face lifting" was the silence over the peasants' rebellions in the South against the Piedmontese-Italian government, after 1861. These popular uprising were not only repressed in blood, but misnamed "brigands wars" (Hearder, 1983:240). See also Cammarano, 1995:48-49.

[24] Coupled with this there was internal migration, usually seasonal. Tuscans (especially men) traveled annually to Corsica, Sardinia, and Calabria. These are often *carborari* (coal makers) and shepherds. Inside Tuscany there were seasonal migratory movements from the northern part of the region to the southwestern plains of the Maremma. This also facilitated the contacts among central Italian poets and the diffusion of lyrics, poems, and themes of the *Contrasti*.

[25] These unbalances, which are at the base of the *Questione Meridionale* (Southern Question), are still present today. Levy, for example, writes: "If the average GPD [gross domestic product] in the European Community in 1991 equated 100, the GPD of Northern and Central Italy was 122, that of the South 68.9. ... In 1991 unemployment stood at over 15 per cent in Sicily, Calabria, Basilicata, Campania and Molise. In most of Piedmont, Lombardy, Emilia-Romagna and the Veneto it was below 5 per cent" (1996:3).

northern regions the property of the land was subdivided more equally than in southern Italy, where the land belonged to a few powerful families (Bodnar, 1985:27; see also Fichera, 1981). The new Piedmontese administration reinforced, rather than ameliorating, these imbalances (Montroni, 1995:415-418). The crisis was aggravated by the First World War. But the turn of the century saw also the organization of the first unions and of the socialist-democratic party. Under the leadership of Giolitti, moreover, the right of vote was extended to all males (women would have to wait until 1945, after the fall of fascism).

On the 28th of October 1922, Mussolini entered Rome, taking power through a coup d'état. He became dictator in 1925, suppressing freedom of the vote and eliminating all political adversaries. The regime lasted in Italy for twenty years, and led the state into a colonialist war against Ethiopia in 1935, then into the Second World War in alliance with Germany. Mussolini's rule ended in 1943, when the king Vittorio Emanuele III formed a new government (in exile), which broke the alliance with Hitler and joined the Allied Forces. Immediately afterwards the Germans occupied Italy. In the next two years there was war on Italian soil. The Italian Partisan army freed parts of northern Italy, while the other allied armies moved north from Sicily and freed all of southern Italy and Tuscany. In 1947 the Italian Republic was created.

According to Levy, "the Fascist regime had left Italy in 1945 divided between a North radicalized by civil war and the Resistance and an Allied-occupied monarchist and largely conservative South" (1996:4). In the successive decades, a political-economic division of Italy in three sectors became increasingly evident: a conservative, economically poor and underdeveloped South; a "red" and economically prosperous Center;[26] and a prosperous and highly industrialized North, of more variously distributed political allegiance. In the past two decades, the North has seen the emergence of strong separatist movements.

. *II. b. National Historiography and the Role of the Intellectuals.*

If nations are "imagined", then historians, through historiography, seems to have an important role in this imagination. The Italian nation state since its beginning upheld a partial version of Italian

---

[26] The central regions, Tuscany and Emilia-Romagna in particular, have traditionally given the majority of their votes to the parties of the left.

history, that was part of the political project of creation of the new nation. The historian Harry Hearder notices that "until comparatively recently most Italian nineteenth-century history was written by sympathizers of Cavour and the moderate party who succeeded in imposing their solution to the Italian Question" (1983:295).

Bruno Tobia argues that "historiography between 1860 and the beginning of the eighties, which was 'politics in act,' wanted in great part to consciously assign to itself the task of building an image of the *Risorgimento* process able to produce an active consensus around the result of that process: the unitarian and constitutional monarchy" (1995:453; my translation). According to this version of history the "Italians," united in Roman times then divided by the barbaric invasions, longed for centuries to be united again (see for example, Sir J. A. R. Marriott, 1931:3). The occasion finally came in the nineteenth century, when the patriots of the *Risorgimento* were able to convince the king of Savoia to help them unify Italy. Backed then by the popular masses, these courageous patriots were able to free Italy from foreign domination.

An example is the following description of "Italian history," by the historian Arthur J. White (1944:2): "Her military spirit was decayed: unity she had none: and the little states into which she was divided, so fertile and genius in the Renaissance, were a fatal weakness in the face of the great Powers now taking shape beyond the Alps. For a century and a half she lay inert while France and Spain fought for possession of her unprotesting body." The fusion of nation images with gender images (nation, female, passive) is here quite interesting. If on one side there is "lady Italy" to be united, on the other there is the Piedmontese Kingdom "the most virile of all her states" (White, 1944:8) to take care of it with its "hardy race of soldiers" (White, 1944:9). The Piedmontese conquest is seen as a mission (Tobia, 1995:454).

The history of Italy was seen as a teleological process that tended toward the necessary outcome of unity in one nation. The historians discussed at great length the reasons why unity was not achieved before, like in other "nations" (see for example Marriott, 1931:10; who find the obstacles in Physiography and in the temporal control of the Church), but they did not actually contest its necessity. This "history" not only assumes a pre-existence of Italians to the formation of the nation, but also neglects to address the issue of language, so that people are left to imagine that an Italian standard language has always existed, and that everybody in Italy speaks it and spoke it in the past.

The educational system had a large role in the creation of the Italian nation. Probably the most influential thinker here was Francesco De Sanctis. In his *History of Italian Literature* De Sanctis constructed an "Italian" moral history on the basis of the idea "that the history of literature could be the history of the Italian civil greatness, that the delineation of Italy's literary profile could mark the characters as well of what had tightened it together before unity" (Tobia, 1995:460). De Sanctis was also a minister of Public Education in the new government; thus his political program and his historiographical program must be seen in connection.

Historians shared their role in the *imagination* of the nation with intellectuals and artists. Among them the poets Josué Carducci and Alessandro Manzoni, to whom I will return. I want to mention here that the new state invested a lot of resources in the arts. Innumerable monuments were built in the cities, glorifying the heroes of the new nation. The names of plazas and streets were changed, books extolling the patriotic qualities of the "Italians" were written (most famously *Cuore* by Edmondo De Amicis), and festivities and celebrations were created (Tobia, 1995:495).

II. c. Tuscany Today.

Tuscany today is an economically prosperous region, which is highly industrialized. Politically, it has been governed since World War II by the Communist and Socialist parties (Rotelli, 1980). Economically, the region has seen major changes in the post-war period. At the end of the war, the agrarian sector was dominated by sharecropping (Pratt, 1994). In the following decades, the number of people employed in the agrarian production has been steadily diminishing (Revelli, 1977). With it, there has been a phenomenon of urbanization and the development of industry. In northeastern Tuscany the abandonment of the countryside has been quite drastic in the mountains. In the plains, instead, most of the land has been converted to nurseries for the intensive production of flowers and ornamental plants. These nurseries have brought wealth in particular to the province of Pistoia.

III. Regionalism and Ethnicity.

Regional and local identities as well as interests have had an influence on the development of the Italian nation state. As I wrote elsewhere (Pagliai, 1995a:22):

Italians at the turn of the century did not have a strong sense of national identity. A few decades before, the nationalist M. D'Azeglio had stated that Italy had been "made" in 1861 (unified or conquered, depending on the point of view), but the Italians did not exist yet.[27] The felt reality was instead the presence of the various local cultures and their individuated identities and languages.

Similarly Levy writes:

Since the Italian nation-state was a relatively recent development, arising from the fortuitous combination of European diplomacy, Piedmontese initiative and nationalist conspiracy, older varieties of vibrant localistic or regional identities were suppressed but never completely eradicated. (1996:3)

An "ethnic revivalist" period started in Italy in the eighties. It stressed regional culture/ethnicity and took at times racial overtones. To understand this new development we need again to look at history, as well as at more recent events. The last two decades of the millennium have seen two important phenomena. The first was the arrival en-masse of immigrants from countries outside the European community – in particular Arabs, South-Saharan Africans, Eastern Europeans, Chinese, Filipinos, Albanians, and more recently Indians. The other has been the emergence of separatist movements, especially in northern Italy. These are the various *Leghe* (Leagues) which converged during the 1980s in the *Lega Nord* (Northern League). Both phenomena have determined a growth in racist feelings both against other Italians and towards immigrants.

The Northern League, for example, from the beginning has produced a series of racist claims regarding the "innate superiority" of the Northern Italians. In the official rhetoric of its leaders the Northern Italians are presented as strong, indefatigable workers, who have built a rich region. The Southern Italians are stereotyped as lazy and always depending on welfare which, in turn, is said to be based on the work of the Northern Italians.

The rhetoric of this politically defined ethnic identity utilizes a folklorist account. Folklore can be easily utilized to support a

---

[27] His is the following famous maxim: "Italy is made. Now we have to make the Italians."

museological, "ad exempla," view of what a culture is. The *Lega Nord* highlights some images inside history. The first regards the origins of the Northern Italian people, the Celts. Other images are taken from the medieval period. The symbol of the Northern League is a warrior in medieval armor, with a raised sword and the shield. This represents Alberto Da Giussano, one of the heroes of the legendary "Oath of Pontida." The legend reports this oath as the origin of the *Lega Lombarda*, which in 1176 won the battle of Legnano against the emperor Frederick the I, who was then ruling Italy. This victory resulted in the independence of the northern state-cities from the empire.[28]

This collapsing of history tends to negate or hide the differences among the various cultures of Northern Italy, and to heighten the differences (often mitigated, giving the changing boundaries and migration, commerce and reciprocal influence, etc.) against Central-South Italy. This discourse does not take into consideration the cultural contacts and blood mixing accelerated especially in the past one hundred years. Here we see the desire to fix both the self and the "other" in a stable and stabilizing identity. The boundaries are clearly cut: us and them, where "them" can become the enemy. The use of folklore to such ends is not new in Italy. The fascists already promoted this way of understanding popular culture, and stitched together triumphal celebrations of Italianness and fascism (see Franceschini, 1983:43-44).

By looking again at history, then, I will proceed to reanalyze these images of ethnicity based on regional belonging. In fact the Italian regions (see figure #2), far from representing preexisting culturally

---

[28] These images create an almost hallucinogenic state in which the immigrants are seen as a growing danger: the origin of all evils (Taussig, 1987:196). Myths and fantasies about the innate criminality, etc. of the Africans or the Albanians are affirmed as real by the Lega Nord, concretized through that image: the war started one thousand years ago. In this case, history has really been "collected in a focal point" (Taussig, 1987:199). Through the use of these images, the Lega Nord is in the process of creating an ethnic memory. This had to underline the communality of all Northern cultures. Both the Celtic identity and the legend of the "Oath of Pontida" answer this need. Not only, but it is a memory in respect to which the Lega has already assumed the position of depository and custodian. As Connerton shows, this move is extremely important to create a legitimating base for the Lega's future power. In fact, "images of the past commonly legitimate a present social order. It is an implicit rule that participants in any social order must presuppose a shared memory" (Connerton, 1989: 3).

homogeneous units, were instead "invented" by the new national government, pretty much as centrally dependent administrative units.

Figure #2: Italy and its regions.

These administrative regions did not coincide with historical regions, nor did they follow the boundaries of preexisting states. Only in 1970 were they reorganized so to give them some autonomy, albeit a quite limited one. Carl Levy writes that: "Regional government was not established in Italy until after the Second World War and except for the special regions, most of Italy did not experience regional government until the 1970s" (1996:4). As Adrian Lyttelton notices, at the time of the national unification:

> In spite of the claims that could be made for regions, in terms of a shared political past, or of a dominant model of social relations, it would be hard to argue that they were the primary focus for identification, either at the popular level, or among the literate classes. ... But it is also significant that the evil which Italian patriots had fought went under the name not of regionalism but 'municipalism.' Underneath the surface of the territorial states of the modern period, the vitality of the city-state tradition survived powerfully (1996:35).

According to Lyttelton the few preexisting regions, namely Tuscany, Lombardy, Piedmont and Veneto, "had been shaped by the action of a dominant city. One can think of regionalism as a force radiating out from the capital city and diminishing in intensity as one moved away from it" (Lyttelton, 1996:33). The situation in Tuscany was partially different. A Tuscan state had existed since the Middle Ages, and its boundaries were pretty much left untouched in the new region.[29] This, however, does not mean (as I will show more in Chapter 5) that local municipal identities were less felt in Tuscany than elsewhere. John Davis also agrees that: "the true historical locus of identity and loyalty in Italy has been more localized – the city, the village, the community" (Davis, 1996:54).

The interests of the municipalities, then, and the rivalries among then, must be taken into consideration to understand the events before and after the formation of the Italian nation state. One important thing that emerges is that different parties, with different interests, were taking part in this creation: national (monarchic or republican), regionalistic (along the lines of the previous states) and urban/local interests. While the "centralists," who wanted a strong central state on the model of the French one, won in the government, the other political pressure groups did not disappear, but through often-unofficial ways, they kept shaping the nation until the present.

As the monarchist state and the fascist state had been highly

---

[29] In fact, after the unification Tuscany, given the strength and recognized modernity of his previous institutions, obtained at first special status as a region. Namely it did not adopt the organization model of Piedmont but kept its own, including its penal code, mining laws, appeal court, and bank system (Lyttelton, 1996:42).

centralized, so was the Italian Republic after 1947. Inside such a centralized state, municipalities kept their power through the action of the local leaders. Thus municipalism persisted in the Italian state, except that now, "the most effective channel through which personal appeals reached the bureaucracy was through the local deputies" (Lyttelton, 1996:45). In a certain sense, then, the national state, at least at first, was strengthening rather than weakening the local identities. As David Hine (1996:112) writes: "Local leaders became political entrepreneurs defending local interests inside national parties."

Municipalities form a strong pressure group even today, often mediated by the action of a political party, which thus comes to cater to particular local interests (as well as or rather than ideological/national ones). An example can be seen in the evolution of the communist party in Tuscany. The Italian Communist Party was originally quite centralist and nationalistic, but later on it shifted its position to uphold a federalist view. As it received a good part of its votes from the "red belt," the central regions, especially Emilia-Romagna, Tuscany and Umbria, the PCI was obviously pressured to cater to the interests of Central Italians (including Tuscans), its major constituency. In a certain way, it "regionalized" itself.

It is this differential politicization of different areas in Italy that in the past few decades, has slowly created a sense of regional identity (see also Hine, 1996:116). As the Tuscans find their voice vis-a-vis the nation through the parties of the left, a regional identity comes to coincide with a communist political identity.[30] This is an identity that is at the same time regional and political. People in Tuscany may perceive themselves as Tuscan partially *through* a common political allegiance that they share, namely toward the left. They may also feel this identity as in contrast to other regional identities *because* those other regions *do not* share the same political allegiance.[31]

---

[30] In the same process, aspects of Tuscan culture may come to be influenced by leftist ideas.

[31] I recently found what seems to be a confirmation of this idea in a *Contrasto* that I found published on the review Toscana Folk (Londi, Tonti and Landi, 1997:30-33). The theme was "Tuscany, Emilia-Romagna and the Northern League." Done by three poets, it thus opposed two regions among themselves and against a political party (with strong regional allegiance in the North). The development of the *Contrasto*, instead of discussing any cultural distinctions, instead is completely focused on politics, with Tuscany and Emilia-Romagna praising each other (instead of attacking each other) and both professing a leftist

In the nineties, in turn, in Tuscany the parties of the left (Socialist Democratic Party and Communist Refoundation) have adopted a more positive attitude toward ethnic revivalism. After the victory of the right in the Italian government elections in 1994, for example, ethnic identity has been used by them to underline the difference between the "red" central Italy (Tuscany, Umbria and Emilia-Romagna) versus the rest of the nation.

We see then a complex interaction between political ideologies, nationalism, and ethnic identities, which in turn shows how many models of national formation and nationalism are inherently simplistic. These models tend to see the nation as a total and totalizing unit and fail to recognize the divergences, contrasts and continuous renegotiations that shape them.[32] In the Italian context, the centrifugal interests of the municipalities always offered a check to the power of the centralized government of the state. The unification and formation of the Italian nation state was a complex phenomenon, where dissident voices, as well as the more dominant ones, contributed to the shaping of events and where local interests and customs continuously played a role. Lyttelton writes: "Apart from the vast areas of peasant hostility or indifference to the new state, the town hall in most cases continued to be the primary focus of political competition, and even class conflict took intensely provincial forms" (1996:49). In the same way, as I will show, the local languages maintained their relevance in everyday interactions. In this light, then, I now turn to a discussion of the "creation" of the Italian language.

IV. Languages Spoken in Italy and their Varieties.

There is quite a bit of misunderstanding today, both in Italy and elsewhere, as to the status of the languages spoken in Italy. This is partially due to the enduring and widespread tendency to call these languages "dialects" – a term used often as a pejorative – both in everyday conversations and often, unfortunately, in the schools as well.[33] Instead, as Anna Laura Lepschy *et al.* make clear: "These

---

stance and attacking the Northern League. Being Tuscan thus seems to be equated with being communist, this in turn means sharing an affinity (which may be lived as identification) with Emilia-Romagna, the other "red" region, against a conservative North/Northern League.

[32] This has also been noticed by Silverstein (2000) and Errington (2000) in their criticism of Anderson's and Gellner's views of nationalism.

[33] This general, institutionally upheld, ignorance of the Italian languages, can be

Italian dialects are not derived from Italian, nor are they varieties or adaptations of the national language. On the contrary, it is Italian which is based on one of the dialects (i.e., Florentine), or rather, on the standardization of its literary variety of the fourteenth century" (1996:70).

Thirty-two different languages are spoken today in Italy.[34] Some of them are found only in Italy, while others are currently spoken in other nations as well. Some of them (called *allogene*) originated elsewhere.[35] I will use the plural "Italian languages" to refer to these languages. I will reserve the term "Italian language" (singular) to refer to the official national Italian language only. I will moreover distinguish between a standard variety of the Italian language, officially taught in school and which is used in writing and in the mass media, and the other varieties of the Italian national language. If we take "dialect" in its linguistic definition of "geographical variant" of a language, we can identify the following "dialects" of the Italian national language: Tuscan, Abruzzese, Pugliese, Umbrian, Laziale, Central Marchigiano, Cicolano-Reatino, Aquilano, Molisano (Grimes, 1988; see also Appendix C).

Another source of confusion is the use of the term *dialetto* (dialect) to indicate both the various Italian languages, their varieties, *and* the varieties of the Italian language. There are several reasons that make the use of the term "dialect" inadequate: 1) It has been used in a pejorative sense. 2) It implies the primacy of the "standard." 3) It implies the existence of a primary, stable language (but, as argued by Lippi-Green, 1997, everybody has an accent). 4) The definitions of "dialect" vs. "language" is uncertain even among linguists, so that it has been suggested to consider a "language a dialect with an army and a navy."[36] This in turn shows how the definition of language is usually

---

seen as part of what Irvine and Gal have called a process of "erasure", namely "the process in which ideology, in simplifying the sociolinguistic field, renders some persons or activities ... invisible" (2000:38).

[34] It is important to underline that the areas where these dialects are spoken do not correspond necessarily with the boundaries of the Italian regions. See Appendix C; also Grimes, 1988:464-468.

[35] I am not considering here, the languages spoken by the 1,500,000 (estimated) immigrants living in Italy today. Unfortunately (and significantly) no adequate surveys are available regarding them.

[36] This definition, who is part of the lore of Linguistics, is variously attributed to Max Weinreich or Haugen.

political rather than linguistic and often connected to nationalism and other ethnic politics.

Milroy and Milroy have suggested that a "standard Language" is "an idea in the mind rather than a reality – a set of abstract norms to which actual usage may conform to a greater or lesser extent" (1991:22-23; quoted in Lippi-Green, 1997:41). As Silverstein shows in his recent analysis (2000:121) of Anderson's theories about imagined nations, standard languages are "imagined" and then enforced through social institutions and social practices.

There are strong ideological reasons behind the research for the standard language. As Rosina Lippi- Green states: "In spite of all the hard evidence that language must be variable and must change, people steadfastly believe that a homogeneous, standardized, one-size-fits-all language is not only desirable, it is truly a possibility. This language does not exist *in fact*, but it certainly does exist as an ideal in the minds of the speakers" (1997:44, italics in the original). Lippi-Green gives the example of the Standard English that, according to the dictionaries, would be the language of the educated. She notices that:

> The *uneducated*, who by the dictionary definition must constitute the greatest number of native speakers of English, are even less represented. Perhaps there is no way to write a dictionary which is truly descriptive in terms of pronunciation; perhaps it is necessary to choose one social group to serve as a model. Perhaps there is even some rationale for using the 'educated' as this group. But there is nothing *objective* about this practice. It is the ordering of social groups in terms of who has authority to determine how language is *best used*. Clearly, the rationale for this ordering derives at least in part from the perceived superiority of the written language (1997:55; italics in the original).

Thus I opted to consider a language as a set that includes a certain number of varieties, including often (but not necessarily) a standard one.

V. History of Italian and the "Question of the Tongue."

V. a. The Origins.
In Europe, the divergence of the languages spoken by the people from written Latin (probably already started in Roman times), continued throughout the Low Middle Ages, giving origin to the various Romance languages. The Italian languages also diverged and

formed in this period, as we can glimpse from the few but important documents from the time which have survived (see Bruno Migliorini, 1975). After 1000 AD, in the Italian peninsula, these documents multiplied, indicating a growing need to find expression in a native language which was now deeply different from Latin. Various literary traditions also began to emerge. Among them, a Tuscan one, represented by the poets of the *Stilnovo* (New Style, between 1280-1310), who first opted to express themselves in the Florentine popular idiom, rather than in Latin. Among them was Dante Alighieri, whose masterpieces greatly contributed to Florentine predominance over other literary languages.

By the beginning of the fourteenth century, the "vulgare Toscano" is seen as the literary language to be preferred to Latin by literate people both in Tuscany and outside it (Migliorini, 1975:12-13), including Dante (De Vulgari Eloquentia & Convivio, 1303-1307c.). After Dante, literate people from all over Italy started to adapt their writing styles to the Florentine ideal, often fusing or assimilating to it elements of their native languages. In the 1300, therefore, an "Italian" language (shared only by highly educated people plus the Tuscans) began to form. Other important writers use it in their works, in particular, Francesco Petrarca and Giovanni Boccaccio. In 1348 Petrarca started the publication of the *Canzoniere* (Migliorini, 1975:14). In 1349-1353c. Boccaccio wrote the *Decamerone* (Migliorini, 1975:14). These became two fundamental texts of Italian.

V. b. The Question of the Tongue.

In the following centuries, the so-called *questione della Lingua,* "question of the tongue," began to develop. In 1515 Trissino rediscovered Dante's *De Vulgari Eloquentia.* On its base, Trissino started a debate with Agnolo Firenzuola (in 1524), soon involving other humanists and writers like Valeriano, Oreandini (on the side of Trissino), Martelli and Tolomei (Migliorini, 1975:29-30). From its beginnings (at the beginning of the fifteenth century), this *Questione* revolved around two possible alternatives: Italian should be equated to the living language spoken in Tuscany; or Italian should remain closer to the model (by then three hundred years old) established by Dante and the literary tradition of the 1300. The use of the Tuscan language was defended, among others, by Tolomei, who published his theses in *Il Cesano* (Migliorini, 1975:30). In 1525 the Venetian Bembo published *Prose della Volgar Lingua* (Prose of the Vulgar Tongue), arguing instead for the use of the language of the great poets of the fourteenth century. In 1532 the final edition of the *Orlando Furioso* by Tasso followed the norms of Bembo (Migliorini, 1975:32).

In 1582 the *Accademia della Crusca* was created in Florence (Migliorini, 1975:42), with the intent to study and preserve the Tuscan language as a base for the Italian language. It privileged archaism and for this reason was criticized since the beginning by various scholars and literate people, like Beni and Tassoni (Migliorini, 1975:45). In this period the supremacy of Tuscan was not yet well established, as various scholars would prefer other dialects like, for example, the one spoken in Bologna (Scaligeri della Fratta, 1630) (Migliorini, 1975:47).

In 1747 Gasparo and Carlo Gozzi founded the *Accademia dei Granelleschi*, which supported the use of XIV century's Tuscan as Italian (Migliorini, 1975:56). Between 1763 and 1765 Baretti and Verri (the creators of *Il Caffè*, the first Italian newspaper), instead, spoke against the pedantic use of Tuscan in favor of "a simple and sincere style and language" (Migliorini, 1975:58). In 1785 Cesarotti expressed the need to enrich Italian with the contribution of the various dialects (Migliorini, 1975:60). In conclusion, for centuries what was to be considered as "Italian language" remained a rather controversial concept. There was no general agreement among the scholars and each of them would practically create their own version of the language, despite the repeated attempts at standardization.

The discussion, which up to that point had remained a literary diatribe, picked up new importance during the romantic period, with the emergence of nationalistic movements. In 1817-24 Monti, in producing an Italian vocabulary, disagreed with the conservative positions held by the *Accademia della Crusca*. Niccolini in 1818 started wondering what role the people would have in the formation of the Italian language (Migliorini, 1975:64). Finally, we had the opinion of the writer and poet Manzoni (1827) who upheld the use of the spoken Florentine variety of Tuscan as a base of Italian. It seems then that at this point, the imitation of the classic, which had received preference in the past, was no more felt to be adequate enough to serve as "national language."

Although Italian had been used in some Italian kingdoms since the sixteenth century,[37] it is only after the unification of Italy as one nation that the "question of the tongue" gets in the top agenda of

---

[37] In 1560, Italian began to be used in Italian Savoy in administration (Migliorini, 1975:39). In 1729, in Piedmont, it was ordered that Italian be taught in school together with Latin (Migliorini, 1975:53).

Italian politicians. At this point, in fact, it became necessary to choose and define a language for the new nation. In 1859, the Casati Law was passed, providing for the creation of public schools. In 1868 the minister Broglio nominated a commission to study the situation regarding the Italian language, calling Manzoni to participate in it, together with a committee of Florentine scholars (Migliorini, 1975:69).

Even this "task force," at first, failed to establish an agreement among the scholars. Manzoni and his followers thought that the Florentine dialect of Tuscan should become the national language (De Mauro, 1970:88). A second group, among whom was the poet Carducci, proposed that the literary Italian, developed from Tuscan but never spoken, should be used (De Mauro, 1970:327). A third current (including Ascoli, D'Ovidio and De Sanctis) wanted to take elements from the various regional languages and create a new language from their fusion. They finally agreed, toward the end of the century, for a middle ground between the first two solutions (De Mauro, 1970:330). However, as Tullio De Mauro notices: "the effective practice of the schools happened outside these opposed programmatic schemes" (1970:89).

V. c. Illiteracy and Scholarization.

At the birth of the Italian state, only few well-educated people knew Italian. It was practically a dead tongue, by admission of its scholars themselves. De Mauro informs us that already Gozzi "had defined Italian as 'a dead language' laying 'in the thousands of written volumes' and that was learned 'as all dead tongues,' through its study" (1970:14, quoted from Bobbio, 1951; my translation). De Mauro continues writing: "The situation had not changed much in the years of unification. The primacy of Italian was already at that time a certain and sure data, but only on the cultural and political plane, not on the factual linguistic plane" (1970:14). Thus was the "paradox of a language celebrated but not used and, in a sense, a stranger in its own land" (1970:14).

In the first census of the new Italian nation in 1861, 78% of the population was illiterate (De Mauro, 1970:36). But how many of the remaining were barely literate, namely had just a basic knowledge of the alphabet? In 1862-63 only 0.8 % of the population was being instructed in junior high school and high school. According to De Mauro, we can assume that these people knew how to speak Italian (De Mauro, 1970:42). To them De Mauro adds those Tuscans and

Romans who were not completely illiterate, concluding that: " in the years of national unification, the speakers of Italian – far from representing the totality of Italian citizens – were slightly more than six hundred thousand over a population of more than 25 million individuals: barely 2.5% of the population" (De Mauro, 1970:43).[38]

Although in 1877 the Coppino Law had made primary education obligatory (Migliorini, 1975:70), at the beginning of the twentieth century, illiterate people constituted more than half of the population (De Mauro, 1970:91). And here we need to keep in mind that literacy only meant basic knowledge of the alphabet in most cases, and that instruction was generally limited to two or three years of primary school. The effective use of the Italian language in speaking, according to De Mauro (1970:99), must have been even more restricted, probably only to those who were able to study at least at the level of junior high school.

Moreover, the teachers themselves often had a limited command of Standard Italian and they would code-switch to other Italian languages and dialects (De Mauro, 1970:93). De Mauro states that: "As a consequence, the action of the elementary school had an effect principally in the sense of weakening the dialect, of leading the teachers and the pupils toward italianizing forms of dialect ... or toward regional varieties of Italian that, especially from the phonological point of view, had to be strongly polarized toward the dialect" (1970:93). Moreover, an ideology that saw the correct way of speaking as a reflection of written language ("speaking like a printed book" is a common expression meaning "to be a good user of the language") found its diffusion in the schools. This, according to De Mauro: "favored the verbosity, namely the adoption, by both the pupils and the teachers, of crystallized stereotypical formulas" (1970:104).

This situation started to change after the first quarter of the twentieth century, due to historical forces not directly related to the educational system. The mass media had a large role in shaping a "common tongue." The programs on the national radio started in 1924, while the first broadcast of the national TV (*Radio Televisione Italiana*, or RAI – "Italian Radio and Television") was aired in 1954. The diffusion of the cinemas and movies were also important.

On the political side, after the advent of fascism, Mussolini's

---

[38] See De Mauro for a further discussion of illiteracy in Italy from the unification until today, 1970:37 and fol.

dictatorship progressively restricted the use of dialects. The nationalistic program of the regime was oriented toward the creation of a homogenized Italian language. This linguistic ideology can be seen emerging also in the campaign, launched by the regime in 1932, against the use of foreign words, which were prohibited in 1941-42 (Migliorini, 1975:76). In Italy, fascism "tried to introduce forced assimilation of linguistic minorities, including the italianization of placenames and surnames" (Lepschy, 1996:76). In the new democratic republic after WW II, two other important factors contributed to the spread of the Italian Language: the obligatory military draft that brought together young males from different regions; and finally the substitution of Italian for Latin in the catholic ritual after 1965.

V. d. The Situation after 1950.

From the preceding analysis, it appears that the formation of present day Italian has been much more dynamic than generations of planners would have wanted or expected. The national survey (Doxa) conducted in 1991 shows that 36% of the population use the "dialect" with everyone inside the family (while only 34% uses Italian with everyone inside the family), and 23% uses the "dialect" only or mainly outside the family as well (while 48% use only or mainly Italian in this situation). According to Lepschy et al., "Italy is now a largely bilingual country" (1996:75), and this seems to be a rather stable situation.

What happens to the various Italian languages vis-a-vis the imposition of Italian? It seems that there is convergence and hybridization that can be seen over a continuum. At one side of the continuum we find the original language, let's say Lombard. At the other side we find Italian. In the middle of the continuum we find an Italianized form of Lombard, and a "Lombardized" form of Italian. Thus:

Lombard ← Italianized Lombard – Lombardized Italian → Italian

An important thing that emerges is that a given phonological, morphological, syntactical or semantic element may belong to several of the varieties along the continuum (see also Alleyne, 1988:137).

We can consider the 1950s a turning point after which there is a steady convergence of the Italian languages toward Italian. At the same time, Italian keeps developing and incorporating elements of other Italian languages. As Mervin Alleyne states, referring to the case of the evolution of Jamaican English, "When two languages are mismatched, second language learning is unidirectional: speakers of the subordinate language learn the dominant language but not vice versa. ... The lower languages undergo drastic change as a result of either borrowings from the dominant language or to losses in inner form as a result of growing disuse. The dominant language, however, ... changes drastically when acquired as a second language by speakers of the lower languages" (1988:121).

According to Alleyne, language loss happens at the same time in the "inner form (structural)" and in the loss of "domains (functional)" of use (1988:125). Still the lower language keeps influencing the shaping of the "dominant" language as a "substratum influence" (1988:129). Referring to the case of Jamaican English, Alleyne states that: "This has culminated today in the existence of language forms that are still difficult to assign to an idealized language system and that can perhaps best be seen as differential degrees of continuity of African structures in the acquisition of English" (1988:129).

Alleyne adds that the resulting language: "is best understood dynamically, as a 'becoming'" (1988:121). The same could be said for the way Standard Italian and the Italian languages are spoken today on a continuum. Of course there are obvious historical and social differences between the Jamaican case and the Italian case. Standard Italian cannot be seen as the language of the "dominators" as English was in Jamaica. Still, Standard Italian is definitely and politically chosen to be the hegemonic language, and as such imposed through the educational system, the economic system, the mass media, etc.

To return to my previous example, while the speakers of Lombard diminished in number after the 50s, "pure" Italian is used in writing but spoken more in theory than in practice, except by the mass media. "Italianized Lombard" is practically the contemporary form of Lombard that has been influenced by the spreading of Italian literacy. It has borrowed many words from Italian, etc. (here following the fate of any dominated and colonized language). "Lombardized Italian" is the form of Italian spoken in Lombardy, namely "Italian with an accent." This is a variety of Italian (some would prefer the word "dialect"), and it is the one that Lombard people will adopt when speaking to Italians from other regions. A growing number of Lombard people will also use this as their first language in talking to each other, especially the younger generations in the urban areas. The linguist Luciano Canepari writes:

The 'standard' pronunciation of Italian, namely the one of those who have learned it voluntarily (like the professional speakers on radio and television, and the majority of the actors) is generally not used by the majority of Italians, who instead use a pronunciation more or less connoted by phonetic characteristics, especially regional ones, depending on the language learned in infancy. Very often, this is the local *dialect* (while often Italian is 'learned' in school), or a form of *regional Italian* more or less marked (especially at the phonic level, but for sure also lexical and morphosyntactic) (Canepari, 1979:203; my translation; italics in the original).

According to De Mauro, the limited use in writing of Italian throughout the centuries had influenced its phonological, morphological, grammatical and semantic characteristics in peculiar ways (De Mauro, 1970:27-28). Thus Italian changed very little since the fourteenth century. Usually new elements were added to old ones, creating a high polymorphism (De Mauro, 1970:28-29). A result has been "an iperthrophy of synonyms in some semantic fields" (De Mauro, 1970:29), due to the maintenance of alternative terms (no one of which could ever be selected negatively through usage, as would happen in spoken languages). At the same time other semantic fields remained relatively poor and underdeveloped. The Italian of the last century, for example, was missing terms for plants and flowers, for the crafts (De Mauro, 1970:30), for family life and household items, and for the most "colorful" language (swears, insults, vulgarities, etc.). In all these cases, the various dialects or Italian languages would be used.

In the last decades, as Italian has been spoken by more and more people, it has absorbed lexical and grammatical forms from the "dialects", thus becoming more colloquial and less based on a written system. This according to Lepschy, has "reduced tolerance towards all-too-widespread pompous, bombastic rhetoric, and favoured the development of a clearer, simpler, and more spontaneous linguistic usage" (1996:75).

VI. The Tuscan Situation Regarding Language.

The case of Tuscan is particular, so I will spend a few additional words here. I have already described how the Italian literary language emerged from Florentine Tuscan starting around the thirteenth century. From this point, the two began a process of divergence, so that by the middle of the nineteenth century, the language spoken in Tuscany was quite different from the Italian literary one (which at this point, as we have already seen, was practically a dead tongue, or better, an intellectual lingua franca). This difference also accounts for the *querelle* among those scholars who wanted to use Tuscan as the national language, using it to "revitalize" Italian, and those who wanted to stick to the literary form.

After the imposition of Italian as the national language, I have shown a process of convergence toward it of the various Italian languages. Tuscan seems to converge as well, although various scholars indicate that there seem to be a contemporaneous convergence in Tuscany toward the Florentine variety. This process, quite interesting in itself for the student of language maintenance and change, seems to offer in turn an avenue of resistance against assimilation to the Italian standard. The choice of Florentine, according to the linguists is logical and expectable in consideration of the preeminent political and cultural role of Florence (as capital) in the Tuscan region.

Due to its association with Standard Italian, Tuscan has partially shared in a hegemonic atmosphere. Because of this, Tuscans (and others) prefer to use the term *vernacolo* (vernacular) to refer to Tuscan, rather than *dialetto*. The choice of the word is not particularly appropriate. In fact, in common linguistic use, this term is reserved for indicating the language spoken by an oppressed minority, as a result of conquest or colonization. A second meaning is the language of the home and thus connected to the informal context. This would in turn point to a situation of diglossia, in which Tuscan would be the informal variety. This is absolutely not the case, as Tuscan is used in Tuscany only, and there, also in very formal contexts. In sum, I prefer to consider Tuscan another variety of the Italian language.[39]

There are several sub-regional linguistic variants of Tuscan (Bini, 1974; Giacomelli, 1975). These are clearly heard and recognized by the locals and allow the people to discern each other's provenience with high specificity. According to the *Carta dei Dialetti d'Italia* ("Map of the Italian Dialects;" by Pellegrini, 1977), the "dialect areas" in Tuscany include:

---

[39] For a list of characteristics of the Tuscan variety, see Appendix C.

- Fiorentino
- Senese
- Occidental:
    Pisano/Livornese/Elbano
    Pistoiese
    Lucchese
- Aretino
- Grossetano/Amiatino
- Apuano

The varieties included in my research have been mainly the Fiorentino and the Occidental, with their internal sub-varieties. Florentine norms have long expanded to the rest of Tuscany (Giacomelli 1984/85:124), given the cultural prominence held by Florence, and its linguistic prominence, standing as the original model for the Italian language.[40]

This division is far from definite. The proliferation of possible varieties of Tuscan is practically limitless. The more we bring the magnifying glass of linguistic analysis to any of these varieties, the more they seem to subdivide into further varieties. The boundaries established between the one and the other, thus, are quite arbitrary. It would be much closer to reality to talk about a continuum, which articulates differently according to what we are looking at in a particular moment: phonological, morphological, lexical and grammatical continuums do not necessarily correspond. Hence it is practically impossible, in the majority of the cases, to affirm with certainty that code-switching between one variety and another is happening at a given time. In my data, for example, a poet may produce a particular phonological change. But can we say that this is code switching? Or is it rather a way in which the poet deploys

---

[40] Professor E. Tuttle, Dept. of Italian, University of California Los Angeles. Personal communication. What is even more interesting, is that various studies seem to indicate an acceleration of the rate of 'Florentinization'' of the Tuscan dialect in this century (Agostiniani & Giannelli, 1990; Giannelli, 1989). Namely, at the same time during which pressure was applied from outside (through Scholarization first and the mass media later) to abandon the Tuscan dialect in favor of the standard dialect of Italian. This 'Florentinization' then, seems to have acted as an instrument of symbolic and linguistic resistance. It could be seen as a tendency to create an internal standard of Tuscan that could be opposed more strongly to the Italian encroachment.

language to obtain certain artistic effects? Or just a way for him to obey the demands of the metric and rhyme? These questions cannot really be answered, no matter how much analysis we deploy to find an answer.

A final note regarding linguistic ideologies of differentiation: Tuscan is usually characterized, both by Tuscans and by outsiders (other Italians) through the aspiration of the sound /k/. Among Tuscans, other differences are noticed, like the aspiration of the /k/ (done by the Florentines) versus its complete dropping (done by the Pistoiesi). Performers will imitate or suppress these sounds to represent characters from certain cultural groups. A "nationally" recognized grammatical characteristic of Tuscan,[41] is the reduplication of pronouns: "*a me mi*" (literally "to me to me"), instead of just "*a me*," or "*mi*." Inside Tuscany, other differences are emphasized (e.g. *andorno* [they went] and *irono* [they went]). Lexical markers are of course numerous and readily available at the conscious level in the mind of the speakers. They are thus amply used by the Tuscans to distinguish the various Tuscan cultural groups.

VII. Conclusion.

Linguistic Anthropology today has begun to acknowledge the importance of history. The larger macro-context of language use, once almost completely disregarded, is also receiving growing attention. In this chapter, I have tried to depict an image of Italy and of the Italian language, to serve as a background to understanding the verbal art genre of the *Contrasto*.

At the same time, I have started to analyze the way in which political ideologies and linguistic ideologies are interrelated. While a relationship between the standardization of Italian and the formation of the Italian nation state appears obvious, different ideologies regarding language were present in the mind of the Italian politicians at the turn of the century. The interplay of these ideologies gave origin to the complex reality of today's language use in Italy. As Graham Pechey puts it: "Any sociopolitical project of centralization or hegemony has always and everywhere to *posit itself against* the ubiquitously decentralizing (centrifugal) forces within ideology" (quoted in Dentith, 1995:104).

In the formation of the Italian nation state, nationalistic ideologies

---

[41] See Appendix C.

shared the ground with municipalistic ones, and both in the end shaped the reality of the state. This in turn shows how important, in theorizing about nationalism, it is to pay close attention to the context. The history of the emergence of a particular nation cannot be taken as the "truth" of state formation and national formation. Caution is necessary, and an attention to history and local interests is imperative.

Finally, I have shown how the Italian ethnic "problem" has been coterminous with the Italian language problem. The new immigration and the emergence of the Northern League have led to the emergence of an idea of region as cultural unit, all but absent one hundred years ago. In the next chapters, I will examine how language, politics, ethnic identity and ideology are at play in the performance of the *Contrasto*.

3
UNDERSTANDING THE *CONTRASTO*
AND THE *POETI BERNESCANTI*

*I love all the arts that can still remind me of their origin among the common people,
and my ears are only comfortable when the singer sings as if mere speech had taken
fire, when he appears to have passed into song almost imperceptibly (William B.
Yeats, 1961, Essays 223).*

I. Introduction.

In many anthropological studies of art, there has been the unstated
assumption that oral artistic productions are "simpler" than literary
ones. This simplicity, then, has been often (and dangerously)
associated with the "simpler minds" of the common people. I will
show in this chapter that far from being simple, the *Contrasti* are a
highly complex genre. This complexity has multiple layers that include
the metric, melodic and structural systems, the use of language, and
the ideological system. Moreover, the creation of *Contrasti* is a highly
intertextual production, which extends back through more than 1,000
years of oral and literary history.[42]

Another problem with the view of the oral process as "simpler" is

---

[42] While orality and literacy have been considered two separate spheres (almost
two separate worlds), the analysis of the *Contrasti* points toward their
interrelations. This is not to negate the fundamental differences between oral
and written processes. Instead, I want to point to the coexistence of the two
systems, which both shape (through the different systems of linguistic ideologies
connected to them) the evolution of the genre of the *Contrasto*.

the idea that oral artists are some sorts of "clones," all reproducing and repeating established formulas and memorized texts (almost like folk computers, as one *poeta* once jokingly noticed). This in turn has led scholars to focus more on the process of "oral memorization" (see for example Cirese, 1988) and to ignore the creativity of the single artists, as they are shaped by their life histories, and their unique personalities.[43] Although the scope of this dissertation makes impossible an extensive treatment of each of the artists I have worked with, I will give a brief portrait of them in this chapter.

Scholars have often seen artists as asocial beings, living at the margins of society.[44] The relationship between the artist and society is much more complex than could be guessed from that assumption. In recent years, various works by anthropologists have started to doubt the idea that "creativity" belongs at the margins of a society, in the liminal (or liminoid) spaces. Smadar Lavie, Kirin Narayan and Renato Rosaldo, in their introduction to the book "Creativity/Anthropology" (1993), affirm that their intent is to reintegrate creativity into the "mainstream" of culture, freeing it from allegations of marginality. The folk artists, through performance, focus the trends that run through the larger society. They offer them to public awareness and discussion. Verbal art as "reflexive" process, proposes an image of what "things" are, of what they are not, and of what they could be.

In this chapter, I will start by giving a portrait of the *Poeti Bernescanti*. Proceeding in the same vein as chapter 2, I will then narrate the history of the *Contrasto*, which will have to be understood against the background of the Italian and Tuscan history. Following this, I will discuss the structure of the genre and how language is used in it. Finally, I will address in more depth two important elements: context and audience.

II. The Poets (A Brief Portrait).

On the 13th of June 1997, I went to see a performance by the *cantastorie* Realdo Tonti. I had found him thanks to the help of Donella Petrucci, the secretary of Communist Refoundation and friend of my father. I had

---

[43] There are notable exceptions. For example the works included in the edited volume "Anthropology/ Creativity," (1993).

[44] Kroskrity (1993:110-111) argues that contemporary Sociology and Social Sciences have often disregarded the active and creative contributions of the various individuals to the society. Their personal emotionality and life histories have been disregarded.

called him, and he told me about his performance. So I went, and my mother came with me. (From my fieldnotes, 6/18/97)

After months spent trying to contact the Poets, these were the only fieldnotes I wrote about my first encounter with Realdo and the first of his performances that I recorded. I was overwhelmed. I could not write, and trusted my camera for a record.

The poets are the light in our everyday darkness, the blessing of the Muse seeding in the hearts of the people. The poets can see through us, like through a transparent glass. And still when I called Realdo on the phone the first time, I had no idea who or what I was going to meet. When I arrived in Tobbiana, I had never seen his face. I was more than a bit uncomfortable, putting up my camera on the tripod. I always wonder what miracle makes people accept its presence. But I would hide my fear behind a stern face of professional behavior, fumbling with the lenses and the microphone, until finally Realdo came to shake my hand and we smiled to each other. He was calm as if used to being observed and studied. After all he was a performer and an "interesting subject" to tens of professors before me. Well, what I suppose he did not expect is that an anthropologist is after all an aspiring member of your family. An anthropologist will not stop after videotaping or interviewing, but will try to become part of your life.

Realdo is well described by his name ('King Aldo'), regal. He could have been a king of ancient times, a tall and big man, with a powerful voice. He is also a kind person, down to earth and ready to concede a benevolent smile. I was soon captivated by his continuous efforts at introspection, his frequent reflections on the self, and the incredible depth of his mind. And then his shying away from any imposition of that depth with his friends makes him so beloved by many.

Realdo Tonti is a man in his sixties. He was born and lives in Agliana, a small town in the province of Pistoia, with his wife Livia and one of their daughters. He worked most of his life as a factory worker, in the textile industries of Prato. When I first met him, he was still working, although he is now retired. As an artist, Realdo has a rare versatility, and he is known both as a *poeta* and as a *Cantastorie* (Storysinger). Today he is one of only two poets left in the province of Pistoia (the other is Nello Casati[45]). Realdo performed as a

---

[45] I remember the first time I met Nello, that after shaking my hand he told me: "Here is the hand, soft and pale, of a person that works with her mind." His hands by contrast were callous and deformed by a life of hard work on the land. Yes, but his mind has wings that mine will never have.

Cantastorie since he was a young man, but dedicated himself to singing *Contrasti* only relatively late, toward the end of the 1970s. He has sung with several poets, inside and outside Tuscany, and he is today quite renown. For the past decade, he often sang together with the poet Altamante Logli. In the last two years, he has been singing more often with two other young poets, Gianni Ciolli and Gabriele Ara.

Altamante Logli is a seventy-eight year old man with the energy of a child, and sometimes a temper to match. He is a short man with small penetrating eyes, and a smile that makes you wonder if he is really fooling you about something; a little man, with a heart as big as the world. I could not help but love him at first sight. Altamante is like an adopted grandfather for the group of young people who follow him in all his performances, and soon for me too. Good natured and mellow, he becomes a true tiger on the stage, a poet with a fast and aggressive tongue that can give quite a bit of trouble to any adversary.

Altamante lives in Scandicci, in the province of Florence, together with his wife Bruna, his daughter and her husband, and one of his grandchildren. He was born in 1921 in Luicciana, a small village on the Pistoiese Mountains. Since he was a small child, he worked as a shepherd, and later as a lumberjack. After World War II, he started working as a factory worker in the Rex industries, producing large home appliances.

During his long career (since the 1930s), Altamante sang together with some of the most illustrious poets of this century, like Gino Ceccherini, Elio Piccardi, and Mario Andreini. But his lifetime companion was Florio Londi, an older and exquisite poet, who unfortunately died in the summer of 1997 (he had retired from singing before I started my research). Altamante is still very active today. He performs with Realdo Tonti, but also with Gianni Ciolli, with the actor Carlo Monni, and occasionally with another young beginner, Ettore Del Bene.

Of the many other poets I have met or whose performances I had the opportunity to listen to during my fieldwork, I will mention just a few, whose verses and/or ideas are found in this dissertation. No less important are those that I, due to the limits of this text, will have to forego mentioning. Two young poets, Gabriele Ara and Gianni Ciolli started performing *Contrasti* (on stage) during the summer of 1997. Because of this, I had the occasion to see their ability change and progress, and their poetic style evolve, through the next two years. They are today, to the best of my knowledge, the only two poets active in the province of Prato. In contrast with the previous generations of poets – who were illiterate or had received only basic schooling – these young beginners have a higher than average level of school education.

Gabriele Ara, a man in his thirties from Prato, although at the beginning of his career as a *Poeta Bernescante*, has considerable experience as a performer, street artist and theater actor. He is an artist with a sweet voice and a vast knowledge of artistic genres. He often intersperses the singing of *Contrasti* with other songs, including contemporary popular ones and older folk texts. Gabriele has studied philosophy at the University of Florence. Together with his wife, Siliana Fedi, he has formed the folk music group "Octava Rima."

Gianni Ciolli is the youngest of the poets, still in his twenties. He graduated in mathematics and is now pursuing a post-graduate degree. Ciolli started singing at the beginning of the 1990s,[46] after becoming fascinated by a poetic performance. He exercised improvising verses in private, among friends, almost as a game. In the summer of 1997, the great occasion came for him when he had to substitute for an absent poet, and "walked" the stage together with Realdo Tonti. Since then, his performances have multiplied quickly, and from the position of "disciple" he is now becoming a stable companion to Realdo.

Finally, I want to mention two poets from the province of Grosseto, in Southwestern Tuscany, who I had several occasions to record, since they often travel to Northeastern Tuscany to perform. They are Elidio Benelli and his young "disciple," Liliana Tamberi. Liliana is the only female poet I have met. She is also a rock and pop singer, whose strong deep voice captivates the audience. Elidio is a famous older poet (born in 1921), with a perfect rhyme. He is a particularly quiet and suave person.

III. History of the *Contrasto*.

The form of the *Contrasto* as it is today is supposed to have existed since the fourteenth century.[47] This kind of poetry was then widely present in the repertoires of minstrels, bards, storysingers and other itinerant artists. Similar forms of verbal duels have also existed throughout the millennium in Tuscany and in other parts of Europe.

---

[46] Although his interest in other kinds of written poetry dates much further back in time, since his high school years.

[47] I rely here only on written sources, which testify to the presence of a correspondent oral tradition.

Traditions of verbal dueling, sung poetry, or improvised poetry, often with political overtones, are present throughout the Mediterranean. Examples are Bedouin poetry (Abu-Lughod, 1986), Greek and Southern Italian lamentations for funerals (Caraveli, 1986), and Yemenite poetry (Caton, 1990). In Latin America there are forms similar to the *Contrasto*, of Spanish origin (Chechi, 1997:13). In this sense, the *Contrasto* can be seen as belonging to a Mediterranean cultural area.[48]

Compositions in the form of a "dispute" or "contrast" were quite common in the Middle Ages. Documents attesting to the presence of forms of verbal dueling between two "figures" or over a theme, are found in Italy since about 1090, when we have a document where the Provencal poet Rambaldo of Vaquerais, writes a Contrast between a knight and a woman (Migliorini, 1975:5). Among the themes were religious ones like "Christ and Satan," philosophical kind of *disputatio*, and others that are similar to themes still performed today, like "The Dead and the Living," or "Mother and Daughter." Particularly common in this period were the "Love Contrasts," namely arguments among lovers (either wanted or unrequited) (see also Franceschini, 1983).

There are different theories regarding the origins and formation of the "octet," a stanza including 8 verses in hendecasyllables,[49] that follows the structure ABABABCC (Tuscan Octet) or alternatively ABABABAB (Sicilian Octet). The Tuscan octet appears for the first time in a written text, used by the poet Giovanni Boccaccio in the *Filoloco*, about 1336, and in the *Filostrato*, dated 1335. According to Guglielmo Gorni (1978:88-89), Boccaccio created the octet by modifying a similar metric form that had been used by Cino Da Pistoia. Thus Gorni theorizes a completely Tuscan origin (Boccaccio and Cino were Tuscans). On the other side Aurelio Roncaglia (1952) thinks that the octet originated in France and was then brought to Italy during the French domination, to be finally acquired by Boccaccio (Gorni, 1978:84). Others, like Alessandro D'Ancona and Pio Rajna, hypothesized an older origin of the Octet among the

---

[48] It is interesting to note that themes similar to those discussed in the *Contrasto* have been found in archeological documents in Babylon and Sumer (Chechi, 1997:54).

[49] Concerning the hendecasyllable, it seems that its presence is attested in the Mediterranean (Greek) area since the VI-VII century BC. According to Chechi (1997:9; also page 35-36), it was used at that time by Sappho.

Italian popular strata and in the context of the religious or troubadour compositions,[50] to be witnessed in the presence of similar metric forms at least since Dante's time.

It is indeed notable how much attention Italian scholars have given to trying to identify the origins of the Octet, and in particular, to try to establish if it originated in Italy or in France. Of course the question that interests me is why it is so important to know about the origins of the Octet, and what is at stake in accepting one theory or the other? This in fact can lead to uncovering linguistic ideologies shaping the scholastic enterprise. I will come back to this in chapter 7.

The *Contrasto* is attested to have existed in Tuscany since the fourteenth century. In this period Antonio Pucci was active, leaving us several written *Contrasti*. A particularly important document is the *Trattato de li Contrasti* (Treatise of the Contrasts) written by Gidino da Sommacampagna around 1381-84. Here we find a description of the genre that could largely apply to the contemporary forms as well. This description specifies that the *Contrasto* must be done by two poets defending different positions, alternating one stanza each, such stanza being either an Octet or Sextet in hendecasyllables, with the first six verses alternating and the last two ending in a different rhyme (see also Franceschini, 1983:22-23).

From the fifteenth century the figure of the poet who "sings while improvising" starts to distinguish itself from the other kinds of performers (like minstrels and storysingers). Interesting in this regard is the *Certame Coronario*, from the 22nd of October 1441, where 8 poets dispute the theme of "true friendship" (Migliorini, 1975:18). In this case in fact we can deduce that the poets were improvising, or that at least the idea of poets improvising was present. The name *Poeti Bernescanti* (lit. "poets of Berni's style") is derived from the name of the Tuscan writer and poet Francesco Berni, who became quite renown in the seventeenth century for his "burlesque and satiric compositions" (Franceschini, 1983:30). In the seventeenth century the poets began to "chain" the octets, so that the first verse of an octet rhymes with the last verse of the preceding octet.

It is common for the *Poeti Bernescanti* to know and use a repertoire of epic poems, including not only the major ones, like the *Orlando Furioso* by Petrarca, or the *Aeneid* of Virgilius, but also less known operas. Among them are the *Orlando Innamorato* by Boiardo, the

---

[50] In this case various regions have been alternatively proposed, especially Tuscany and Sicily, as the "motherland" of the Octet.

Morgante by Pulci, published in 1482-83 (Migliorini, 1975:23) and the *Malmantile Riacquistato* by Lorenzo Lippi (a burlesque poem) published in 1676 (Migliorini, 1975:50).

In this century, the *Contrasto* became more and more used in markets and public places. Then, with the disappearance of the daily markets, it tended to become a pure performance done on stage for entertainment purposes. As such, it came to be perceived more as a form of art than as a form of interaction that could be used by anybody. At the same time, it is done by fewer and fewer people, who become "specialists" of the art.

Finally, I want to mention the presence of women among the poets. Women performers were common until the beginning of the twentieth century. Female poets were met by the first scholars and travelers who gathered *Contrasti*. Among them Montaigne, who met the peasant poet Divizia, and Tommaseo, who left us some of the texts created by Beatrice Di Pian Degli Ontani. From the beginning of this century, though, the number of female *poeti* diminished drastically. Today there are only few of them left. These changes would merit a separate study in themselves.

IV. Metric and Melodic Structure.

The *Contrasti* are formed by a series of chained octets. The octet can be taken as a recognizable unit, or as a turn in a poetical conversation, defined by its internal structure as well as by the melody. Each turn has a certain length that usually varies between 30 seconds to more than one minute. Each octet is composed of eight verses of 11 syllables (hendecasyllable[51]) (example 1, line 1). The first six have a *rima alternata*, "alternating rhyme" (ABABAB, see example 1, line 1-6) the last two have a *rima baciata*, "coupled rhyme" (CC, see example 1, lines 7-8).

The rhyming part starts from the syllable on which the last stress of the verse falls. The octets are chained; the ending rhyme of the first has to be the same as the beginning rhyme of the next.

---

[51] Although not all the verses respect this rule, most of them are indeed hendecasyllables. The number of syllables in each verse can be modified by the way it is performed. The melody, for example, allows a multiplication or reduction of the number of syllables through pausing, division of the diphthongs, elision, or melodic prolongation of vowels.

(1)

(Realdo Tonti)

    1 / 2 / 3 / 4 / 5 / 6 / 7 / 8 / 9 / 10 / 11

1-A *C'é/ le/ bel/ lez/ ze/ ve/ di/ le/ piú/ ra/re*
     There are the beauties, you see, the most rare

2-B *o quella l' é la tera degli amori*
     oh, that is the land of loves

3-A *doe si coltivano cose-e molto rare*
     where the rarest things are cultivated

4-B *o specialmente delle rose e fiori*
     and especially roses and flowers

5-A *o li non avrai delusioni amare*
     oh there you will not have bitter delusions

6-B *o dove che si incontrano gli amori*
     where loves are encountered

7-C *invece te che abiti a Scandicci*
     instead you, living in Scandicci

8-C *e tu ti trovi sempre ne pasticci.*
     you always find yourself in a mess.

The coupled rhyme signals the other poet that his turn has arrived. Notice, in example 2 below, how Gabriele Ara begins by using the same rhyme "left" by Realdo Tonti in his last verse (INI). Here, the choice of the rhyme is a delicate matter. "Difficult" rhymes will spell sure trouble for any poet except the most skillful ones. The concatenation of the rhyme makes each of them answer to the preceding one and creates the need for the following one.

(2)

Octet 1 (Realdo Tonti)

C 8 *gli stessi ladroni pigliavano 'kattrini*
     the same big thieves were taking the money

Octet 2 (Gabriele Ara)

C 9 *E ora fa i patti con quegli assassini*
     and now you make accords with those assassins

The closure of the octet, from the stand point of meaning, is given in the last two verses, where usually the poet makes his most important point, at the same time challenging the other poet to answer. The special significance of the last two verses is underlined by the increased response of the audience (laughter and/or applause). Although the audience can laugh throughout the octet, it is at the last two verses that the laughing increases. At this point, also, the audience may applaud.[52] Applause is a strong sign of agreement and enjoyment. In the last two verses we often find the crudest remarks and insults (see example 2 above), and frequent switches to an informal register. These too tend to result in a laughing response from the audience. Thus, here the cleverness of the poet is proportionally related to the outrageousness of the verbal attack.

The melody as well tells when a turn is about to finish. In melodic terms, the eight verses can be divided in two sections. The melody in the first four verses is repeated in the second four verses. This division also reflects a division in the development of the theme. In the first four verses, the Poet usually "answers" to the preceding octet. In the second four verses, he develops his own argument. In general, the tempo in the second four verses is more sustained and quicker than in the first four verses, drawing naturally toward the closure.[53]

If we consider the two blocks of the octet, we can also notice acceleration from the first to the third verse (and from the 5th to the 7th) with a deceleration or dilatation in the 4th (and 8th) verse. According to the ethnomusicologist Maurizio Agamennone: "The acceleration of the verses ... coincides with the elaboration of the sense and growth in the narrative (and emotional) tension, which distend themselves in the partial resolution of the sense and in the melodic semi-cadence of the 4th verse. The contraction of the tempo increasingly stringent in the verses 5th to 8th favors the fluidity of the expression and leads directly to the conclusion. The segmentation of the tempo of the octet coincides thus with a crescendo of the

---

[52] Indeed the lack of laughing here is in some way a signal of failure to entertain or obtain an agreement from the audience. This is complicated by the fact that the Poet may be doing the part disliked by the audience. In this case laughter is a sign of great success, while its absence is acceptable.

[53] Variations are present and depend on the individual style of the artist, from the difficulty of the theme or of the rhyme, as well as from other contextual factors. Moreover, regional differences are detectable. The rhythm changes, becoming faster, as the poets get more and more absorbed in dueling, especially when it gets "rougher." Gianni Ciolli, a young "apprentice" Poet, called my attention to the fact that changes in the length of the verses are meaningful and can be analyzed.

expressive pathos whose apex is the closing in the coupled rhyme with which the poet leads his exhibition to an end" (Agamennone 1988:24).

The melodic expansions are also significant. The longest expansion usually happens at the end of the first verse. Here, it may also have the function of giving the poet some time to recollect his thoughts and find the right rhyme. Inside each verse, the melodic expansions usually follow the metric (syllables, accenting), with longer or vibrating sounds, sometimes dividing syllables to follow the rule of having eleven of them in each verse. The major melodic expansion usually falls between the next to the last and the last syllable.

V. Language in the *Contrasto*.

The language use of the poets is quite complex. It includes Italian as well as the varieties of the Tuscan dialect. There is mixing of codes and registers, with various degrees of formality, plus the use of the poetic variant of Italian. As Fabrizio Franceschini notices: "The aulic register, linked to the higher literary tradition, has a notable importance. ... The other fundamental [stylistic] register is the *Berni*'s one in a strict sense, linked to the comic-realistic and satiric tradition" (1983:63; my translation). Other characteristics of the poets' use of language include the deployment of archaisms and particularities that can be considered as belonging to the genre. These include particular formulas and insertions of special lexical elements.[54] Moreover, the language includes an extended use of metaphors, similitude, and allusions. Clemente *et al.* write:

> It must be remembered that Tuscan folk poetry, in its oral tradition, is never properly in dialect. ... The blending of dialectal and literary elements originates at times from the presence of some written archetype but, more generally, from elements typical of the Tuscan linguistic situation: the absence of bilingualism, and thus the copresence of only one inclusive codex of elements e.g. more or less rural, etc. We just need to think of the variability of the usage of the full or truncated infinitive (*andare* [to go] and *andà* [to go]), of the strong or weak participle (*porto*

---

[54] Franceschini again notices that, "In accordance with the thematic of the *Contrasti*, sectorial languages must be utilized, like the political-trade unionist one, the sport one, the scientific one, etc., while the characterizations of the personages themselves involves particular lexical and linguistic choices" (1983:63; my translation).

[carried] and *portato* [carried]), of the *un/non* [not], etc., to the intrusion of Florentine re-determinative pronouns even in text coming from elsewhere, to understand how folk poetry draws from a conspicuous number of variants. These are notably flattened in their diatopic, stylistic and sociolinguistic character, to facilitate the composition, especially in reference to the respect for the metrics (Clemente, Fresta and Giannelli, 1982:73, my translation; italics in the original).

The poetic language of the *Contrasto* thus allows a high degree of semantic and grammatical creativity. The language of this genre disparages and ignores the common rules governing grammar and phrase formation in Italian. The linguist Luciano Giannelli calls it "a-grammatical" and "polymorphic" (Giannelli 1988:48-50). The prominence given to the sound, to the internal organization of the genre itself against the constraints of grammar, is striking. Even the semantic use is particular. The poet can create new words whose semantic meaning is null and at the same time reconstructed by the listeners, often through assonance of meaning (we will come back to this again in chapter 4). Giannelli concludes that

> An element of consistent presence in the production of the octets is that of the infringement of the rules of everyday language. ... The motivation is again to be looked for essentially in exigencies of the versification. ... This does not exclude that these elements end up corresponding also to a character proper to the genre, and to satisfy again the condition of autonomy of the poetic language indicated by Jacobson (1988:58; my translation).[55]

In chapter 2, I discussed how an Italian language was selected, standardized and imposed in the new Italian State after the national unification. Contrary to the nationalistic desire for "one, standardized, tongue," the poets operate a sort of "de-standardization" of language. Their "tongues" multiply.[56] They continuously create new words, change them, or recover ancient words that have lost their meaning

---

[55] Still, although the poets, in searching for the right rhyme, may at times sacrifice meaning in favor of the poetic function, this is always valued less positively than the ability to follow both the poetic and the referential functions.

[56] As proper for the ancient prophetess, the Sybil, inspired by the Gods. In fact the poets also, as I will show better in chapter 4 and chapter 7, see themselves has inspired by the Goddesses, the Muses.

over the ages, to then attribute to them new meanings. Standardizations are politically unstable operations. As Silverstein writes: "Linguistic practice ... under standardization is an essentially contested order of sociocultural reality" (2000:124). Thus the *Contrasti* can be seen as one of the forces operating toward this destabilization or, in Bakhtin's term, as centrifugal forces.

According to Bakhtin, centrifugal and centripetal forces are operating in society, whose conflict can never be resolved. Alessandro Duranti describes how "the centripetal forces include the political and institutional forces that try to impose a variety or code over others. ... The centrifugal forces instead push speakers away from a common center and toward differentiation" (1997:76). To these is to be reconnected the notion of heteroglossia, or the many voices in a person's speech, that represent "the co-existence of socio-ideological contradictions between the present and the past, between differing epochs of the past, between different socio-ideological groups in the present, between tendencies, schools, circles and so forth" (Bakhtin, 1981:291).

Poetry is indeed a centrifugal force. According to the poets, the "poetic license" overrides the need for using the standard or even expressing themselves through a "commonly understood" language.[57] In a certain way, it is up to their audience to learn, to become knowledgeable enough to be able to understand them. This prospective effectively overturns the dominant idea that language use should be first of all intended to make yourself understood. It also overrides the necessity of a "standard." In this case, the poets' linguistic ideologies propose their own rules, that may be at odds with those accepted in the national, institutionally upheld, view of "good language".

The language of the *Contrasto* negates the "standard," it negates language as a pure means of communication. The poets often invoke the Muses at the beginning of their performance. As I will discuss again in the next chapters, through this invocation the poets construct language as sacred and magic. Through the invocation of the poetic license, at the same time, they construct language as free from rules. They deploy to its maximum the flexibility of language, its capacity to still carry meaning when flexed, replenished with external elements, filled with threads of meaning in verses that only respond to each

---

[57] I will discuss this further in chapter 7.

other after an unpredictable numbers of turns. The poet thus makes manifest and brings to its extremes the heteroglossia present in language.

The poets reinvent language in song, and at the same time, they reinvent the poetic language itself. I will come back to this in chapter 7, when I will discuss the ways in which the poets redefine art itself, by constructing an "ars poetica" that is at the same time an upholding and a negation of "Art" as defined by the Italian nation state and imposed through its educational institutions. The poets in the end show to their public that language, poetry and art are something you can play with, something that "ain't necessarily so."

VI. Context.

VI. a. The Relevance of the Study of Context.

To understand verbal art performances, it becomes necessary to go past the analysis of a text, to the study of a culture. A central tenet of the ethnography of speaking is the fundamental place that it reserves to the study of *context*, which had been almost completely disregarded in non-ethnographic research on language. Dell Hymes affirms that: "two ... considerations will be essential – the performance as situated in a context, the performance as emergent, as unfolding or arising within that context" (1981:81). As such, context becomes a fundamental variable in the search for meaning. Again in Hymes' words: "One needs to investigate directly the use of language in contexts of situation, so as to discern patterns proper to speech activity, patterns that escape separate studies of grammar, of personality, of social structure, religion, and the like" (1974:3-4).

Among Hymes' followers, Bauman and Briggs (1990) call our attention to the connection between performance and sociocultural and political-economic contexts. Here, it is evident that the word "context" may in reality refer to a series of different things. A first distinction can be made between a micro and macro context; but far from solving the problem of definition, such a distinction complicates it. Where are the boundaries between micro and macro contexts to be found? Briggs notices that the definition of context seems to be regressing indefinitely. The number of things that can be included in it can be expanded to include practically anything. But then, he argues, the concept seems to loose heuristic value (1988:14 & fol.).

This problem had also been perceived by Gumperz (1992), who suggested substituting the study of context with the study of the "contextualization cues." In this way context is defined in the course of the communication, among the participants. It becomes a process, continuously redefined, maintained or changed by the speakers (Bauman & Briggs, 1990:68). According to Bauman & Briggs: "Contextualization involves an active process of negotiation in which participants reflexively examine the discourse as it is emerging, embedding assessments of its structure and significance in the speech itself" (1990:69).

Following this definition of context as process of "contextualization," Bauman has analyzed the contextualization of a text by other texts, or of a discourse by other discourses (1992b:140), namely "intertextuality." In his study of the internationalization of folklore (1993), he introduces the concepts of "decontextualization" and "recontextualization," thus bringing the discussion of context beyond the level of interaction, to address the influence of macro-context on meaning. Practices of decontextualization and consequent recontextualization are imposed on the oral text in the moment it is written down, and /or translated, and brought to the attention of audiences (through publication) different from the original one that the narration intended to reach. It is clear to Bauman that each of these decontextualizations and recontextualizations modifies the meaning of the text. They destroy the original context, and thus the original meaning, and build a new context, and thus a new meaning (1993:267).

This bears particular importance for my research, as I am proposing these texts to an audience very distant from the one for which they were created. Sensitive to this problem, I have tried to give as much detail as I could regarding the original context of the performances. Of course, this alleviates but cannot eliminate the issue. In writing down texts that were supposed to just disappear into thin air, I am assuming responsibility, especially toward the artists themselves. If published in Tuscany, these *Contrasti* I have gathered may some day modify the genre itself in unforeseen ways.

As Bauman talks about the nationalization and internationalization of folklore, it is evident that the context to which he refers is also a national and international one, thus stretching the notion of macro-context to its limit. At this level, the connection of verbal art to particular political and ideological discourses becomes evident. Bauman notices that folklore is thus extended: "to the construction and reconstruction of the nation-state and the international cultural order" (1993:267). We should not forget, anyway, that even at a micro-contextual level each performance of an oral text, in a way, transposes it to a new context, thus changing or modifying its meaning.

Charles Goodwin and Duranti (1992) present a notion of context as "frame," that surrounds and furnishes the key to interpret a particular event (1992:3). In this formulation, language itself becomes part of the context, meaning "the way in which talk itself both invokes context and provides context for other talk" (1992:7). Goodwin and Duranti affirm that, "Context is thus analyzed as an interactively constituted mode of praxis" (1992:9). This idea, in the study of performance, could be associated with the notion of "intertextuality."

Language and context, then, appear to be in a reflexive relation with respect to each other (Duranti, 1992c:87). Notice that this can be seen as parallel to the reflexive relation existing in a society between performance (as a form of artistic expression) and the macro-context (socio-political, etc.). In fact Duranti himself proceeds to further theorize a "dialogue" (or reflexive relationship) between words and social reality (1992c:89).

Interesting is also Lamont Lindstrom's vision, according to which "context is a field of power relations. It is not, however, a frozen field. ... People can contest the context, by evoking available alternative or competing discourses" (1992:102). This suggests that context can be negotiated and that relationships of power and resistance are inherent in context (1992:104). This implies that connected to performance there is a negotiation of truth (as interpretation of the social context) and moreover, questions of authority: who can perform? Who can tell the "truth" about context?

I need to underline that context can be seen as differing in kind, and not only in inclusiveness. For example, aside from the socio-political context, a historical context could be taken into consideration, with fundamental effects on the performance. Indeed, the performing artists are often using a traditional repertoire, and the stories they tell may refer to different historical periods. A look at history has shown recurring trends, differences among them and developing tendencies. The present cultural revivalism in Tuscany, thus, was seen as the background to the forces that concurred in the creation of the Italian nation.

VI. b. The Context of Tuscan Verbal Art Performances.

In the last century and until the 1950s, dueling poets were a common scene on the plazas and in the marketplaces of Tuscan cities and villages. They used their art to gather people, to whom then they would sell various goods. After World War II, with the disappearance of the daily markets, this "economic function" of the *Contrasto* was lost. The contexts where the *Contrasti* are most commonly performed today are public festivals and events.[58] In Tuscany today, there are festivals organized by the various district units of the parties, the traditional *Sagre*, that center in country villages, around a particular seasonal food or produce,[59] the religious festivals, organized by the parishes; and new festivals of revivalist flavor, born from the more recent attempts to recover and reinforce various traditions.[60]

Most of these festivals take place during the warmer season, and are usually done in an open area, a plaza or a large field (see figure #3). In the festival there is a restaurant, booths selling various products and books, game booths, and a stage area (see figure #4), in front of which there is an open space, where concerts, dancing, and eventually political conferences are done, together with the traditional performances. Sometimes there is a wooden dance floor. All or most of these structures can be temporarily built for the festivals (see figure #3).

The most common of the festivals are those organized by the parties of the left. The *Feste dell'Unitá*, "Festivals of Unity" in Tuscany (and in general in central Italy), are not just the feast of a political party, but a real cultural institution. After the split of the Partito Comunista Italiano, or PCI (Italian Communist Party), at the beginning of the nineties, the various local sections of the party were also split. Some of them passed to the *Partito per la Rifondazione Comunista*, or PRC (Party for the Communist Refoundation), the other stayed with the newly renamed *Partito Democratico della Sinistra*, or PDS

---

[58] Although *Contrasti* may also be performed in more private occasions, like marriages. I witnessed several spontaneous *Contrasti* among poets during dinners, often following the public performances. I never had the occasion, unfortunately, to record any of them.

[59] The most common are those for the gathering of the grapes and the production of wine, between September and November, and the gathering of chestnuts, between November and December.

[60] These are often organized by the local Chambers of commerce, or other associations. Often the funding may come from the city council.

(Democratic Party of the Left). While the PDS kept organizing "Festivals of Unity," the PRC changed the name of its feast to *Festa di Liberazione*, "Festival of Liberation."[61] Although the names changed, the people, the places and the festivals remained pretty much the same.

> *These festivals are part of the Tuscan landscape in summer, and they have been part of my life so deeply that I despair to be able to capture all of what they are in a few paragraphs. As a kid, I would wait in earnest for June, when the festivals start, to go to them with my parents. The festivals' cheap food allowed us to eat out more often, and there was music and entertainment. My parents and their friends were with us, and in the enclosed space of the festival arena, I was free to run around with the other kids. The red flag displayed made me proud of belonging to a "communist family," something not easy to feel in everyday life otherwise. My parents would explain to me the meaning of the posters showing the injustices of the capitalist system. Then we would dance to the rhythm of the ballroom music on the central floor. There were shops as well, selling crafts from distant and exotic "paradises of the working class" like Russia, China and Cuba. After I grew up, for a long time I did not go to those festivals anymore, not until.........*

Figure #3: Festival of Unity in Spedalino, July 1997.

---

[61] After the name of their main newspaper *Liberazione*, "Liberation." The Festivals of Unity also take their name from the PDS's main newspaper, *L'Unitá*, "The Unity."

The festivals have changed little in the past two decades. The most radical political accents were starting to be lost already in the eighties: there are fewer political debates, more pizzerias; more discos, fewer political shows and posters. The festivals organized by the parishes are very similar to those of the parties. The food, the games, the performances (and often even the people) are the same. The speech of the priest substitutes for the political addresses, and the location is more often in the area near the church. Both kinds of festivals are similar, because they take the model from the *sagra*, which also includes similar elements.

Figure #4: Festival of Unity in Spedalino, July 1997.
The dancing area.

For the poets, performing at the festivals means being able to adapt to any kind of distressing circumstance. The places are noisy, and the audience may be only partially seated, or just pass by, coming and going. The stage may be uncomfortably huge, too far from the audience, or absent. The lighting may leave them in darkness or shine in their face to the point of blinding them. The microphones and speakers may be old or broken, and occasionally may produce their own deafening "performance" of hissing, screeching and shrieking. Part of the art of being a poet, then, is to be able to improvise solutions to these problems.

Apart from the festivals, other events may request the presence of the poets. In recent years, the poets have been called to perform occasionally at local radio or TV stations. On two occasions they were also invited to perform for the students at the universities of Bologna and Rome. More importantly, since 1992 a yearly "gathering" of poets has been organized in the town of Ribolla, in the province of Grosseto. Here, several poets, coming from all over central Italy, can perform for an attentive, seated audience, a situation very different from the noisy chaotic flow of people in the festivals. The meeting in Ribolla is an important occasion for the poets to meet, renew old acquaintances and, sometimes, organize for further encounters.

VII. The Audience(s).

My focus on performance requires a redefinition of the role of the audience as well. The audience co-performs with the artists (Fretz, 1995:96). Rachel Fretz writes: "The narrator and listener voices interconnect in a performance much as in an animated dialogue – sometime alternating, but often overlapping" (1995:99). Thus artists and audience influence each other (and each other's performance). As Renato Rosaldo shows in his discussion of Ilongot storytelling, a narration develops through the dialogue between teller and the audience, who take the specific roles of "active interlocutors" (1986:129). Through this dialogue not only does the storytelling unfold, but its stylistic features are also created.[62] The audience not only co-constructs performance, but also co-constructs the artist, in the sense that they relinquish to him/her the power to represent them. The artists and the audience, then, stand in a reflexive relation respect to each other.[63]

The poets often address the audience directly in their singing, asking for an agreement, a judgment, or an alignment. Sometimes they engage a person in the audience in a short dialogue. The audience can also request a particular story or a particular genre of performance. They may, for example, request a sentimental song from a poet, a *Contrasto*, or a song in Tuscan or in another language. The audience also gives various kinds of feedback, including evaluations,

---

[62] Rosaldo writes: "The back-and-forth verbal play they engage in requires a skilled narrator and an adept interlocutor, both of them cultural insiders" (1986:129).

[63] This reflexivity contributes to situate the artist in a central, not marginal position in the Tuscan society.

interpretations, or "identifying responses" with respect to the characters themselves, etc. (see also Fretz, 1987:306-307) and, of course, laughter and applause. "Warmer" audiences may interact more with the poets, ask for particular songs, jokes, or themes of *Contrasti*. Sometimes they may even intervene and get on the stage to try some personal number (a song, music, some octets).

Figure #5: Performance of *poeti* in Migliana, July 1997.
Seated audience.

If we see context as "contextualization," then we see that the artist has to consider the knowledge that the audience has of the context itself (especially the macro context). Namely, the performers can assume a certain degree of knowledge from their audience. They can then deploy this "assumed knowledge" in their performance. This is well illustrated by Keith Basso's description of Apache stories, as they are connected and evoked by the saying of names of places[64] (Basso, 1988; also see Basso, 1990). This assumption is connected, as I demonstrated elsewhere (Pagliai, 1995b), to the creation of a sense of common identity.[65] As Robert Georges writes:

---

[64] In certain cases, the pronunciation of the name can actually substitute the performance of the story itself (Basso, 1990:145).

[65] I will go back to the discussion of identity and place in chapter 5.

Everything human beings say and do when they assume the contrastive, but complementary, communicative roles of narrator and listener is an integral part of the event generated by their interacting; and this includes what they say or do in terms of such identities as those rooted in their sex, age, religious affiliation, ethnicity, occupations, etc. ... For individuals involved in narrating are always much more to each other than just narrators or listeners (1981:251).

It is important to notice also that the audience is not homogeneous. There are various kinds of audiences, and each of them can have a different role with respect to the performance (Goodwin, 1986). Altamante Logli and Realdo Tonti, for example, have a group of closer "fans" that accompany them to all the performances. Many of them are young people, and they included, in 1997, some of their disciples who, by 1998, had started to perform with them. The "fans" are "experts" in the genre, and they have often helped me during my fieldwork. They guided me and directed my attention toward important elements of the *Contrasti*.

Figure #6: Audience at the Festival of Unity in Florence, July 1998.

There is then an audience who sits and listens throughout the poets' performance (see figure #5). They may include older people, who are usually well acquainted with the genre, but also younger people and children, for whom this can be the first time they are exposed to *Contrasti*. The children more often move and play around, paying little attention to the performance. Especially when the performance takes place in an open space, there are passersby who may stop and listen for a while, often standing at the borders of the area. The use of vulgarities and insults in the performance, for example, may momentarily draw in more people, as passersby stop to hear what the whole thing is about. Finally, there are people working in the nearby bars and restaurants, who usually listen as well, while attending to other activities (for example in figure #6, it is possible to notice people passing by, and other people working in the booths).

The audience can also be divided into "supporters" and "antagonists" with respect to the performance. During the *Contrasto* the audience may be polarized in favor of one of the two personages described. In a theme "Berlusconi vs. D'Alema" – Berlusconi being a right wing politician, D'Alema a left wing one – held at a Festival of Unity, for example, the audience strongly favored the poet impersonating D'Alema. They laughed and applauded much more often to his octets, than to the octets of the other poet. Finally, let's not forget that the audience can be a possible (next) narrator. For example, when more than two poets are present, there can be interaction between the poets on the stage and other poets off-stage (who are momentarily part of the audience).

I believe that in the interaction between the artists and the audience(s) as co-performers, and in the multiple contexts in which they are embedded, lies an important key to understanding the social impact of verbal art. Not only is the performance created in the interaction between speaker and listeners, but also, through this interaction, a certain social reality is upheld or criticized, a social organization can be legitimated or delegitimized.

VIII. Conclusion.

In this chapter I have discussed the elements that define the genre of the *Contrasto*. In doing so, I have touched some of the parts that compose Hymes' SPEAKING model, and which are at the base of an ethnographic approach to language. These elements included the setting or context; the participants, namely the performers and their audience; the norms, namely the structure itself of the *Contrasto*; and finally the instrumentality, which in this case I saw as the particular use of language. As a further element, I have added a brief history of the genre, as I believe it can shed light on its present significance. At this point, the readers should have a clear perception of the complexity of the genre, and a portrait of the artists, the *Poeti Bernescanti*.

Next, to breathe life into the portrait, I pass to the analysis of the *Contrasti* themselves. I will start, in chapter 4, from a discussion of the

Contrasti of political argument. As I proceed in the analysis, it will become more and more clear that there is a connection between this art form and the regional and national political spheres. Such a connection, I believe, will in turn justify the amount of space that I have dedicated in describing the Italian historical, ethnic, political and linguistic situation.

4
IN RHYME I WILL ANSWER YOU:
THE POETICAL CONSTRUCTION OF POLITICS[66]

A work of art is authentic or true not by virtue of its content (i.e., the "correct" representation of social conditions), nor by its "pure" form, but by the content having become form. ... The truth of art lies in its power to break the monopoly of established reality (i.e., of those who establish it) to define what is real. (Herbert Marcuse, 1978:9)

I. Introduction.

Verbal art can be a political instrument, an instrument of legitimization or de-legitimization, of established norms or power groups. It can shape the way of thinking of the communities where it is produced and performed. Language, in verbal art, can "embody alternate models of the social world" (Gal, 1989:349). In the *Contrasto*, we find a dramatic representation of ideological and political divisions present in Tuscan society. The *Contrasto* also upholds or attacks political relationships and political views, thus contributing to defining and constructing the political sphere, and furnishing a dialectical approach to the definition of social realities. At the same time, the complex structure of the genre protects the artists by creating for

---

[66] A previous version of this chapter, with the title "In Rhyme I Will Answer You: Verbal Fights and the Poetical Construction of Politics in the Tuscan Contrasto," was published in the Proceedings of the Seventh Annual Symposium About Language and Society-Austin. Texas Linguistic Forum 43, 2000:153-163.

them a "poetic space of freedom" where they can express their ideas.

There is a long-standing debate in the study of political oratory, regarding the use of formal language. This debate originated in Maurice Bloch's discussion of the use of formal language to uphold the power structure present in a society (1975). Bloch's idea has been lately revisited and partially criticized by Judith Irvine (1979) and Duranti (1994). In the course of this chapter, I will come back to that discussion, to show how my data contradict Bloch's theory and furnish a confirmation of Irvine's and Duranti's ideas.

To understand verbal art as political action, we have to step out of the Western notion that sees the artist as marginalized in society, and art as a contingent, separate realm abstracted from politics. Studies like Caton's work with Yemenite poets (1990), or Alton L. Becker's work (1979) on Javanese Shadow Theater (Wayang), have shown that the artists can become a means of expression of voices and trends present in the community itself, and can work to reinforce or oppose these trends. A. L. Becker writes that in the "national elections the most powerful public statements against the government were done by dalangs [the actors in Javanese Shadow Theater], using just this technique" (1979:228). In a similar vein Caton writes: "It is significant that the epithet 'able to solve problems' extends to the conception of the poet, who is an analyzer and solver of pressing issues" (1990:246).

In the Tuscan culture, the artists take a central place. They are not at the margins of the cultural space. As such, they assume a "responsibility" in their performances, which is not just aesthetic, but moral and political.[67] This in turn exposes the artists as possible political targets, especially in the case that s/he expresses ideas that "offend" the established power in the society.

II. The *Contrasto* as a Political Genre: A Few Historical Notes.

Political themes are traditionally among the most common group of topics in the *Contrasto*. I recorded a large number of them. Similar *Contrasti* have been collected and published by other authors[68] as well, sometimes by the poets themselves.[69] Their diffusion can be

---

[67] Here I refer to Hymes' and Bauman's definitions of performance as "responsibility" (See Hymes 1981:11).

[68] See for example Bencistá, 1990. Also, Franceschini, 1983.

[69] See for example the book edited by Bencistá (1994). This includes texts by the

connected to the general political involvement of the poets themselves. The poets have often been fervent political activists and political speakers. This is attested both in the work of other scholars and emerges in my fieldwork. We learn, for example, from Pietro Clemente (1988:14) that he found handwritten *Contrasti* among documents regarding the participation of the sharecropping peasants in the social unrest after the Second World War. Franceschini writes that the *Contrasto*:

> Follows the development of the political movements between the end of the nineteenth century and the period after World War II, at times expressing the levels of the 'common sense' solidified among the popular strata, at times becoming itself an active instrument in the formation of the collective orientations. In the phase of the organization of the Leagues and of the peasant movements, the greatest Tuscan improvisers are League-leaders and agitators who make poetical ability a powerful instrument of ideal conquest and of organization (1988:45; my translation).

This tradition probably goes back further than it is possible to prove given the lack of documentation. Poems in octets that expressed the voice of the poor or destitute have been found, which can be dated to centuries ago.[70] Indeed, as the poets are attuned to and in continuous dialogue with their audiences and communities, poetry can be a key to understanding the way Tuscan people feel toward the events in the Italian and International political spheres.

An example is the *Contrasto* between "Peasant and Land-owner,"[71] a well known and often quoted theme, one of those that belong to the general folk tradition and are often learned as well as improvised. This *Contrasto* is an interesting rendering of some of the basic ideas derived from the Marxist *Manifesto*, which imbued the ideology of the Italian Communist Party. In regard to this Clemente writes: "The *Contrasto*

---

poets L. Banchi, E. Benelli, F. Benelli, R. Benigni, V. Cai, G. Ceccherini, E. Collodi, A. Giuntini, N. Grassi, N. Landi, A. Logli, F. Londi, N. Masi, B. Mastacchini, A. Melani, A. Puleri, E. Romanelli, S. Rubegni, L. Staccioli, L. Tamberi, R. Tonti, D. Turini, L. Vietti. Also, the poet Mauro Chechi's book, 1997: *Come si Improvvisa Cantando (Storia e Tecnica sull'Uso di Versi e Rime)*.

[70] A "*Contrasto* between the poor and the rich" has been found dated in the XVII century (see Franceschini, 1983:76).

[71] With some variations, including the more recent "factory worker vs. owner."

presents ideological ambiguities which are then progressively overcome until the poetry conveys explicit affirmative statements" (1988:14; my translation). Del Giudice writes about it: "Since it is a vehicle of *folk* expression, it is not surprising that it is this class that is vindicated, that is, the poor over the rich, the simple over the sophisticated, the *contadino* [peasant] over the *padrone* [owner]" (1995:75-76; italics in the original).

An indirect proof of the political importance of the *Contrasto* is given by the censoring of the poets during the fascist period. Under that tyrannical regime, the poets were controlled and often silenced.[72] Altamante Logli, who lived many of these events in first person, remembers the verses with which the famous poet Gino Ceccherini described the situation under fascism:[73]

> *e alla bocca ci s'avea i sigilli*
> and our mouths had seals
> *per via di ella razza poo bona*
> because of that bad sort of people [the fascists]

The political themes in particular where prohibited, or allowed only under the surveillance of the fascist authority, with the direct goal of exalting the works of fascism. To this end, the "dueling" part of the *Contrasto* was eliminated and substituted instead with series of celebrative octets sung by only one poet. As Franceschini notices, in this imposed monologic form the *Contrasto* loses the capacity to address "the real material and cultural contradictions of a society" (1983:47; my translation).

After the fall of fascism, the poets became associated with the parties of the left, especially the Italian Communist Party. Even in times of democracy, though, the poets occasionally experienced persecution by the police, especially for their political views and their anticlerical stances. For example, Altamante Logli narrates that:[74]

---

[72] Sometimes they were ostracized or threatened, but more often they retired into a voluntary silence.

[73] Quoted from an interview I did with Altamante Logli, in his home in Scandicci (Firenze), on 11/9/97 (code: I 1-A-222). My translation. See also Appendix D.

[74] Quoted from an interview with the poet, in his home in Scandicci (Firenze), on 11/9/97 (code: I 1-B-302). My translation. See also Appendix D.

The cold war came to pass, you understand, there was a period when the Communists were tailed, I mean, these leftist people, right? [...] Yes, that's it, we went through maybe fifteen years, I don't know, democracy was really a regime, right? We were on the brink, by God! You know? We were almost on the brink of the time of the colonels, like in Spain, like it happened in Greece, like at the time there was- Good Lord! In the world there were coups d'état. They tried to do it here too. Because for history, you know, I have a good memory. At every Festival of Unity there were policemen, three or four policemen standing there looking at you. And that really bothered me. [...] The [poet Vasco] Cai of Pisa went on for a long time to refuse- he did not want tape recorders in the rooms. He did not want them because, as he used to say, "When we go away from here, no one knows what has been said.[75]

The Festivals of Unity became a context where the poets performed increasingly often. By the seventies, they had become the most prominent places where *Contrasti* could be heard. In the period of the cold war, common topics of the *Contrasto* included duels between "United States and Russia," or "The West vs. the East." These highlighted the main differences between the two political/economic systems, but also defended or criticized actions taken by these two governments especially in the international arena such as in a *Contrasto* between "Vietnamese and American."

III. Analysis of a *Contrasto* of Political Argument.
To answer the question of how are political relationships and political views defined, upheld and/or attacked in the *Contrasti*, I will analyze a *Contrasto* between two political figures, "D'Alema and Bertinotti."

III. a. Context and Development of the Topic.
At the time of this performance D'Alema – impersonated by the poet Realdo Tonti – was the secretary of the Democratic Party of the Left (PDS). Bertinotti – impersonated by the poet Gabriele Ara – was the secretary of the Party for the Communist Refoundation (PRC). This *Contrasto* can be considered part of a series of similar ones very

---

[75] This in turn was reflected in the attitudes (past and present) of the poets toward the scholars. Because of this distrust, reinforced at times by a lack of clarity in the respective agendas between poets and researchers, I had to gain the trust of the poets myself.

common in recent years, and that pit against each other famous figures of the Italian political scene. These include those between "the Communist party and the Democratic Christian party," "Berlusconi vs. D'Alema," or similar dyads. The recent split in the Italian left has been reflected in innumerable duels between the two parties of the left, etc.

This *Contrasto* is more that 18 minutes long, and spans over 23 octets.[76] It is part of a series of *Contrasti* sung by Tonti and Ara during a performance at the *Festa di Liberazione,* "Festival of Liberation" in Viaccia (see figure #7).[77] The performance itself lasted for more than three hours.

Figure #7: Performance in Viaccia.

After discussing who is taking each part in the first octets, in the fourth octet (see schema #2) Ara/Bertinotti launches his first attack to Tonti/D'Alema. He contests the decisions taken by D'Alema in the government, accusing him of having deluded the governmental coalition of the left, by following the interests and suggestions of the

---

[76] See Appendix D for a full transcription of this *Contrasto*.

[77] In the province of Prato, Italy, 5th of September 1998.

right. Tonti answers in a conciliatory tone. He avoids offences and instead stresses the inevitability of his decisions and the need for the parties of the left to recover harmony and work together co-operatively. From the beginning, the poets refer to events and figures of the present political situation in Italy, showing that they are deeply knowledgeable and attuned to what happens in the political sphere. Indeed, for a poet to be able to develop any topic he must be always aware, informed on the important issues in the larger society, and able to develop opinions about them.

Schema #2: *Contrasto* **"D'Alema Vs. Bertinotti."**

Argument	Octet	Point made by the poet
Opening	1-4	The poets choose their roles.
I	4,6,8	Bertinotti contests D'Alema's decisions in the government.
	5,7,9	D'Alema defends himself: the decisions were unavoidable and the left should try to remain united.
II	10, 12	Bertinotti: PDS abandoned the communist flag.
	11, 13	D'Alema explains the meaning of the new flag.
	14	Bertinotti recalls the history of struggles that the flag symbolizes.
	15	D'Alema argues that struggle did not change things.
	16	Bertinotti accuses PDS of betrayal of the ideals.
	17	D'Alema argues that the changes were necessary, and that there was no betrayal.
	18	Bertinotti concludes that people do not care anymore (for politics) and the government is degraded.
Out of Theme	19,20	Both poets elaborate on the metaphor of the "processed meat"
III	21	D'Alema says that the PRC is internally divided.
	22	Bertinotti accepts that is a problem.
Closing	23	The poets alternate producing one verse each. They reaffirm their initial positions.

Figure #8: The poets Realdo Tonti (left) and Gabriele Ara (right).

Starting from the 10th octet (see schema #2), there is a shift in the discussion of the argument. Ara/Bertinotti brings a new attack to Tonti/D'Alema, accusing him of having lost sight of the goals of communism, and not being a communist anymore. Tonti defends himself by arguing that although the PDS has changed, they are still communists. This argument is quite complex. First, the poets discuss the change of the name and flag (the communist symbols) done by the PDS. Then Ara recalls the history of struggles that those symbols stood for, and the discussion takes an historical turn. At the closing of the 18th octet, Ara accuses Tonti of putting a "mortadella" in the government. The metaphor of the "processed meat in the government" is then carried on for the next two octets (see schema #2), while the poets momentarily lose the "theme line." In the 21st octet, Tonti/D'Alema "re-enters" the topic and this time he attacks Ara by recalling the internal divisions of his party. Ara accepts the criticism and the poets conclude the *Contrasto* with the 23rd octet, reaffirming their different positions.

From the previous synopsis, it is clear that Ara/Bertinotti attacks Tonti/D'Alema much more than vice-versa. To understand this difference we need to consider the context, a Festival of Liberation.

Here Ara, impersonating the secretary of their party, can assume to have the audience already on his side. He can bring attacks that are more direct without the risk of angering them. Tonti is in a more difficult position, impersonating the secretary of the PDS, given the occasionally tense relationship between the two parties of the left. Gabriele Ara's argument reinforces the view of right and wrong political actions and practices held and shared by the audience, and contributes to that sharing. He reinforces their view of reality. More interesting is to understand what Tonti is achieving. Why should the audience enjoy exposing themselves to reasoning that goes against their views?

Why should people make things difficult for themselves? It is a question that has no answer in a "function dominated" anthropological masterplan. Bakhtin spoke of centrifugal forces. But what does that really mean in term of each and every one of us? A bodily need to get out of the uncomfortable clothing of a set culture, or reality, or institution, or maybe hegemony? A temptation to freedom? But then we could ask: who has an interest in avoiding disagreement? Who has an interest in making us believe that all people want is to avoid disagreement? This "simplification" of people is probably one of the main problems of the social sciences. There is an unstated assumption that people like to think "easy," to avoid "difficulties." But we just need to raise our noses from our books and look around, to notice how people like building complexity in their lives. Why then do "we" need to assume a human propensity for "simplicity," for "non contradictory" statements? Why do "we" assume that people cannot "tolerate" or live through contradictions, and even appreciate them?

III. b. Articulating the Split of the Italian Communist Party.

I will now furnish an in-depth analysis of three octets (15-17). As we go through them, remember that this poetry is improvised, so the poets build the argumentation as they proceed. In octet 15, Tonti/D'Alema, defending himself from allegations of having renounced communism, steps momentarily out of the sequence of reciprocal attacks,[78] to address the audience, and possibly obtain their alignment on his positions: [79]

---

[78] This kind of strategy in storytelling has also been analyzed by Goodwin, 1990:244.

[79] For the transcription notation, see Appendix A.

(Octet 15) Tonti/D'Alema

A 1   *O quando si cantava Fischia il Vento*[80]
      O when we were singing "The Wind Blows"

B 2   *ormai gli é un tempo giá passato*
      but now that time has gone

A 3   *e a ricordallo e che n'ho un tormento*
      and it's a torment for me to remember

B 4   *di quel partito che gli era [dannato*
      that party that was damned

(4)   Ara:[((shakes head affirmatively))

A 5   *camicie nere lá spiegate al vento*
      black shirts[81] there, unfurled in the wind

B 6   *e il popolo veniva [ingannato*
      and the people were being conned

(6)   Ara: [((shakes head affirmatively))

C 7   *quando i Partigiani morivano sugli Appennini*
      when the Partisans[82] were dying on the Apennine[83]

C 8   *gli stessi* <u>*ladroni*</u> *pigliavano '[kattrini*
      the same <u>big thieves</u> were taking the money
                Ara: [((shakes head affirmatively))

Tonti uses the octet to tell a narrative, the story of the resistance to fascism in Italy. The story, supposedly well known by everybody present, is suggested rather than narrated in linear fashion, summoned forth through a series of metaphors and emotionally strong images. In this way, the poet evokes emotions more than events. It is after all the mythical past of the Italian Communist Party – the myth of the origin, that underlines the fundamental unity of the left. This unity is foregrounded since the first verse, with the use of the pronoun *si*, "we" (A1), and the metaphoric use of the title of a communist song *Fischia il Vento*, "The Wind Blows." The song also immediately orients the audience toward the story, indicating the participants (who) and the time (when).

---

[80] I believe this was originally a Russian folk song, then adopted by the Soviet party. Translated and rearranged in Italian, it became a symbol of the resistance against fascism.

[81] The name given to the fascist militia organized by Mussolini.

[82] Name given to the civilians who fought against the fascists and nazis in Second World War.

[83] A chain of mountains going from Tuscany to Sicily.

Immediately after, though, Tonti states that the time of the Resistance is gone (B2). By doing so, he is introducing a deconstruction of the myth itself. He interrupts the causative chain: the past is past and does not correspond to the present anymore. Recalling it then becomes painful (A3), but not because of a desire to ideally return to that past (something that may be regarded as desirable for those in the PRC who feel that the party's communist ideals have been corrupted since). That past represents a negative period, in which a "damned party," (B4) the fascists, held the power. It is a past in which the Black Shirts could boast their symbols (the evocation of flags fluttering in the wind – A5). When the people had been tricked to believe in fascism (B6) and those who fought to oppose it were dying, or hiding in the mountains (C7).

Tonti closes stating that the same people who had the power then have the power still (C8). Although unsaid, the logical conclusion is that those fights and deaths were in vain. This is in tune with his general argument in this part of the *Contrasto*, namely that the political views and actions of the Democratic Party of the Left changed not because they abandoned communism, but out of a realization that the previous methods used to bring about social change had revealed themselves useless. Though, in the next octet, Ara turns Tonti's argument against him:

(Octet 16) Ara/Bertinotti
C 9   *E ora fa i patti con quegli assassini*
      and now you make accords with those assassins
D 10 *o meglio é quello che tu senti*
      or better, this is what you feel
C 11 *ti fai i patti e trovi i confini*
      you make accords and set the boundaries
D 12 *insieme a loro compagno o disc- camerati o discendenti*
      together with them comrade- camerati[84] or their descendants

---

[84] The Italian word *compagno* does not properly translate in English. The English word "comrade" includes both Italian words *compagno* and *camerata*, although in Italian they are dramatically distinguished. *Camerata* is used to indicate a person sharing the same dormitory among soldiers. Otherwise, more generally, it applies only to fascists. *Compagno* situated the person as part of the left or as an anarchist. To call a person *camerata* is to call him a fascist, which in this context is a very strong insult.

C 13 *dissi compagni e sbagliai i rini*

I said "comrade" and I erred the rhymes

D 14 *volevo dire porci e malfidenti*

I wanted to say pigs and untrustworthy

E 15 *che se tratti con Prodi*[85] *o Berlusconi*[86]

that if you negotiate with Prodi and Berlusconi

E 16 *di certo nun le trovi tue ragioni*

for sure, you are not going to find your reasons

Ara starts immediately with a direct attack. He steps out of the frame of the story, by resetting the time to the "now" and isolating Tonti with a "you" (verse C 9). At the same time, he compares the past actions to the present "misdeeds." D'Alema is denounced as sharing with "those assassins" (the fascists) the same feelings (D 10). He is equated to them, no more a *compagno* but a *camerata*[87] (verse D 12). In doing so, he is proposing a different interpretation of history: "society did not change, because you, and people like you, betrayed us." He is putting responsibility directly on the PDS. Notice moreover how the negative judgment is reinforced by the use of the term "assassins" (verse C 9; substituted for thieves in verse C 8), which links back directly to Tonti's evocation of the dead partisans. Ara concludes by explaining and justifying his strongly negative judgment. He reconnects to recent events in Italian politics, stating that there is no way to justify (verse E 16, "find your reasons") the negotiations with Prodi and Berlusconi.

Realdo Tonti was portraying the view that the split in the communist party will ultimately do no good for the people, and make the reaching of any goal even more difficult. He indeed stresses the

---

[85] Prodi was then the Italian First Minister. He was put in charge by an alliance of parties that included both the parties of the left.

[86] Ex-First Minister. A businessman that owns the major private TV channels, Berlusconi is one of the richest men in Italy. In the beginning of the 90s, he created his own party, *Forza Italia*, through which he was able to go to the government, although for just a few months.

[87] Here Ara has an interesting slip of tongue, using the word *compagno* and then correcting it in *camerata*. It is a potentially dangerous one, since it could be misunderstood by the audience (as a statement that the two terms are equal, that there is no difference between the two kinds of people) and anger them against him. In fact, he apologizes immediately after (C 13), interrupting the flow of his argument and thus momentarily stepping out of the duel to address the audience directly.

idea that the common enemy is elsewhere. Not only does he express a more moderate stance, but also one that subordinates the means to the ends. Gabriele Ara, in turn, recalls the attention on the importance of the means, indexing a view that finds "wrong" means incompatible with "right" goals. This stance tends in turn to stress ideological differences that become then concrete differences in practice (or "malpractice").

In octet 17, Tonti/D'Alema furnishes a reinterpretation of his own actions which is at the same time a justification of them and an indirect negative judgment of those (namely Bertinotti) who just make "confusion:"

(Octet 17) Tonti/D'Alema
E 17 *Cerco di non fa' troppe confusioni*
 I try not to bring too much confusion
F 18 *o di cercarla la diretta via*
 and to find the direct path
E 19 *come vedi ancor lotto-o contro i padroni*
 as you can see I still fight against the owners/masters
F 20 *voglio dir per la democrazia*
 I mean to say for democracy
E 21 *io nun so' dalla parte dei ladroni*
 I am not on the side of the big thieves
F 22 *l'ho mantenuta quell'idea mia*
 I kept that idea of mine
G 23 *se dell'idee e che ce n'ho la scorta*
 if of ideas, indeed, I have a surplus
G 24 *al mondo gliela vo' dare una svorta*
 I am going to make to the world spin

Having acknowledged the failure of the preceding fights, D'Alema is looking for another "path" (F 18). This statement is extremely layered with meaning. It evokes in fact the political theory of the "third path" to communism proposed first, at the beginning of the eighties, by the then secretary of the Italian Communist Party, Enrico Berlinguer. Thus, Tonti is summarizing the political thinking behind the formation of the PDS: still fighting against capitalism (E 19), but for democracy (F 20) (versus the dictatorship of proletariat). Tonti/D'Alema concludes by stating that his ideas have not changed (F 22), and it is through them that he will finally be able to change society.

All but trivial, these issues reflect the recent history of the Italian left, starting from Berlinguer's formulation. Berlinguer's own vagueness in defining what the "third path" – namely the democratic alternative path toward communism – was has left much to be interpreted for his successors. Some skeptically commented that the "phantom third path" was a skillful way to avoid addressing the contradictions of Marxist thought when applied to the world of "advanced capitalism." We need to understand also which "paths" are excluded in this formulation. One of them is the one of armed revolution, that was at the base of communist/Marxist thought as it became exemplified by the Soviet revolution, and by the FLN (Front of National Liberation). The second path is moderate reformism, as was proposed then in Italy by the *Partito Socialista Italiano*, "Italian Socialist Party." But how can we define the "third path" and translate it into political practice? These were some of the most fundamental questions debated in the Italian left in the eighties, which led to the split of the communist party at the beginning of the nineties. Even after that split, the question was far from being resolved.[88] The proposal of this topic to the poets, then, testifies to the audience's attempt to make sense, and their request to the poets is at the same time a request that they "create" that sense. Next Ara starts to shift to another argument:

(Octet 18) Ara/ Bertinotti

G 25 *Ma sa alla gente cosa gliene importa*
   But you know, people do not care
H 26 *tu sai gli é come dare l'acqua ai somari*
   you know, it is like giving water to donkeys
G 27 *i mass media ti danno questa vorta*
   this time the mass media give you
H 28 *l'opportunitá d'esser quello che appari*
   the opportunity to be what you appear
G 29 *ad un poeta poco gliene importa*
   to a poet this matters little
H 30 *te lo dicevo ora e un é guari*
   I was telling you now, it is not (a trouble)

---

[88] A consequence can be seen in the most recent split in the PRC, that in fall 1998 led to the creation of the *Partito dei Comunisti Italiani*, "Party of Italian Communists" headed by Cossutta.

I 31 *che la sorte é sempre quella*
        but the destiny is always the same
I 32 *al governo ci hai messo la morta[della*
        you put a mortadella[89] in the government
33   Tonti: [((laughing))
34   AUDIENCE: ((general laughing))

Ara depicts a more cynical view of society, where ideas have become useless because people (metaphorically equated to donkeys – H 26 – that in Italian also means "idiots" or "ignorant") do not listen anymore. Reality is now created by the mass media (G 27- H 28). The man Ara filters through the mask of his personage, as he seems to retire from the contest in renunciation. At the same time, he expresses the clairvoyance of the poet, who can see through the veils of the mass media and of power relations, but fewer and fewer people listen. In this light, his closing (I 32) is more a moral commentary on the corruption and brainlessness of politics, than an attack to D'Alema in particular.

The image of the mortadella is a powerful cluster of meanings. Its similarity to "salami" evokes stupidity.[90] Its pink color can symbolize the result of the washing out of the "red" of communist ideals. Its fatty round shape evokes plainness and dullness. As food, it evokes eating, thus selfishly appropriating for oneself, or putting our personal interest ahead of the collective good. Moreover the mortadella is considered a "low standard" processed meat, a cheap food, and its presence in the parliament evokes the general abasement and low standard of the elected representatives there. And of course, the image is extremely funny. In fact the audience, which had been following in silence until now, starts laughing.[91]

---

[89] The *mortadella* is a kind of processed meat, of pinky color. The statement implies that the PDS has substituted the red color of communism for a faded color, namely that they are no more true to the communist ideals.

[90] In Italian the word "salami" indicate a kind of processed meat but also a slow-witted person.

[91] My father, who was also present at this performance, recently furnished me a further interpretation of the "mortadella metaphor." He thinks that the mortadella stands for the political leader Prodi, who was in fact sent to the government with the help of D'Alema. Prodi is from Bologna, the city where the mortadella was first created, thus justifying the association.

IV. The Structure of the *Contrasto* as "Protective Device."
The analysis so far has shown how the dueling poets depict, and thus create, the political arena itself, articulating its boundaries and their arbitrariness. As we saw in chapter 3, the structure of the *Contrasto* is very complex. I believe that this complex, articulated and precise structure must take precedence, because it makes the expression of opinions on social behaviors and political decisions possible and protects the poets who perform such opinions.

IV. a. Political Language and Power.
Language is not just a medium for the expression of power, but it can constitute power. The merit of recalling the attention of sociologists and other scholars on political language as having power or agency in itself, belongs to Bloch. According to Bloch's landmark study on traditional oratory, formalized language reinforces and furnishes a legitimization of the power hierarchy present in a society (1975:22).

Bloch underlines that is exactly the form of the speech that establishes its authority, a form which is directly connected to tradition. Rules for regulating speech making are seen as "effective forms of social control" (1975:6). In formal speeches, like those used in political oratory, these norms become rigid and fixed. Such fixity reduces the possibility for negotiation, thereby reinforcing the authority of those in power (1975:9). Bloch explains this by writing: "It is because the formalization of language is a way whereby one speaker can coerce the response of another, that it can be seen as a form of social control" (1975:20). Bloch notices how formalization often leads the speaker to speak for a social role. This according to Bloch limits the freedom of the individual (1975:16). Though, as others have shown, it can also furnish a way of resistance to authority, especially when the possibility of the person to speak has been already otherwise limited.

A formal system, then, can be read in many directions. Irvine's analysis of formal speech brings this possibility to the forefront. She arrives at the conclusion that the degree to which formality upholds a social hegemonic structure seems to be mediated by the "political ideology, which the formal meeting expresses" (1979:784). Finally, she concludes: "Some anthropologists have argued that it is the very formality of such ritual occasions, which minimize personal histories and focus on the relevant social relationships, that makes the creative transformation possible" (1979:784).

Duranti arrives at similar conclusions in his study of Samoan ceremonial speeches. He writes: "Bloch's argument about the constraining force of formal oratory should be contextualized. It might be accurate for some situations, but not for others" (1994:103). By applying the concept of heteroglossia to these formal speeches, Duranti goes further, and shows how rhetorical art can express many voices, often in contrast and opposition with each other, so that the political arena becomes a field in which power relationships are negotiated and challenged. The challenge is cloaked in traditional formal style.

In sum, as demonstrated by Irvine and Duranti's studies, the presence of exact rules, or norms, and the higher degree of formality of a genre, may not be a limit on freedom of expression and action. A highly formalized structure, on the contrary, may be the safeguard of that freedom. It can be compared to the "veiling" that Abu-Lughod describes for the Bedouin poetry (1996). Conversely, as John Heritage writes:

> The idea that informal language allows more freedom than more formal styles ... is the illusion of theorists who equate conceptual determinacy with determining power. It is not shared by autocrats and dictators who know that open and unbounded sets of rules, backed by force, are just the way to consolidate a set of advantageous social arrangements (1984:209)

Various authors have shown that a fixed structure can furnish a way of resistance to authority. The person can invoke a higher authority, like tradition (Kapchan, 1995) or the divine (Kuipers, 1990) as a base for the right to speak, and cloak resistance in the veils of formality. This is true, for example, for the ritual speech of the Weyewa, studied by Kuipers (1990:167). In the Weyewa, through the use of textual structures, the performer: "creates the conviction he is not speaking on his own, but on behalf of some distant person or spirit" (1990:6). These create an "authoritative" or "authentic" performance (1990:109). In the *Contrasto*, it is the "poetic art" itself that can be invoked (sometimes identified with the "Divine Muses"). It allows the artists to voice opinions on social behaviors and political decisions. This includes bringing attacks to the established political structure,[92] to religious institutions, and to social norms and roles, using offending words that would not otherwise be allowed.

IV. b. Giving the Precedence to the Structure.

Significantly the poets, having to choose between meaning and structure, always opt in favor of the second. So the poetic function, in a sense, has to have the precedence over anything else: over meaning and over emotions. The structure must be preserved, because it is the structure that makes the expression possible and protects it.

Word use follows the needs of musicality and rhyme. Notice for example in Octet 16 (sung by Gabriele Ara), in the words *malfidenti* and *rini* the departure from semantic and phonetic adherence in favor of structural constraints:

(Octet 16 – Gabriele Ara)
C 11 ti fai i patti e trovi i **confini**
    you make accords and find the boundaries
D 12 insieme a loro compagno o disc- camerati o **discendenti**
    together with them comrade- "camerati" or their descendants
C 13 dissi compagni e sbagliai **i rini**
    I said *compagni* and I erred the rhymes
D 14 volevo dire porci e **malfidenti**
    I wanted to say pigs and untrustworthy

(1)   Italian: la rima = the rhyme = female singular
        le rime = the rhymes = female plural
    Gabriele Ara's transformation: i rimi* = male plural
                        i rini* = further modification (C 13)

(2)   Tuscan: malfidenti = untrusting (not trusting)
        Probable intended meaning = untrustworthy (D 14)
    Italian/Tuscan: di cui non ci si puó fidare, menzognero = untrustworthy

In example (1), Ara modifies the gender of the word *rima*, "rhyme," and then modifies it further by substituting "m" with "n" (C 13). Notice how he maintains the agreement between the article "i"

---

[92] This protection does not always save them from the established power, and the poets can tell stories of occasions when they have been harassed, censured or arrested. In the past, as we have seen, the police could interrupt performances.

and the noun. In example (2), Ara's use of the word *malfidenti*, "untrusting" (D 14), if understood literally, makes no sense in the context of his discourse. He has been offending the other party by calling them *camerati* and "pigs," but "untrusting" is not an offence. The logical word here would have been "untrustworthy," which makes sense as part of his general argument, namely that the other party has "betrayed" the communist ideals. He could have used the Italian word *falso* or *menzognero*, "untrustworthy," or he could have used a sentence, like "*di cui non ci si può fidare*," "that we cannot trust." This, though, would have gone against the structural constraints of the genre (rhyme, number of syllables). He solves the problem by using the word *malfidenti*, basing himself, in a way, on assonance of meaning.

The adherence to the structure makes the syntagma of the verses and their semantic adequacy more complex, creating ambiguities of meaning, sometimes of difficult interpretation. Giannelli also notices in this poetry: "the presence of dislocations to the right and to the left. Frequently scissored phrases and rhetorical constructs are then constituted by phrases started by "é che." These procedures combine among themselves to the point of constituting verses of great complexity in the superficial syntagmatic structure" (1988:56; my translation). An example of this can be seen in octet 18, verse H 26.

(3)
(octet 18 – Gabriele Ara)
H 26 *tu sai gli é come dare l'acqua ai somari*
        you know, it is like giving water to donkeys

In example (3) the metaphor of "giving water to donkeys" is quite complex. It is a transformation of a metaphor commonly used in the *Contrasto*, namely: "to give manure to columns." Since columns are not plants, to fertilize them in the hope that they will grow is a useless action, so it is useless to give knowledge to idiots. The new metaphor is created out of the association between "watering" and "fertilizing." In both cases the action of educating is seen as "cultivating" (Latin: colere, culture), or passing the water of knowledge, that can quench the thirst of the person looking for understanding. But, giving this kind of knowledge to donkeys is a useless action.

Notice how the adherence to the structure/rhyme complicates the semantic adequacy and makes the phrase ambiguous. As a matter of fact, understanding this verse and disambiguating it requires the audience to be highly sophisticated in its knowledge of the genre. Still, although the poets, in searching for the right rhyme, may at times sacrifice meaning in favor of the poetic function, this is always valued less positively than the ability to follow both the poetic and the referential functions.[93]

IV. c. Invoking the Structure.

In the following excerpt from an interview to the poet Altamante Logli,[94] he tells of two occasions in which, because of the lyrics he was using he risked getting in trouble with the local police:

> At San Vincenzo, we went to Campole, when the police made us stop singing because we were singing 'De Gasperi versus Togliatti.' The policeman says: 'why are you saying bad things about De Gasperi?' 'Because he says bad things about me!' I told him, right? We are doing the *Contrasto* in poetry, by the Virgin! (Of course)! [...] This happened immediately after the war.

To the policeman's question on why Logli (impersonating Togliatti[95]) is offending De Gasperi,[96] the poet answers that is it because the other poet (impersonating De Gasperi) is offending him. Then he qualifies it by saying that they are doing a *Contrasto* in poetry. "Of course," namely the poet is appealing to the fact (that the policeman should know) that given the structure of the *Contrasto*, which requires each poet to answer the other, there is really no way that he could avoid to say "bad things" about De Gasperi. The poet thus invokes tradition and the traditional genre. He distances himself from his own words, and argues against being held responsible for

---

[93] I am actually not sure I agree with Jacobson formulation. Speech play and rhyme, poetic language in general, seems very referential to me. All of irony, for example, is built on speech play, and I doubt that it can be considered meaningless. Cirese (1988) may agree on this. The distinction may be forceful as poetic language is also referential and referential language is also performed and thus has an attention to the "taste" of the listeners.

[94] Interview held in the poet's home in Scandicci (province of Firenze), on 11/9/97 (code: I 1-B-302). My translation.

[95] Palmiro Togliatti was the secretary of the Italian Communist Party from the end of the World War II until his death in the sixties.

[96] Alcide De Gasperi was a politician in the Italian right, powerful in the period immediately after the World War II.

them. Rather than depicting himself as (political) agent he depicts himself as passive, almost captive in the structure of the duel. The agency, instead, is depersonalized and attributed to the genre itself, of which the poets are merely the contingent "animator."[97] The same happens in a second episode that Logli narrated shortly after the first, during the same interview:

> We went through some bad moments, you know. So, even in poetry, we had to keep it into account, as I was telling you. Once, here in Badia, we were singing 'The Undertaker, the Priest, the Physician, and the Pharmacist.' We were four poets. Suddenly the marshal appeared, and he said- the Undertaker [had been saying] 'I am going to do deep excavations to bury these loafers.' That poet said [this] referring to the Priest. The marshal (then) tells me 'come here!' He tells me 'Why are you telling bad thing about (him), and [why] do you do things this way? I hear you have mentioned that the priest is a loafer and [you say]: I work more. Why are you doing these things?' I say 'But they are not- but they are *Contrasti* in poetry! We are not doing it to really fight, you know?' He says 'But can't you put someone else in that place?' This is what he told me. And someone was about to tell him 'marshal, would you like us to put you in the place of the priest?
> Anthropologist: hh hhhhhh hu hu
> Logli: But I would have ended up in jail! We could not say that!

In this narrative, one poet, impersonating an undertaker, is proposing to bury all priests, that he judges to be useless loafers.[98] The marshal, hearing this, calls Logli, therefore interrupting the performance. Notice how in both this and the previous narrative the policemen are depicted as agents who do not hesitate to use their power in defense of the established hierarchies.[99] The marshal asks

---

[97] It is interesting to notice the parallel, in a completely different context and narrative genre, with the analysis by Capps and Ochs of narratives produced by an agoraphobic woman, describing her anxiety and panic attacks (1995). In both cases the narrator deresponsabilizes her/himself by removing agency onto external, depersonalized forces.

[98] It is a view often heard, in Tuscany, that priests are lazy people, since they do not work "to earn the bread they eat," and are thus a useless element in society.

[99] Notice also how the policemen do not just impose silence, but they question the poet. In this way, the narration sets up a "trial-like" situation in which the poet is put on trial for his words and has to defend himself.

Logli why are they offending the church. Logli answers by informing the policeman that they are doing a particular genre of poetry, namely the *Contrasto*. Then he adds that they are not *really* offending each other. Here again, the poet refuses the attribution of agency by underlining that what he is doing is "fake," it does not belong to the realm of reality, but to the imagined realm of poetry.

Next, as the marshal asks if the poets could do a *Contrasto* without the priest, (namely avoid the political kind of *Contrasto*), Logli mentions that somebody suggests the possibility that the policeman could take the place of the priest. This statement is layered with meaning. First, the speaker seems to offer to the policeman the possibility of further defending the priests by participating himself in the verbal duel. To do so, though, the policeman would have to enter in the same "creative realm" of poetry, and accept its fixed rules, thus renouncing the exercise of his power as an enforcing agent of public morality. This is a dialectic realm where his state-given authority and power would mean nothing. It is a realm where the poets are the authority, chosen and blessed by the Muses themselves.[100] A position where, in the end, the policeman could only lose. It is exactly in this realm, where the power of verbal art reshapes reality and dares to define, display and attack the forces operating in the political arena.

But the challenge to take the priest's place offers itself to at least another reading.[101] Taken in the context of the preceding last verse of the poet, the phrase may mean: "should we bury you instead of the priest?" This is a more direct political statement, one that suggests that the established hierarchies of power, represented and defended by the police, can be subverted and destroyed.[102] Thus, at the same time in which the poet is negating, on one side, his political agency,

---

[100] These poets believe that poetry cannot be learned, but that it is the result of an innate sensibility to the call of the Divine Muses, to which the poets ultimately cannot resist.

[101] There is also a third, more meta-discursive meaning in this narrative. Namely, the phrase may mean: "would you prefer a *Contrasto* in which one of the personage represented is a policeman?" Although that *Contrasto* could not be done at the time of the event, it is in the present time of the interview, that it takes place. In the narratives themselves, in their articulation and construction for the anthropologist/audience, Altamante Logli is presenting the elements and development of a *Contrasto* between "the Policeman and the Poet."

[102] Notice that the anonymity of the speaker in this case and the use of the pronoun "us" in the sentence, transforms the speaker into an anonymous *vox populi*.

on the other, he is reaffirming it.

To recapitulate, in both of these examples, the poet defends his actions in front of the police by underlying the needs of the genre itself. He uses the structure of the verse as an excuse for his words (words that are immediately recognized by the policemen as political actions). The constraints of the structure contribute to make the poet appear as not responsible for what he says.

However, seeing the structure of the *Contrasti* just as a protective device is limiting. I believe, instead, that such a tight structure enhances the poets' ability to use it for their own purpose. Nothing obtains the approval of the public more than the virtuosity of the poet. They appreciate the skill of following the constraints, the ability to bend them, the creativity in overcoming them and the originality in the final result. Thus the verbal duel's potential for social impact resides in the creative potential that performance unleashes, in the possible and alternative realities that it presents to the view. It is, in Schechner's words "the way these [unreal] worlds take concrete shape in time and space, expressed as gestures, dances, words, masks, music, and narratives" (1992:279).

The structure of the genre – its bipolar organization that allows and requires that two opposite voices (or two opposite discourses) may be heard, and both in turn be attacked – allows the *Contrasto* to present always two sides of reality, both now unstable and subjective. More than that, they allow for a continuous affirmation and deconstruction of both of them. The "dialogic" style of the *Contrasto* does not lend itself to "exalt" only one side, and in fact we have seen that it was exactly the dialogic/dueling form that was eliminated during fascism. The poets were asked to sing alone, no more in couples (namely, to uphold only one point of view, not two).[103] In the verbal duel, no truth is *a priori*, each depends instead on the ability of the poet who defends it. The *Contrasti* fuel and exploit the heteroglossic potential of language. Bakhtin celebrated heteroglossia and polyphony, the "plurality of independent and unmerged voices and consciousnesses" in a person's speech (1984:6). In the *Contrasti* the heteroglossia of language becomes transparent as diverse voices emerge from the verses.

Bakhtin had refused the idea itself of "dialectic" as monologic in its tendency to recognize "conflict and contradiction only to resolve

---

[103] See Franceschini, 1983:47.

them ultimately" (Dentith, 1995:44). Contradictions cannot be resolved, because centrifugal and centripetal forces are operating in language, whose conflict can never be resolved. Similarly, there is no consensus built in the *Contrasto*. The final closing of the performances does not propose synthesis, but rather calls for tolerance and for an appreciation of each other's position (and often not even that: most *Contrasti* end in a fight just as they started). Truth is constructed in the context of everyday conversations (so is reality, according to Peter Berger and Thomas Luckmann, 1966). But in performance possible alternatives to truth and other possible realities are proposed. The *Contrasto* always politicizes reality. Not only, but the *Contrasti* name power, they identify friends and foes.

V. Conclusion.

A shared reality is an ongoing accomplishment. People make it happen by engaging in shared practices. Thus reality is "performed" in each of an infinite number of separate instances of participation. The speech play is a mimicry and a display of what in everyday life is the continuous negotiation of reality and its continuous contestation as well. It introduces counter-discourses and contradictions, which reflect the counter-discourses and contradictions present in the social context (see Lindstrom, 1992:103). Lindstrom argues that people's talk: "set truth conditions – a 'regime of truth'; and ... link that regime of truth 'in a circular relation with systems of power which produce and sustain it'[104]" (1992:105). At the same time, in verbal duels disputants "violate principles of quality by insisting on alternative truths" (1992:110).

Gal notices that language is connected to the control over representations of reality, and thus a terrain of conflict (1989:348). In this sense, every *Contrasto*, independently from its topic, is inherently political. It transforms power relationships and political knowledge into a highly dynamic terrain of dispute.

In the dialogue of the poets, in the final absence of a resolution of the confrontation, lies the hidden suggestion that a final truth may just not exist.[105] This can act for the audience as a moral reminder of a

---

[104] Here Lindstrom is quoting Foucault, 1980:133.

[105] There is an underlying belief, shared by the communists, that in a dialogue between peers, truth will have a way to prevail. This assumption is derived from the cultural matrix of Marxist thought itself (in its derivation from Hegelian Philosophy) as well as some of the most resilient ways of organization of

need of introspection, of reanalysis, and doubting. Poetry confronts the audience with voices that, although "perturbational,"[106] request to be heard, becoming suddenly unavoidable cracks in the fabric of reality. It confronts them with the possibility that other views may be just as "reasonable" as your own, and leads them to pass to a different level of complexity in their thinking.

Poetry as action, modifies the political realities that it portrays. The mechanism by which performance can create this structural change is – quoting Bauman – by offering "to the participants a special enhancement of experience, bringing with it a heightened intensity of communicative interaction" (1977:43).[107] This defines performance as both "reflective" and "reflexive." In the first meaning it "mirrors" society, and makes us witness to ourselves. Dramatic performances in general can be extremely powerful in this sense, by the fact that they create an image, thus transforming the audience into witnesses, capturing them deeply into the "frame."

In the second sense, art as "reflexive" furnishes a commentary on society, and thus acquires agency, or pragmatic intent and force. As Kapchan writes: "performance ... not only fabricates meaning in highly condensed symbols ... but comments on those meanings, interpreting them for the larger community and often critiquing and subverting them as well" (1995:480). Art as "reflexive" considers the time dimension and thus the possibility of change. As Briggs writes in this regard: "Performance features do not merely reflect situational factors; rather, they interpret the social interaction, thus opening up the possibility of transforming its very nature" (1988:15). He adds: "performers are not passive, unreflecting creatures who simply respond to the dictates of tradition or the physical and social environment. They interpret both traditions and social settings,

---

Western thought (from dualism, to agnosticism, to Neo-Platonism, to Christianity). This belief asserts that truth cannot be hidden and in the long run will reveal itself from behind the veils of ideology (like the soul will free itself from matter). Such is the teleological project found in Marxism's optimistic belief that the utopian world of communism unavoidably lays ahead. Pollner though notices: "The very conflicts which are mundanely regarded as 'failure' in the perceptual process through which the world is observed and its features brought to formulation may alternatively be regarded as 'evidence' of the absurd and radical subjectivity of the world" (1974:58). It is this "radical" vision that the *Contrasto* brings forth.

[106] In the sense in which Freud uses this word.

[107] See also Peacock, 1968.

actively transforming both in the course of their performances"
(1988:7).

It is participation, in each of an infinite number of separate
instances, that creates the "densely woven fabric of morally
accountable cultural practices" (Heritage, 1984:198). We can say then,
that reality can be "performed," built through practices (participant
frameworks). But, as a reality can be performed, so can its
alternatives. In the *Contrasto*, each poet proposes a different view of
causality, or what motivates people, of what are the facts of human
relationships, including what is the meaning of relations of
exploitation and how they come to be created, and especially, how
they can be changed. The poets in this *Contrasto* do not just present
different views of reality, they also discuss how those realities could
be modified. In this sense the *Contrasto* is also a metapragmatic
genre.[108] The poets dive through the strata of complexity of everyday
reality, and, what is even more important, they bring their audiences
with them.

---

[108] Heritage writes: "the production of an action will always reflexively
redetermine (i.e. maintain, elaborate or alter) the circumstances in which it
occurs" (1984:180). Thus the poets do not just assume a political reality, but they
modify the political realities that they enact. They can maintain, create, and
contest them.

5

I FOUND MYSELF SINGING IN THIS LAND: CREATING IDENTITIES IN PERFORMANCE

I. Introduction. [109]

To view poetry and performance as social action is fundamental to an understanding of how the construction of identity, and the construction of images of ethnicity, happens in poetry. This chapter explores the representation and negotiation of ethnic identity and place in verbal art performances, through the analysis of the *Contrasto*. I show that the Tuscan poets use performance to create images of the self and the other. Language is used to give shape to images of identity.

Pierre Bourdieu (1977, 1990) has emphasized the centrality of *practices* in the everyday construction of reality. In this chapter, I show how particular realities are emergent in (Tuscan) performance, and connected to places and placenames. The poetical *Contrasto*, as improvised, is made and unmade in the moment of performance, and only in performance does it acquire its social relevance. In the same fashion, there is a continuous making and unmaking of images in performances. These images are concretized and reflected in the innumerable repetitions of their representation in the everyday use of language in Tuscany, thus becoming continuously performed.

---

[109] A previous version of this chapter, titled "Lands I Came to Sing: Negotiating Identities and Places in the Tuscan *Contrasto*" was published in the journal *Pragmatics* 10 (1), Winter 2000: 125-146.

II. Ethnicity, Place, Performance.

While working on the *Contrasti*, I started to realize that the definitions of ethnic identity found in anthropological theory were insufficient and unsatisfactory for looking at how Tuscans think about and construct their identities. The word "ethnic" also seemed inadequate. It became more obvious instead, that places – named places – were especially relevant.

The word *identity* is ambiguous. On the one hand, it refers to the person's self-perception. On the other side, it refers to a process of external labeling, such as in the connected process of identification, or attribution of an I.D., of a particular place in a group and in a society. In this second sense, it becomes possible to talk about policies of identification, or categorization, of inclusion and exclusion, of establishment of borders and border crossing.[110] "Classic" definitions of ethnicity see ethnic groups as stable and self-perpetuating social units to which the individual belongs by birth or primary socialization, and which can be defined through sets of *traits*.[111] This model, as Kroskrity has noted, tends to "reify" the concept of ethnicity

---

[110] In this sense Visweswaran (1994) writes that: "identities, no matter how strategically deployed, are not always chosen, but are in fact constituted by relations of power always historically determined" (1994:8).

[111] An example of such lists comes from the Random House College Dictionary (1988): "*Ethnic Group*: A group of People of the same race or nationality who share a common and distinctive culture." Similar definitions have constituted for a long time the base for the study of ethnicity. In all of them an ethnic group is defined by the sharing of something. The problems start when we try to say what is shared. No common agreement exists (and I would say can exist) on this. An example of such lists is Naroll's six criteria: territorial contiguity, language, political organization, ecological adjustment, traits distribution and local community structure (1964). Another example is Smith & Kornberg's definition of ethnic group as "a group that shares common cultural norms, values, and identities and patterns of behavior and whose members both recognize themselves and are recognized by others as an ethnic group" (1969:342). The main problem with all lists of traits is that the ethnic group can be defined through different features on different occasions or by different people. One of the first to realize this was Moerman (1965). His reflections started from the factual impossibility to define who the Lue, an ethnic group in Thailand, are. The point is this: although everybody is able to indicate immediately if a person is Lue or not, the reasons for such identification change. The only solution Moerman could envision was to consider the ethnic group as a pure emic category. Each external categorization, he concluded, tells us more about the ethnic group of the categorizer than about the categorized.

(1993:191) ignoring the space of free decisionality that identity offers to the person, and possibly offering a supposedly objective base to racist and discriminatory claims.

In this fixed definition, ethnicity is defined through boundaries. For example, Fredrik Barth proposed considering ethnic groups as "categories of ascription and identification by the actors themselves," (Barth, 1969:10). Those categories that a group regards as important (*diacritica of ethnicity*) will enter the definition of the boundaries.[112] According to Barth, once the boundaries are established, movements of people through them and relative converging of cultural content between the groups will not diminish for the people involved the feeling of belonging to different communities. Anya Peterson Royce, aware of the presence of a duality in the concept of ethnic identity, proposed the concept of *double boundary*: "the boundary maintained from within, and the boundary imposed from outside" (1982:29). "Objective definitions" of ethnicity correspond to ascription of traits from outside; "subjective definitions" refer to the internal, individual awareness of belonging to a group.

The risk here is to forget that the focus on boundaries is in itself an ideological choice, influenced by Western worldviews and historical events that stressed the importance of national borders, of contours, limits, and forms. The ideological attention on boundary maintenance defines people as people only as long as they remain inside an established boundary, and negates the humanity of those who refuse the boundary, those who trespass them. This in turn, as we saw in chapter 2, is connected to linguistic ideologies that stress the necessity of linguistic homogeneity and standardization (see Irvine and Gal, 2000). Ronald Cohen (1978) notices that every attempt to define an ethnic group by creating a boundary is artificial, and cannot account for the many *situational* transformations of ethnic identity and/or ethnic groups. The idea of situational ethnicity (Cohen, 1978:389) implies that it is constructed in interaction. The person will enact and communicate the particular ethnic identity of the ethnic group that is

---

[112] Barth's model tries to show the arbitrariness, thus the historicity, and the connected reversibility and negotiability of social groups and categories. He affirms that ethnic groups are maintained: "not only by a once-and-for-all recruitment but by continual expression and validation" (Barth, 1969:15). This leaves to the individual a space for agency, even if limited, and thus for redefining the boundaries themselves. Because of this, Barth's model opposes itself to "lists" models.

taken as referential in a given moment/context.[113]

Theories of identity and ethnicity are not free from power relationships. The preference given to one model rather than another has political and social resonance. In Italy today, "traits" definitions are used by separatist movements – like the Northern League, as I discussed in chapter 2 – or associated with discriminatory statements against Southern Italians or recent immigrant groups.[114] They imply a desire to fix both the self and the "other" in a stable and stabilizing identity. For these reasons, I believe it is important to reaffirm the constructedness, the multiplicity, and the instability of social and ethnic identities. Only in this way, we can recover the *centrifugal* potential of identity and the space of free decisionality that it offers to the person as an agent.

Kroskrity has proposed to study "a given social identity in its interrelationships to other available social identities" (1993:209). The sum of the available identities would then constitute a "repertoire" (1993) from which the person can choose. In this model, the individual is seen as an agent strategically using particular identities and actively redefining them and the roles associated with them.[115] This model is in agreement with the studies done by Kroskrity himself on the Arizona Tewa ethnic identity (1993), and with Zentella's ethnography on the New York Puertoricans (1990, 1997).

Similar findings can be seen in the work of Duranti *et al.* with the Samoan Americans in Los Angeles (1995) and in Gloria Anzaldua's writings on Chicano and Mexican American identities (1987). Similarly, I have discussed elsewhere the presence of a repertoire of

---

[113] Joan Vincent affirms that 'political actors, ... when articulating ethnic status, are able to define and redefine the rules of interaction according to their changing interests. Thus ethnic identifications are broadened when greater political mobilization is required, and narrowed when exclusion is sought." (1974:376).

[114] I cannot overstress the way in which 'traits" definitions of Ethnicity are used as a base for ethnic hate crimes and discriminatory behaviors, such as the Holocaust and other attempted genocides. They can be seen at work today in the conflict between Serbs and Albanians.

[115] Kroskrity's model argues that ethnic identity is created in context in everyday encounters and contributes to the definition of the context, and thus of the meaning of the encounter itself. The context limits the number of possible identities among which the person can choose, in the sense that it makes some of them irrelevant or inapplicable, and others salient (these can be both adaptive or dis-adaptive, but anyway salient).

identities in my work with the Italian American community in Los Angeles (Pagliai, 1995a, 1995b, 1996). In all these cases, people can shift among different ethnic identifications. Since natural belonging to a group is no longer a necessary nor sufficient condition to present the self through it, how the presentation of self is achieved and why becomes the new question.[116] As I show below, in the *Contrasti* a repertoire of identities becomes evident in the way the artists choose to represent themselves across contexts.

As identities become contested and are negotiated in performance, so are places. In traditional scholarship on ethnicity a "place" is inhabited by a specific ethnic group (maybe a nation, a region, or more often a ghetto), fixed in the same way in which ethnic groups are seen as fixed and defined. However, the recognition of a repertoire of identities goes against the view of identity[117] as stable/stabilizing. Instead, identities emerge in the context in which they are performed.[118] Places are constituted through negotiations and re-negotiations (see Blu, 1996:198-99). Identities are connected to places, but places can shift. If not like the Wamirans stones, which move around at night (Kahn, 1996:181), they can shift in poetry, through the way the poets call on each of them.

Performance creates places, and places are continuously performed. In every word, in every encounter, we perform being Tuscan, and we perform our belonging to places that are at the same time the depository of us being Tuscan. As the poets tell their stories, they contextualize them by recalling names of villages, cities, or particular features of the landscape. The answer of recognition by the

---

[116] This has also been seen as a problem in Rampton's recent study of language crossing (1998). Though Rampton's distinction between "interactive," "reactive" and "deracinated" ethnicity (with the connected idea of a "true" belonging versus "commodified" belonging) presupposes again the existence of an ethnic group outside or before people's creation of an identification to one, namely before its creation in everyday practices or shared participation into it. This is like presupposing a reality outside of its social construction. Here, Rampton does not seem to have made any theoretical progress and be still abiding to some kind of "trait/fixed" definition of ethnic group.

[117] Here, I focus more on the "subjective" side of identity, although by no means I intend to negate the importance of looking at the "boundary imposed from the outside" (Peterson Royce, 1982: 29).

[118] This emergence, in turn, implies the contextual creation of a shared knowledge regarding the identity itself (its characteristics, boundaries, etc. including possible beliefs in fixed traits).

audience defines a shared memory and knowledge. As Charles Frake writes: "the use of placenames implicates much more than their denotation. In their phonological forms and their semantic suggestiveness, names often become remarkable – worthy of a story – in their own right" (1996:238). Or, expressed in a parallel way by Gerald Vizenor, talking about Native American names and nicknames: "Native American Indian identities are created in stories, and names are essential to a distinctive personal nature" (1994:56). Thus, acts of identity are also acts of naming, or renaming, where memory has been canceled.

Talking about placenames, Basso writes: "Because of their inseparable connection to specific localities, placenames may be used to summon forth an enormous range of mental and emotional associations – associations of time and space, of history and events, of persons and social activities, of oneself and stages in one's life" (1988:103). To give a name is to reconstruct the reality of an object into a dimension of belonging. Vizenor again writes (1994:104):

> Nicknames are personal stories that would, to be sure, trace the individual in tribal families and communities rather than cause separations by personal recognition. Even so, nicknames and stories change, a condition that liberates personal identities from the melancholy of permanence.

Thus a metonymic chain connects names to stories, stories to memories, memories to places, and places to identities. Though, as Vizenor also warns us, stories change, and so do identities.

III. *Campanilismo* in Tuscany.

Provincial identities today in Tuscany are very strong. People tend to identify with the main town, the provincial capital, but also with their village and town and the particular area or valley, etc. These identifications may also create antagonisms. In general, Tuscan towns have been traditionally antagonistic to each other. This antagonism is usually dated back, by the people themselves, to the medieval ages, the time when Tuscany was divided into city-states.[119] As we saw in chapter 2, historically Florence has been the main cultural and

---

[119] Although the antagonism could possibly date back further to the Etruscan time. In fact, it is now known that the Etruscans were also organized in city-states.

political center of Tuscany. Prato was constituted as a province only in the eighties. Before, the territory was part of the provinces of Florence and Pistoia. Both Prato and Pistoia were traditionally subject to the political control of Florence.

The term used to describe this situation, in Italy, is *campanilismo*. This term, which has no translation in English (the Webster suggests "parochialism" but this, I believe, is incorrect), is semantically very similar to the term *nazionalismo*, "nationalism," to which indeed it is compared in conversations in Italy. Nationalism implies an allegiance to a nation, and a series of associated feelings of pride, of belonging, of common history, etc. – but nationalism is also associated with national expansion, encroachments, colonialism, war and domination. The first series of meanings can also describe the term *campanilismo*, with one difference: the focus is not on the nation, but on the city, the town, and the village. In fact, the term etymologically derives from the word *campanile*, "bell tower" (we could think of a translation as "bell-tower-ism"), and makes a clear reference to what could be considered an ubiquitous landmark in Italy: the tower of the main church of the city, town or village.

In Tuscany *campanilismo* takes up also, in part, the second series of meanings of the word "nationalism": the memory of the city-state of medieval times, when "*non c'era posto indoe un facessen guerra*" ("there was no place that wasn't at war" – verse from a traditional sung poem in octets, "*Pia dei Tolomei*"). Notice the word *posto*, namely "place," in this verse. Antagonisms among villages and towns today have lost any violent side, although many elders in Tuscany still remember that rivalries leading to violence were still a common happening at the beginning of the century.[120] The poet Realdo Tonti, for example, recalls that:

Campanilismo is like this. In the past, among towns and towns, for example; here, when I was a boy, if a young man would pass the limit to go to San Niccoló, if he would pass a certain limit he would find himself hit with stones. You know, the ignorance [of the people]. If he was in love with a girl of that town, it was even worse. The evening when he would go in that town, they would do him the worst tricks. It is the same with *campanilismo*. It was like this in the towns. To you it may sound like something difficult to believe. ... You are young. ... Yes, [this was] at the

---

[120] This phenomenon is in some way similar to what Blu describes for the towns in Carolina (1996).

> beginning of this century, but even until the war, even until the 1930, 1935. ... There was *campanilismo* between San Piero and San Niccoló, San Michele.[121] This [would say that] they were better, because they had the soccer team, you see. The other one had the music band. The music band of San Niccoló was better than the one of San Pietro, and so on. This is how it was. Then there were *Contrasti*. ... Better, the poets would win their bread with it..[122]

The antagonism is today expressed only in jokes and blasons, rarely offensive. Blasons are particular forms of stereotyping in which the stereotype is known and accepted by both the in-group and the out-group, and which are defined through oppositions. Thus an identification as *pianigiano*, "plains person," will recall the relevant opposition, namely *montanino* or "mountain person." Blasons are very common in Tuscany and practically every town and village has its own, as shown by the studies of scholars like Paolo De Simonis (1984/85), Giulio Pecori (1975) and Mario Cortellazzo (1984). De Simonis, regarding the Tuscans, talks about a "precise consciousness of the diversity of the other" (1984/85:8-9), even among small villages very near to each other.[123]

Talking about "ethnic identity" is not a common Tuscan experience. I doubt that most people would even understand what the term mean. As Tamanoi writes of Japanese rural women: "Perhaps they had many identities or none at all; 'identity' is just not the way they talk about their living histories" (1998:207-8). Conversations about places, instead, are continuous: the names, the roads to get there, the way people talk "there" and "here," together with innumerable acts of placing people, making sense of their actions, reckoning their *razza* ("race," but in the Tuscan meaning of "family ancestry"). "*Che razza di gente enno lá a X?*" ("What kind of people are those in X?") They will ask me when I come back from the United States. As I shrug my shoulders in the impossibility of an answer, they

---

[121] Villages that today are part of the town of Agliana.

[122] Excerpts from an interview conducted in Realdo Tonti's home, in Agliana, on June 18, 1997. My translation. For the original transcripts in Tuscan Italian, see Appendix E.

[123] Important oppositional identities in the area under study are the one between the city and the countryside. Examples are: Florence versus the rest of its province, the plains versus the mountain, and the juxtaposition between Pistoia and Prato. These are also reflected in several *Contrasti*.

will answer with the proverb: *"tutto il mondo é paese"* ("the entire world is a town," or "the entire world is made out of towns").

In the performance of the *Contrasto*, the articulation of "repertoires" of ethnic identities depends on several factors, including the context, the audience, the negotiated meaning of the event, and the individuality of the artists. All of these factors, in turn, come to be reshaped by the performance itself. As Bauman has shown,

> Performance, like any other form of communication, carries the potential to rearrange the structure of social relations within the performance event and perhaps beyond it. The structure of social roles, relations, and interactions; the oral literary text and its meaning; and the structure of the event itself are all emergent in performance (1986:4).

In the *Contrasto*, identity itself can be seen as emerging in performance. The analysis of this genre, thus, underlines the active role of the individual in choosing and enacting a "repertoire" of identities.

IV. Tuscan Identities as Connected to Place: Places Named.

In the *Contrasto*, the contestation of each other's presentation and claim of identity passes through the metonymic association of the person (self and other) with places. These places can be named, hinted at, evoked through metaphors, and they are actively constructed and deconstructed. The act of naming, then, in verbal art performance, becomes fundamental and can furnish a key to understanding a Tuscan vision of things. The Tuscan repertoire of identities could be articulated in a series of places, to which the person can claim or be claimed as belonging. Belonging itself, in turn, is articulated in terms of "knowing" or "being known," naming or being named. Names then become part of the way the claiming gets done.

At the beginning of a performance, the poets usually sing a series of "opening octets" in which they introduce themselves and greet the public. While they introduce themselves, the poets situate (identify) themselves each time in relation to the audience, the setting, and the other poet(s) present. This is the first of a series of layers of identity that they portray and of which they are invested during the *Contrasti* (often indissolubly mixed as well with their own identities as artists and as persons).

The identity chosen can be portrayed through many means (for example by using particular varieties of the Tuscan dialect). Here, I focus on the conscious verbal self-identification in the opening octets. Here, in fact, we can see the connection between place-names and identity. The poets rarely present themselves as "being Tuscan" in their songs. Identity instead is connected to towns, villages, valleys and mountains, monuments and historical events and legends. The poet whose "self-identifications" I will discuss here is Altamante Logli.

Schema #3, Altamante's Repertoire of Identities.

Repertoire of Identities	Place where he has invoked them	Setting
- Apennine Mountains - Mountains - Cantagallo[124] - Migliana [125]	- Migliana	- Local feast
- Florence (city)	1) Papone[126] 2) Lido di Pandoiano[127]	1) Festival of Liberation 2) Local traditional feast
- Scandicci[128] - Tuscan	- Florence	- Festival of the ARCI[129]
- Political identity: communist	- Papone	- Festival of Liberation

As shown in Schema #3, Altamante identified himself, in different performances, alternatively as Florentine, from Migliana, from Scandicci, from Cantagallo, from the Apennines, etc. (see also Figure #9). Only once he identified himself as Tuscan, during a performance in Florence, notably at an event organized by a national association, the ARCI (Italian Recreational and Cultural Association). He would otherwise refer to the particular Tuscan sub-groups or sub-

---

[124] Small town in the province of Pistoia, on the Apennine mountains.

[125] Small town in the province of Prato, on the Apennine mountains.

[126] Village in the southern part of the province of Pistoia.

[127] Village in the province of Livorno.

[128] Town on the outskirts of Florence.

[129] *Associazione Recreativa e Culturale Italiana,* "Italian Recreational and Cultural Association."

cultures.[130]

Figure #9: Map of north-eastern Tuscany.

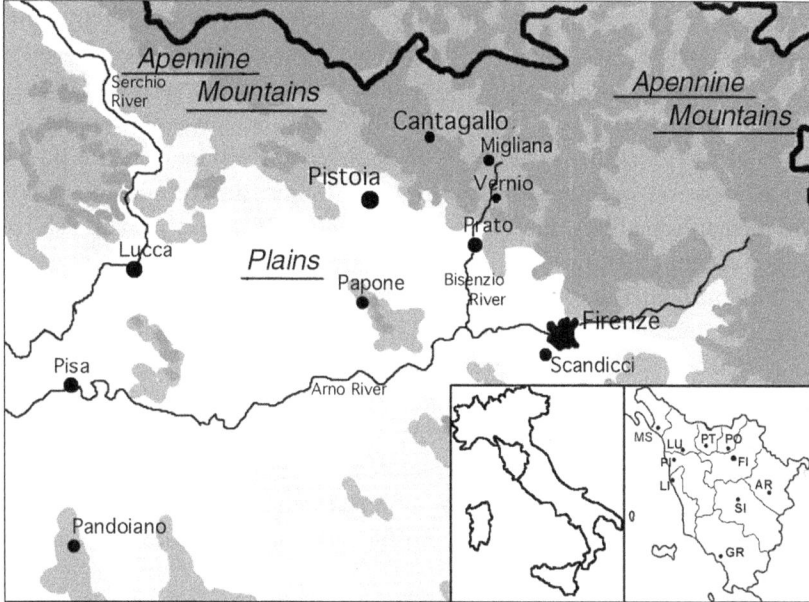

Naming indexes local knowledge. It affirms the presence of a relationship. The poets call in places as witnesses of their ability to belong to those places/identities. If they can name places, they can say that they are part of them, that they have that identity.[131] The identity declared by the other poet is also relevant. Usually poets tend to propose different identifications from each other. Thus, when singing with Realdo, who often associates himself with the province of Pistoia, Altamante would rather not declare himself from Pistoia. This seems to set the base for subsequent oppositional role-taking.

The connection that the Tuscan poets build with their audience

---

[130] Of course, this might have been different if he had found himself outside of Tuscany (he performed many times in Lazio and once in Emilia) or outside of Italy (he performed in Switzerland), but I lack data for those occasions. Insight can be used, anyway, by comparing him to another poet, Mariani, from Lazio, whose performance was recorded in Tuscany. Mariani actually never presented a Lazio identity, but rather his sub-cultural group in Lazio. He also declared himself akin to the Tuscan people.

[131] This idea I share with Ms. Sepa Sete, since it was formed though a dialogue with her.

through their performance is fundamental. It is important to remember that the members of the audience are co-performers (as seen in chapter 3). Artists and audience influence each other, and both a reflective and reflexive relationship is established among them. The audience usually requests the particular topic of the *Contrasto*. They may furnish various kinds of feedback, including evaluations, interpretations (see also Fretz, 1987:306-307), laughing and applause. They can even address the poets in rhyme.[132] The fact that the poets often insist on participation, on the possibility for everyone to "take the microphone," on the "we are here for you, to do what you ask us to do," is enlightening.

The performance is created in the interaction between speaker and listeners, and through this interaction a certain social reality is upheld or criticized; a certain representation of identity can be legitimated or delegitimized. According to Heritage (1984), an objective reality exists so far as people agree on it. It is the ability of the poets in performance to obtain the agreement of the audience on the identities that they portray themselves or about themselves, that makes the poets part of their public. The identification can be contested, as I will show later.

It is in the moment that the people accept the poets as part of them that the poets become able to express the audience's voice. The people recognize the poets and thus recognize the poets' ability to express their (local) voices. They recognize the poets by accepting the performance and by co-constructing it. As Georges writes: "Everything human beings say and do when they assume the contrastive, but complementary, communicative roles of narrator and listener is an integral part of the event generated by their interacting; and this includes what they say or do in terms of such identities as those rooted in their sex, age, religious affiliation, ethnicity, occupations, etc." (1981:251). Thus, the Tuscan ethnic identities and the communities to which they refer are *imagined* in the dialogue between the poets and their public.

The poet portrays the identity that allows him to feel closer to the

---

[132] As I discussed in chapter 3, the audience is not homogeneous, but there are various kinds of audiences, and each of them can have a different role in respect to the performance (Goodwin, 1986). Moreover the people in the audience have an influence on each other's performance as audience (Goodwin, 1986). The audience can also be divided into "supporters" and "antagonists" in respect to the performance.

audience. For example, in Migliana (see schema #3) Altamante creates an association though a series of towns in the Apennine Mountains. When this is not possible using an ethnic category, he uses class identities, professional identities, or others. For example in Papone, a small village in the southern part of the province of Pistoia, the setting being a Festival of Liberation, he prefers to identify himself through a political identity, as communist (see schema #3). This declaration of affiliation to the audience is revealing. These artists are not "heroic" figures. They escape from the hegemonic definition of the artist as hero; they share the same life, problems, unsettling questions, common sense, or limits of their audience. They do not stand out against the background of their communities, but find in their communities their strength and their voices. The relationship of the Tuscan poets with their audiences situates them close to the heart of the social network.

V. Place and Identity as Negotiated in Performance.

In performance, the poets contest places and their definitions. Places are constructed and reconstructed in the *Contrasto* (see Blu, 1996:199). Metaphors of places overlap through the octets like realities overlap over the landscape (Blu, 1996). Places (towns) become contested sources of identification, discursively constructed, thus pointing at contestable and unstable identities.

I now turn to the analysis of a short excerpt from a *Contrasto*, done toward the end of the performance in Papone[133] (8th of August 1997; see figure #10). The context was a Festival of Liberation, taking place in the large courtyards of the local *Casa del Popolo* ("house of the people"). At the northern side of the building, there was a large paved space where, in other evenings, dances would be held. On one side stood a small stage erected for the occasion, and paraded with red Communist flags. This stage was used for musical groups, theater, political speakers, or other performances. At the other side of the paved dance ground, under the trees or along the side of the building, were the lines of the chairs where the audience sat. From the bar inside the building, voices and noises of dishes being washed created a droning accompaniment to the poets' singing.

---

[133] Papone is a village near the town of Lamporecchio, in the province of Pistoia, but very close to the border with the Florence province, and separated from Pistoia by a chain of Hills, the San Baronto. It is also high country, over the hills themselves.

Figure #10: Altamante Logli (left) and Realdo Tonti (right) in Papone.

The performance had started quite late, around 10PM. In part for this reason, the audience was smaller than usual. The *Contrasto* I am analyzing was the last performed, at about 11:30PM, when only a small audience (about 45-50 people) remained. Because of it, the poets were getting ready to quit their rather short performance (not nearly as long as the customary two or more hours). The remaining audience had been instead requesting to hear something more. The *Contrasto* started as a "closing octet," then developed into a *Contrasto* of "plains vs. mountains" and then "city vs. countryside." The poets' indecision may explain why they start the closing octets, but then they end up doing another *Contrasto*.

In this *Contrasto* (spanning over 21 octets), the poets switch and shift among several Tuscan identities, and contest the other's identity as well as those attributed to the self by the other person. Altamante had started his closing octet, evoking his travel back to Scandicci (see Figure #9), where he lives. Realdo also evokes the travel back to the plains (where Pistoia is located). At this point, Altamante produces a third octet attacking Pistoia (octet #3):

(Octet 3) Altamante[134]

A 1 *Torna a s- Pistoia lá in quell'accquazione*

Go back to Pistoia, there, in that stormy downpour

2   Realdo: *<He! Ho! Ora comincia (vai)!>*[135]

He! Ho! Now you start (go on)!

B 3 *torna lá nel mezzo ai <gineprai>*[136]

go back there, in the middle of those tangles of troubles

A 4 *io ritorno alla mia abitazione*

I go back to my abode

B 5 *<che a Pistoia un ci> tornerei mai*

since I would never go back to Pistoia

6   AUD?: (   )

A 7 *c'é la paura po' dell'infezione*

there is also the fear of the infection

B 8 *e poi ci sono tanti paretai*

and then there are so many tangles of walls

C 9 *ci son delle giornate tant' amare*

there are some days so bitter

C 10 *a forza sí di mosche e di zanzare.*

by force, indeed, of flies and of mosquitoes

11   AUD: ((laughing))

12   AUD?: *[(e infatti) ce l'ho*

(and in fact) I have them[137]

13   AUD?: [Ha! Ha! Ha ha ha ha!

Notice that Altamante uses characteristics of the environment, its rainy and humid weather, and recalls the fact that in the past the area had malaria (line A 7: the infection). Belonging to Pistoia, thus, is metonymically connected to sickness. The verses evoke ugly weather, unhealthy waters, and a general sense of a place where you cannot

---

[134] See Appendix A for a list of transcription conventions. Notice that I transcribe sentences spoken by other than the singer by indenting them and indicating the name of the speaker, followed by a colon. These sentences are also numbered, although they are not part of the octet.

[135] Note the audience's laughing response to Altamante's first verse (signified by the brackets, see Appendix A). It underlines the passage from the closing octets to a new *Contrasto*, at the same time recognizing and encouraging it.

[136] Literally, *gineprai* means "bushes of juniper," but it is generally used in its idiomatic sense of "troubles from which it is difficult to extricate oneself."

[137] Referring to the presence of flies and mosquitoes, very common in summer.

avoid feeling uncomfortable: the tangle of bushes (B 3) become a tangle of walls (B 8): ravines and an inhospitable place. A place where people live in fear, where the days are bitter in the continuous siege of the mosquitoes (themselves carriers of malaria) and the flies.

The harshness of Altamante's attack is proportional to the authenticity of the portrait. Talking about Kaluli song, Steven Feld writes: "Its evocative power depends not on the quantity of detail of places named, but on their connectedness, on the extent to which they map a place narrative that emotionally resonates with personal, biographical, and historical self-consciousness" (1996:125). Notice, for example, the comment from a person in the audience (line 12), confirming the presence of flies and mosquitoes. The plains used to be a swamp. They were slowly drained over almost two thousand years by the peasants. Pistoia's original hamlet was built on the swamp itself, like a pile-dwelling. The name, Pistoia, comes from the Latin *pistores*, people stamping their feet, making the land solid with that movement. It evokes for me the image of an unstable soil, continuously on the verge of sinking back in the swamp from which it was stolen. Altamante's derision of such an effort creates a powerful attack, and evokes powerful memories. Realdo defends Pistoia and attacks Scandicci in turn. In doing so, he creates another powerful image of Pistoia:

(Octet 4) Realdo
C 14 *C'é le bellezze vedi le piú rare*
  There are the beauties, you see, the most rare
D 15 *o quella l' é la tera degli amori*
  o, that is the land of loves
C 16 *doe si coltivano cose-e molto rare*
  where the rarest things are cultivated
D 17 *o specialmente delle rose e fiori*
  and especially roses and flowers
C 18 *o lí non avrai delusioni amare*
  o there you will not have bitter delusions
D 19 *o dove che si incontrano gli amori*
  where loves are encountered
E 20 *invece te che abiti a Scandicci*
  instead you, living in Scandicci
E 21 *e tu ti trovi sempre ne pasticci*
  you always find yourself in a mess

22   AUD: [((scattered applause))
23   AUD: [((laughing)
24   AUD?: (..........)

Realdo cancels the image of a painful past with that of a prosperous present. After the Second World War, there were many changes in the cultivation of the Pistoiese plains. The end of the sharecropping economy was associated with the development of nurseries. The humid climate makes the plains an ideal place for the production of flowers and ornamental plants. In Realdo's verses, these flowers that cover the land become a symbol of love. Suddenly, Pistoia is a sunny colorful heaven. As Karen Blu writes: "how the land is to be construed, interpreted, and used is very much a matter of negotiation and often contestation" (1996:198).

The land as constructed resonates and indexes realities of economic change and exploitation. The layers of human activity accumulated over the soil of the plains: the slow draining of the swamps, the cultivation, and then the recent changes that led to the construction of the nurseries that today bless Pistoia with flowers, money and cancer (from the chemical pesticides used). Old illnesses and new ones: in the performance, the history of our Tuscan land passes in front of us audience. Each verse is a memory.

Scandicci, in turn, is an industrial town that boomed after the Second World War from a small agricultural center; today it is fused with Florence and constitutes one of its suburban areas. Although Realdo does not describe Scandicci, the single mention at the end of the description of Pistoia already hints at the juxtaposition between the beauty of Pistoia and the ugliness of Scandicci. The juxtaposition is all in one word, the "instead" (E 20) that opens the two final verses. But Altamante, instead of picking up the challenge of defending Scandicci, proposes for himself a new identity as "mountain person" (*Montanino*), an inhabitant of the Apennine mountains:

(Octet 5) Altamante
E 25 *Ma -o son- ((coughing)) son venuto da le castagne e ricci*
    But I came from the chestnuts and the husks[138]

---

[138] The Chestnut trees that cover the Apennine Mountains, are an important symbol for the people living in them. They also furnished an important staple food. The chestnuts are gathered and cooked in various ways or ground to make flour, from which a sweet bread is done.

F 26 *dove nasce i Bbisenzio sopra l'Appennino*
   where the Bisenzio River[139] is born over the Apennine
27   AUD: ((laughing))
E 28 *l'acqua colava giù da que' renicci*
   the water was dripping down from those sliding sand deposits
F 29 *e ti bagnò i' ssolo poverino*
   and soaked your soil poor one[140]
E 30 *voglio vedere ome ti tu spicci*
   I want to see how you can unstick yourself
F 31 *son nato fra la ch- fra i ccastagno e i' biancospino*
   I was born between the chestnut tree and the hawthorn
G 32 *a Pistoia tu fa' di' mmormorio*
   in Pistoia you have to grumble
G 33 *tu bevi l'acqua dove piscio io*
   you drink the water where I piss
34   AUD: ((laughing))
35   AUD: ((scattered applause))

This switch leads the confrontation from one between Pistoia and Scandicci, to one between the Mountains and the Plains. Here, naming is substituted by metaphors, which in turn presuppose common knowledge, or common memories. To the cultivated flowers of the plains, Altamante juxtaposes the wild flowers and trees of the mountains (F 31). The pure, running water of the Bisenzio River (F 26), decaying in its downward movement (E 28), becomes the polluted, motionless waters of the plains. Notice how the effectiveness of the poetry depends in great part in the ability to isolate the core elements of each construction of place, and attack those elements.

In the following octets (#6 through #13),[141] Realdo attacks the Mountain people in turn, identifying Altamante with the town of Cantagallo (see Figure #9). Altamante then attacks Pistoia. Later (octets #14 through #21) Realdo shifts the theme by associating Pistoia with Florence, thereby contrasting the city with the countryside, and ends up claiming a Florentine identity. Thus in the

---

[139] See Figure #9.

[140] The swampy plains receive their waters from the Apennine Mountains.

[141] Not presented here. Please see Appendix E for a complete transcription of this *Contrasto*.

end the poets switch their initial identifications around. The switch does not happen without opposition from Altamante. This can be seen better by looking at three octets (#14, #15 and #18) where Realdo starts (#14) and then completes (#18) the switch:

(Octet 14) Realdo

A 36 <*Si vede l'ignorante [come é scortese>*
It can be seen how the ignorant is impolite
37   AUD: [((laughing))
38   Altamante: *[ndiamo si va via (.......). Ora un vó via piú*
come on, let's go away (.....). Now I won't go away anymore
B 39 *tu l'ha messa la firma di mmontanaro*
you put your signature as hillbilly
A 40 <*guardatevi intorno>* *nel nostro paese*
look around in our country[142]
B 41 *ndove gli é un'arte di ppiú raro*
where there is an art of the most rare
A 42 *voglio dí di Firenze, i ppistoiese*
I mean Florence, the area of Pistoia
43   Altamante: *(che c'entra) Firenze (......)*
(what does) Florence (have to do with it) (......)
B 44 *e ora tu lo ngolli [boccone*[143] *amaro*
and now you will swallow a bitter pill
45   Altamante: *[(parlá di Firenze) (.......)*
(to talk about Florence) (.......)
C 46 *dimmi te i piazza di ddomo e i Bbargello*
tell me, the plaza of the cathedral and the Bargello[144]
C 47 *un tu gl' ha visti ncima a Diavello*
you did not see them on top of Diavello[145]
48   AUD: ((laughing))
49   AUD?: (bravo)
50   AUD: ((scattered applause))

---

[142] Addressing the audience.

[143] *Boccone* literally means "mouthful of food" or "bite of food."

[144] The museum of Bargello, one of the most important in Florence.

[145] This reference to Diavello is only partially clear to me. It seems clear that he is referring to a mountaintop with that name. Unfortunately, I do not know its exact location.

Realdo starts by labeling Altamante as an ignorant hillbilly (A 36- B 39). This is the first part of what is going to be shown soon as a dichotomy between the uncivilized country-folk versus the civilized urbanite. In fact, immediately after, Realdo addresses the public asking them to look around themselves, to notice the artistic heritage of the region (A 40- B 41). Notice that he uses the pronoun *nostro*, "our," together with the term *paese* (A 40), namely "country" or "town," thus theorizing a unit that includes him (as Pistoiese) as well as the audience (Papone is situated between the provinces of Pistoia and Florence – see Figure #9) in this address. Then in the fifth verse (A 42) he makes explicit reference to Florence and Pistoia. By mentioning Florence, he is presenting the second term of the dichotomy: the urban space. The closure is highly humorous: the beauty of art, symbolized by the cathedral and the museum of Bargello (C 46), cannot be found on top of a mountain (C 47). The answer of the audience is one of roaring laughing and approval ("Bravo" in line 49.)

Notice that Altamante, at the mentioning of Florence, starts objecting (lines 43 and 45). As an experienced poet, I think he already knows what is coming. Claiming Florence is to claim a powerful ally, especially when the association is done through art. More than a Tuscan capital, Florence is often felt by Tuscans as the world capital of art. As such, it is also the homeplace of all poetry. To claim Florence is to empower one's poetical ability. Rather than attacking Florence, Altamante at this point refuses Realdo's claim to a Florentine identification:

(Octet 15) Altamante
51 AUD: [((still laughing after previous octet))
C 52   [*Ma sentite i cche dice sto zimbello*[146]
             But listen what he is saying, this laughing stock
53   AUD: ((laughing))
D 54 <*vo mettere*> *Pistoia con Fiorenza*
    he wants to put Pistoia with Florence
C 55 *io dio gli é malato ni ccervello*
    I say that he is sick in the brain
D 56 *oppure gli ha poca* <*intelligenza*>
    or he has little intelligence

---

[146] *Zimbello* is literally a "decoy," often a bird or in the shape of a bird.

57   AUD: ((laughing))

C 58 *io parlavo d'i mmonte morto bello*
    I was talking of the mountain very beautiful

D 59 *indoe gli é nato la mia residenza*
    where my residence was born

E 60 *se porto un pistoiese in piazza Signoria*
    if I bring a Pistoiese in the Signoria Plaza[147]

E 61 *l'acchiappahani se lo porta via.*
    the dog-catcher would carry him away.

62   AUD?: [Nooo! ((laughing))

63   AUD: [((lots of laughing))

64   AUD: ((applause))

65   AUD?: (tu sta' in filo) (gli attacca) Pistoia, é?
            (you are in trouble) (he is attacking) Pistoia, right?

Altamante bases his attack on the presupposed impossibility/ absurdity of making a comparison between Pistoia and Florence. He thus reinterprets Realdo's attempt to build an association as an attempt to make a comparison (D 54). Then, he re-establishes his own claim to talk of the beauty of the mountain: since he was born there he can claim residence (D 59) – thus he can speak for it (C 58). In turn, the claim of a Pistoiese to talk for Florence is derided: Realdo is compared to a dog in the central plaza of Florence, less than human, carried away like a madman (E 61). Altamante thus contests Realdo's right to "name" Florence, to call the city as witness to his argument. The negotiation of identity happens on multiple levels: the construction of the image, and the claim of belonging. Altamante also escalates the violence of his attack, to which the audience answers in various ways. They laugh and applaud (lines 53, 54, 56, 57, 63), but they also express recognition of the strength of the attack (line 62), or seem to comment on Realdo's position (line 65). In the next two octets (#16 and #17),[148] Realdo reaffirms his allegiance to the plains, and Altamante again contests the possibility of an association with Florence. Then, in the third octet, Realdo brings about his strongest argument:

---

[147] Florence's central plaza, where are the Museum of *Palazzo Vecchio*, "Old Palace," the connected Uffizi Museum, the Loggia of Orcagna, and the Marzocco Fountain.

[148] Not presented here. See Appendix E.

(Octet 18) Realdo

70   AUD?: *Ovvia!*
            That's it!

A 71 *Ecco tu l'ha scoperte*[   ] *<le tue carte>*
      There! You have discovered your cards

72   Altamante: [*ndiamo si va via per Dio*]
                        let's go away, by God!

B 73 *se se' nato laggiú sull'Appennino*
      if you were born far there on the Apennine

A 74 *io nacqui lo sai da un'antra parte*
      I was born you know in another place

B 75 *vicino a i ssolo quello fiorentino*
      near to the soil, the Florentine one

A 76 *e gli é lí che gli é nata tutta l'arte*
      and it is there that all art is born

B 77 *ma te non lo sapevi* [   ] *pove[rino*
      but you did not know it, poor one

78   Altamante: [*(c'era Cino)*] [*Cino (......)*]
                        (there was Cino)[149] Cino (.....)

C 79 *finché un venivi ni ssolo di Pistoia [e Ferenza*
      before you came in the soil of Pistoia and Florence

80   AUD?:   [(......)]

C 81 *anlon- ancor nun lla sapei la differenza.*
      you did not know the difference yet

Here Realdo first recalls attention to Altamante's previous statement to be born on the mountain (the Apennine, line B 73). Then he claims to be born near Florence (line B 75). Notice that Realdo does not really inform us as to what he means by "near." Thus he is able to turn the table against Altamante: as Altamante had claimed the ability to speak for the mountain since he was born there, so Realdo was born "near" Florence. All art was born there (A 76): indirectly this means that since Altamante was born elsewhere, he cannot be a very good artist. Excluding Altamante from Florence, as artistic touchstone, is to disempower his poetic ability.

In the *Contrasti*, the insults that the poets level at each other are

---

[149] Probably referring to the medieval poet Cino Da Pistoia, who lived in the 13th century; Cino was part of the *Stil Novo*, "New Style," and friend of Dante Alighieri. Here Altamante seems to be suggesting to Realdo a possible ending of the verse, and a possible defense of Pistoia.

quite heavy. However, while the insult exchanged offends the personage, the poet remains untouched and calmly smiling. For example, in line #2 of octet #3, Realdo greets the beginning of Altamante's attack with a "go on." He will wait and give the other time to finish, and then he will take his turn at offending. What is at stake is not actually loosing face for having been offended, but loosing face for not having been able to answer to the insult appropriately and destructively while following all the dictates of the genre. The public itself is very sensitive to the way emotions are displayed by the poets. They will laugh a lot at the insults the poets give to each other, commenting on their ability to effectively counter each of them. However, the public will stop laughing if they perceive that the rage is true.

The attack in octet 18 (A 76), though, is one that questions the poet's ability *as a poet*. As such, it is a very dangerous attack, one that threatens to enrage, and thus reveal, the person behind the personage. Perhaps for this reason, the last verses are full of ambiguity: Altamante did not know (B 77) – but what? That Realdo was from Florence, or that all art is born there? The next verse also has a double meaning: it may make an indirect reference to the fact that Altamante moved to Scandicci later in life; alternatively it refers to the fact that to learn about art (to understand the difference – C 81) he had to come to the cities. The last verse may mean that only by coming to the cities he would understand the difference between Pistoia and Florence, but also the difference between art and non-art. Notice how during this octet, differently from the previous ones, the audience does not laugh at all, thus showing their perception of Realdo's dangerous attack.

Contesting the name taking of the poet is contesting his ability to identify with a community. Accepting the name taking is to accept his belonging. The poets continuously rename themselves, and call the audience to witness their ability to rename themselves as part of those places. They call on places as witnesses of their ability to recall stories, memories, to belong to those places, to claim those identities.

The artist, in this process of identification, can become, be seen and speak as a series of cultural *personae*, each in turn representing a particular version of the world. These personifications are not just constructed in performance but co-constructed in the dialogue between the artists and between them and the audience. The audience relinquishes or bestows on the artists the power to speak for them, about them, and especially <u>from</u> them (as part of them).

This co-construction is the base for the establishment of a reflexive relationship between artists and audience. In this reflexive relationship, portrayals of the essence of particular social identities are offered (presented) and at the same time attacked, praised, derided, offended, deconstructed, reorganized and *imagined*. The audience, through their co-performance can accept, refuse, negotiate those images. Bauman affirms that "Performance is formally reflexive – signification about signification. ... Performance may be seen as broadly metacultural, a cultural means of objectifying and laying open to scrutiny culture itself, for culture is a system of systems of signification" (1992a:47). Each poet disturbs the constructed objectivity of the portrayal of identity proposed by the other. The *Contrasti* are powerful, also because one poet is always going to shake the reality that the other poet is constructing.

As people share the same places, they can have different definitions of them. Each of these definitions implies a reality, so that realities are overlapping. Tuscan places are created historically; they are sediments in these definitions of places. There are layers to Tuscan places. The poets actively deploy each of these layers in their presentation of different definitions of the same places. Not every Tuscan shares the same definitions of the places they live in. It is this non-sharing that the performances underline. They lay bare the contradictions, but they do so with a smile. They challenge the ability of Tuscans to say "this is our place," and they invite the audience to join them on a more complex level of thinking.

Having shown the importance of "place" in the definition of identity, I stated that places are also "performed," or emergent in performance. As Edward Casey notices, "places not only *are*, they *happen*" (1996:27, italics in the original). As the landscape is constituted in speech acts, the connection between the landscape and peoples is also constituted (see Basso, 1996:54). "Thus represented and enacted" writes Basso, "places and their meaning are continuously woven into the fabric of social life" (1996:57). This also implies that performance allows play with each other's reality, a game that can be highly destructive, as the duel of the *Contrasto* can be destructive. Poets insult and humiliate each other as well as their audiences. The freedom of rethinking ourselves is not (and maybe cannot be) free from a bit of stinging pain, that at times may make us grind our teeth in the middle of a laugh. But, would the absence of that sting make us happier, or just more bored and dull people?

VI. Conclusions.

The *Contrasti*'s complex structure has, ingrained in itself, the elements that make it so important in showing contested identities. Its bipolar organization allows and requires that two opposite voices (or two opposite discourses) may be heard, and both in turn may be attacked. Thus, ethnic identity in the *Contrasti* is always shifting, bipolar or multipolar, dual or multiple, and defined in opposition to others. The *Contrasti* mine at its root the sense of the absoluteness of a particular identity, showing to the public how it lies in the eye of the beholder. Identity is revealed as constructed, multiple, unstable.

As recent waves of immigration are changing the ethnic makeup of the Italian nation, many Italians have started to question themselves on their cultural and ethnic identities (see chapter 2). The arrival of immigrants is often seen by the scholars as the moment of starting, the cause of the overlapping of different realities on the landscape. I have tried to show that the overlapping has always been present. It is part of the way people construct their vision of things, not just a phenomenon of modernity or postmodernity. It is not something due to a supposed anomic condition of present times. The contradictions do not take place on a substrata that once was uncontradictory (the pristine unity of one people). Recognizing the necessity of the overlapping of realities, then, can be a first step toward creating new memories together, landmarks that bear our joint names. An old view is still lurking in the background, one that would like to see a happy state in the absence of diasporas and displacements. However, displacement can be a powerful strategy, and the contestation of place can be done with a smile. The Tuscan poets continuously displace, replace and "emplace" themselves. By doing this they augment their power. Deplacing and re-emplacing are strategies that create the universality of a certain discourse; they are strategies of power and empowerment.

While waging their ethnic wars with words, Realdo, Altamante and the other poets offer to their public the possibility to see the relativity of ethnic divisions. What is important is that we, the public, can laugh together about them, and as we listen to the praises and the offenses, we reflect on the various sides of our selves. Tuscan people need their poets today more than ever, as shown by the renewed interest in this ancient genre. They ask the poets to discuss new topics that witness to the need of making sense, of finding a place for other cultures in the constellation of relevant Tuscan identities. Once each portrayal has been in turn constructed and deconstructed, what the public is left with is, in Realdo's closing verses (Octet #20), the final refusal of the individual to be bounded by birth or other presumably obligatory identities:

> *fin da i' momento che siamo nelle fasce*
> since the moment we are swaddled
> *l'artista un si sa mai ndove nasce*
> no one knows where the artist is born

6
SINGING GENDER:
WOMANHOOD, IDEOLOGY AND POWER

A woman cannot "be;" it is something which does not even belong in the order of *being*. It follows that a feminist practice can only be negative, ... at odds with what already exists so that we may say "that's not it" and "that's still not it" (Julia Kristeva, 1980:137).

I. Introduction.

Many *Contrasti* require the poets to impersonate women. Examples are *Contrasti* between "mother-in-law and daughter-in-law," "wife and husband," "wife, husband and lover," "nun and prostitute." These *Contrasti* are important because they shed light on perceptions of gender in Tuscany. Perceptions of gender identity and gender roles are connected to particular (political) ideologies, and particular (political) positionalities.

In this chapter I will first analyze the way the *Contrasto* re-presents power hierarchies among women, and women as powerful protagonists in society and family. Then I will explore the connection between these portraits and the political ideologies upheld by the artists (and reflected by their audiences). I will show how the *Contrasto* depicts women's roles, and how women poets uphold or resist these depictions. To be able to address these two issues, I need first to discuss some views of gender and of womanhood.

II. Gender and Womanhood.

"Gender," like "woman," is an ideological construction. According to Kondo: "Rather than expressing some essential gender identity, full and present, "woman" is a named location in a changing matrix of power relations" (1997:41). Similarly, gender definitions are culturally and historically created. Consequently, concepts of gender need to be carefully scrutinized.

All too often feminist anthropology seems to follow the assumption that the definition of gender and of gender relationships shared by the Anglo-middle-class-American-sub-culture should be valid everywhere.[150] The most important criticism of it, in this case, can come from women who belong to other cultures, who do not recognize themselves in this vision, and who feel they have little in common with Occidental women. Aiwa Ong (1988) warns that Western feminists are often using Western standards to evaluate the position of women in different cultures. Although they may affirm that they share common problems, for American feminists, non-American women remain a depersonalized *other*. Western women tend to lump together all of them in categories like "third world women," etc. They "seek to establish *their* authority on the backs of non-Western women, determining for them the meanings and goals of their lives" (Ong, 1988:80). They pretend to take a role of guide. At the same time, the status of non-Western women is analyzed, judged and graded in accordance to Western values.

This has had the consequence of hiding fundamental differences among women in Western countries as well. Thus Tuscan women have disappeared under the category "Western." No less than males, feminist anthropologists have <u>used</u> the "other women" to sustain and prove their points of view, thereby arriving at a "substitution of understanding of women as cultural beings by an elaboration of feminist theory" (Ong, 1988:84).

In the past decade, the accumulation of critical studies on gender (and "womanhood") has led to a reshaping and transformation of these concepts. On the one hand, linguistic anthropologists, like Ochs, have stressed gender as a form of identity, that the person can display, underline, hint at or hide together with other kinds of identity, like social or ethnic identities, etc. According to Ochs (1992), gender

---

[150] See Ortner's recent discussion of the theories that propose the universality of male dominance over women (1989-90). See also Goddard (1994) for a discussion of the construction of the image of the "Mediterranean" woman.

is connected with the way the "self" is presented in various occasions, namely with the communication of identity. Thus, gender is not an essential quality of the individual. It is indexed and formulated as the result of an active choice (even if influenced by culture, which always reduces the number of possible choices). Gender falls in the repertoire of *social personae* available to the individual.

On the other side, feminist thinkers like Denise Riley and Jill Dubisch have questioned the existence of "women" as ontological beings. Riley affirms: " 'women' is historically, discursively constructed, and always relatively [sic] to other categories which themselves change" (1988:1-2). She warns that "all definitions of gender must be looked at with an eagle eye, wherever they emanate from and whoever pronounces them" (1988:2). According to Riley, a solution could be in considering "women" an unstable category (1988:5). Dubisch (1995) starts from a concept of gender as performed, already proposed by Garfinkel (1967:134). She adopts Michael Herzfeld's idea of a "Poetic of Manhood," (1985) proposing a "poetic of womanhood" (Dubisch, 1995:206). Gender as performance becomes expressive, but also creative, and thus transformative (1995:204).

One important corollary of the universal vision of womanhood in Western feminist writings has been the assumption of the universal oppression of women perpetrated by males. This in turn is based on the assumption that "gender belonging" is a self-evident, innate, and stable quality of the person.[151] In this sense, "gender" is an objectified category. The supposed oppression of "woman" by "man" is then based on the idea that there is such a thing as "man" and "woman," and moreover, that a person will remain of the same gender at all times.

As Chandra Mohanty notices: "The assumption of women as an already constituted, coherent group with identical interests and

---

[151] The tendency to see gender as fixed speaks loudly about our own cultural tendencies. Foucault is illuminating in this case, when he explains how, in the past century, homosexuality was transformed into a fixed quality of the person: "Nothing that went into his [the homosexual] total composition was unaffected by his sexuality. It was everywhere present in him. ... It was substantial with him, less as a habitual sin than as a singular nature. ... The sodomite had been a temporary aberration; the homosexual was now a species" (1978:43). The same absolutism as an explicative principle has been attributed to gender, both in common sense and in the anthropological studies.

desires, regardless of class, ethnic or racial location, or contradictions, implies a notion of gender or sexual differences or even patriarchy that can be applied universally and cross-culturally" (1997:258). But to take "women as a category of analysis" implies the existence of women as a homogeneous group before the analysis itself (Mohanty, 1997:259). Mohanty continues: "The problem with this analytic strategy, let me repeat, is that it assumes men and women are already constituted as sexual-political objects prior to their entry into the arena of social relations" (1997:261). Like in the case of the studies on ethnicity that I discussed in chapter 5, people are assumed to belong to categories, but the categorization itself is left unanalyzed.

Having considered gender as "performed" (Dubisch, 1995) and "womanhood" as an unstable category (Riley, 1988), pointing the finger, as Mohanty notices, to a supposed (ghostlike) "international male conspiracy" is simplistic and misleading (Mohanty, 1997:257). What we need instead is an analysis of the local conditions of imposition of particular oppressive structures, or hierarchies of power. The relevant question then becomes, in Dolores D'Argemir's words, "how discourses regarding gender are linked to forms of hierarchy and power that transcend sexual difference" (1994:221).[152] Following, I show how definitions of "womanhood" (and "manhood") are connected to particular (political) ideologies.

While looking at gender in the *Contrasto*, I realized that in this case, enacting a certain gender identity is often coterminous with enacting a certain gender role. To a multiplicity of gender identities corresponds a multiplicity of gender roles, which in turn corresponds to a multiplicity of social roles (including, notably, kinship roles). Gayle Rubin argues that: "Far from being an expression of natural differences, exclusive gender identity is the suppression of natural similarities" (1975:180). In her criticism of heterosexuality as an "institute process" (1975:180), she notices how the gender of a person is always defined also on the base of particular sexual and kinship roles. This means that a person is always "somebody's sexual"[153] (1975:181). I would argue that a woman is never just a woman, but always a "woman" as defined by particular kinds of cross/same

---

[152] D'Argemir warns that anthropologists, by emphasizing particular aspects of gender, may "reproduce the dominant *models of representation* and *language* through which social relations are expressed" (1994:209; emphasis in the original) thus creating or reinforcing gender stereotypes, instead of undermining them.

[153] A opposed to "heterosexual," "bisexual," "homosexual," etc.

gender relationships. Rubin concludes that: "we are not only oppressed *as* women, we are oppressed by having to *be* women, or men as the case may be" (1975:204).

My analysis of Tuscan verbal art shows that a person is never just "man" or "woman" but a man or a woman in a specific social relationship, which in turns entails a certain position in terms of power. This means that it is no longer possible to look at gender or sexuality without considering contextually relevant power and politics. Moreover, the concept of gender itself no longer refers to dichotomies (or even triads) but to a multiple number of positions.[154]

III. Singing Women into Power.

As Sarah Meacham notices in her work on Japanese women,[155] powerful women are more interested in upholding and reinforcing traditional gender roles, imposing them on less powerful women (for example young women), than in destabilizing them. Thus they take an active role in the construction of social hierarchies that at the same time are connected to ideologies that relegate women to an inferior position in society. The African-American feminist writer Alice Cooper, writing at the turn of the century: "saw patriarchal power revealed in the imperialist impulse, but she also saw that that power was nurtured and sustained at home by an elite of white women preoccupied with maintaining their caste status" (Carby, 1997:333).[156] I believe that this observation can be generalized to women in positions of power in general. It is an error to believe that these women may have the same interests and agendas of less powerful women.[157]

---

[154] This is something that the studies on sexuality have already begun to uncover, especially in regard to "queer" sexualities. But it needs to be applied to any form of sexuality, and it needs to be exported from a discourse on desire to a discourse on power.

[155] Personal communication.

[156] Thus recent studies of the role played by Western women in colonial history (Chaudhuri and Strobel, 1992) are introducing an element of breakage in the traditional feminist masternarrative that sees women as natural allies of each other, innocent victims of male patriarchy.

[157] Even considering women of different social class in the same category as "woman" is in itself deceptive, since it hides the realities of differential power among them. Rather than focusing on a supposed lack of women's consciousness of their own oppression as women, the problem is a lack, as

We need then to pay attention to the construction of power hierarchies among women. Gender hierarchies are connected to economic, age and social hierarchies. Thus we need to look at their intersection with power, economic class, family, status and age hierarchies. As Visweswaran suggests, we need to displace "gender from the center of feminist theory, ... starting from a consideration of how race, class, or sexuality determines the positioning of a subject" (1994:75).

What I wrote so far should not be taken as a negation of the existence of power inequalities between people identified as "men" and "women" in particular social contexts. It is instead a call for a deeper understanding of those contexts, and for a more complex understanding of gender categories. In particular, in this section, I want to put into focus three issues: 1) The differences in power between one woman and another – or one man and another – is often more vast than the difference in power between women and men. 2) How powerful women may actually gain from remaining subordinate to powerful males, since this means that they can exercise power over subordinate women and men. 3) The ways in which women oppress each other.

In the *Contrasto*, as we saw in the previous chapters, the hidden "bricks" of social reality become "unveiled." Given its dialogical/oppositional structure, it is a privileged place for the representation of contradictory views of social realities, including gender realities. When I started to study the *Contrasti* involving female personages, I started to realize that the disputes among them often involved power. This is no surprise, since a *Contrasto* has the declared goal to demonstrate the superiority of one side over the other, or of one vision of reality over another. In the same way, I found different visions of gender and gender roles being at stake in these disputes. Not only, but as the personages themselves were never just "women," but "women-in-relation-to" somebody or something (for example with respect to kinship systems), these *Contrasti* offered an image of those relationships, an image that highlighted struggles for power

---

Cooper well understood, of class and racial consciousness of particular groups of women. In Cooper's case, she is referring to white women. Middle class feminists like to think that the oppression comes from males (that automatically absolves them from any further need to acquire a class consciousness). The category "woman" or "womanhood" may actually help justify this hierarchy and be fundamental in the maintenance of the present power structure.

inside them.

IV. Contrasting Women: Mother-in-Law Vs. Daughter-in-Law.

One of the most common themes in the *Contrasto*, and one that pits women in a kinship relationship against each other, is the one called *la Suocera e la Nuora*, "Mother-in-law vs. Daughter-in-Law." I present an analysis of two of them here. The first was performed by the poets Altamante Logli and Realdo Tonti, while the second was sung by the poets Elidio Benelli and Liliana Tamberi.

The theme of the fighting *suocera*, "mother-in-Law," and *nuora*, "daughter-in-law," is very ancient, probably centuries old. Thus, it refers to a family and kinship structure that, although common in Tuscany in the past, is almost completely absent today. This structure included patrilocality, which was particularly diffused in the Tuscan peasant family.[158] In this extended family structure the daughter-in-law went to live in the household of her husband, thus finding herself under the direct authority of the Mother-in-Law. The daughter-in-law was, in this traditional family structure, also a laborer:[159] not just a reproducer, but a producer. As such, she could really be considered at the lower end of the power hierarchy in the family.

In the *Contrasto*, as I will show, far from accepting her status of inferiority, the daughter-in-law opposes by any means the right of the mother-in-law to order her around. In this battle, the mother-in-law and daughter-in-law manipulate images of womanhood and gender roles. Again, the *Contrasto* opens to scrutiny reality as crafted.

IV. a. Setting the Topic: Family and Kinship in Trouble.

The first *Contrasto*, sung by Realdo Tonti and Altamante Logli, was performed at a Festival of Liberation in Papone, on July 8, 1997. I

---

[158] In the past, the predominant form of organization of the household in Tuscany was the extended family. This form was common in Italy in general, but not unique (see Kertzer and Saller, 1991). Today the nuclear family is the most diffused, and this is connected to the general urbanization and abandonment of the countryside after the Second World War. The residence can be matrilocal, patrilocal or, especially today, neolocal. The form of kinship is cognatic.

[159] The harmonious family, where everything is in place, would be one in which the mother-in-law treats the daughter-in-law like a daughter. As with "sisterhood," "motherhood" can hide the reality of the possibility for exploitation.

have already given a description of this context, since it is the same as that of the *Contrasto* I analyzed in chapter 5. This *Contrasto* was requested by the audience and performed relatively early in the night, around 11PM. In the first four octets, the poets had decided who was going to impersonate each character. Then in the 5th octet, Altamante entered his personage (the mother-in-law) and started the "duel:"

(Octet 5) Altamante/Mother-in-law

A 1 *sento che un sentimento bello e li raffiora*
   I feel that a beautiful sentiment is reappearing on the surface

B 2 *si vede che gli ha tanta sempatia*
   you see that she has so much sympathy

A 3 *io son contenta d'avella una nora*
   I am happy to have a daughter-in-law

B 4 *e che presto la venga in casa mia*
   and that soon she may come to my home

A 5 *ma se la si intendesse fa camora*
   but if she should intend to make trouble

B 6 *co una pedata te la mando via*
   with a kick I would send her away

C 7 *se l'avesse un sistema un po' balordo*
   if she had a system of behavior a bit foolish

C 8 *speriamo e si vada poi d'accordo*
   let's hope then, that we may get along

(8)   AUD = ((sparse applause))

Altamante starts by portraying the relationship as harmonious, but already in the second four verses (5-8), he is foreboding the possibility of its disruption. The mother-in-law affirms that she is ready to love, as long as the daughter-in-law does not "make trouble," by trying to impose another "system" (verse 7) namely another order if things. This already foreshadows a hierarchy of power, one that the daughter-in-law is warned not to try to disrupt. The answer of the daughter-in-law is similarly oriented, at the beginning, toward the possibility for a harmonious relationship:

(Octet 6) Realdo/Daughter-in-Law

C 9 *non voglio dí che la lingua io mi mordo*
   I do not want to say that I am biting my tongue

D 10 *o socera ti sei pronunciata*
   mother-in-law you made your statement

C 11 *l'intenzione ce l'ho d'anda' d'accordo*
   I have the intention of getting along
D 12 *anche se <u>in casa tua</u> sono arivata*
   even if I have arrived in your house
C 13 *peró una cosa vedi ti ricordo*
   but one thing, you see, I remind you
D 14 *ormai um pohino é che ne sei invecchiata*
   now you have become a bit old
E 15 *e ora te lo dó un pensiero ardito*
   now I'll give you a daring thought (something daring to think about)
E 16 *tra moglie- tra la nora- tra il mmarito e la nora <u>un ci mettere i ddito</u>*
   <u>don't put your finger</u> between the husband and the wife[160]
17   AUD = ((sparse applause))

Realdo/daughter-in-law also starts by proposing the possibility of a harmonious relationship with the mother-in-law. A relationship, though, that he hints is already hindered by the mother-in-law's previous statement (D 10). The daughter-in-law restates the mother-in-law's words in verses 11 and 12, namely the intention to get along and the agreement on the fact that the house belongs to the mother-in-law (D 12). In the second four verses, though, her tone changes, as she hints that the mother-in-law has gotten old (D 14). Although unstated, the conclusion to be drawn here is that the mother-in-law is too old, thus she may be unfit to lead the family. The daughter-in-law concludes by warning that the mother-in-law should not try to have control over the relationship between her son and the daughter-in-law (E 16).

Thus the daughter-in-law refuses the right of the mother-in-law to exercise her power on the relationship between her son and the daughter-in-law. Moreover, it is a statement that affirms the primacy of the marital relationship over the kinship system of descent. This implicitly negates support to a family structure that recognizes the center of power inside the family in the linear (agnatic) relationship. It is interesting to notice that this possible "disruptiveness" of the marital relationship with respect to the agnatic kinship system has been extensively studied, in the context of the Bedouin culture, by Abu-Lughod (1986). The daughter-in-law is not simply affirming herself and her power inside the family but, as will appear better as we

---

[160] Italian proverb exhorting people to keep out of the personal business of married couples.

proceed in the *Contrasto*, she is destabilizing the family structure itself, and acting within it as a centrifugal force.

As the *Contrasto* progresses, both poets escalate the reciprocal attacks. The mother-in-law threatens to use her power inside the family to throw the daughter-in-law out of it, as we can see in the following example/verses from octet #7 and from octet #9:[161]

> (Octet 7) Altamante /Mother-in-law
> G 23 *cerca di avé rispetto in casa mia*
>   try to show respect in my house
> G 24 *sennó dopo tre ore tu va' via*
>   otherwise after three hours you will go away
> (24a) AUD? = [ha ha ha ha ha
> (24b) AUD = [((scarce applause))
> (Octet 9) Altamante (Mother-in-Law)
> A 33 *guarda donnuccia io te lo do un consiglio*
>   look silly woman! I give you a counsel
> B 34 *quando tu sse' venuta sotto i mmio tetto*
>   when you have come under my roof
> A 35 *m'araccomando un allungá l'artiglio*
>   I recommend you, do not extend your claws
> B 36 *e guarda se tu porti di rispetto*
>   and see to show respect

Here the mother-in-law fights to keep and impose her power on the daughter-in-law, whom she sees as threatening (having claws rather than hands suggests rapacity – A 35). She requests a "respect" for her authority from the daughter-in-law (B 36).

IV. b. Language Use: Powerful Speech.
If we look at language use in these first octets, we will find several elements associated with what linguists call "powerful speech."[162] Among them, I want to focus on the following:

---

[161] The daughter-in-law, in turn, in octet 8 (not presented), complains of the disrespectful treatment she is receiving from the mother-in-law.

[162] I am referring to the studies by linguists and linguistic anthropologists who have been looking at the construction of hierarchies through conversational practices, and studies of cross-gendered speech.

1) Bald directives.
2) Use of insults.
3) Use of possessive pronouns.
4) Use of threats.
5) Use of pronoun "I."

These elements can be used, quoting from Candy Goodwin: "to build, and display to each other within the details of their talk, a distinctive type of social organization, one in which participants are pictured as aligned toward each other in an asymmetrical, 'hierarchical' fashion" (1990:77). Many of these elements can be found both in the mother-in-law's and in the daughter-in-law's speech,[163] indicating that they are trying to actively realign their hierarchical positions with respect to each other.

First, we find the use of strong, unmitigated, and thus face threatening directives (like orders). An example is, in octet #6, the injunction "don't put your finger" (E 16), namely do not interfere in the marital affairs. In octet #7, there is the only slightly mitigated order "try to show respect" (G 23), reiterated again in octet #9 (B 36). Still in octet #9, there are two more orders: "look" (A 33) and "do not extend your claws" (A 35).

Second, there is the use of verbal insults, and insults used as address terms, together with a demeaning description of the addressee. For example, in octet #9, the mother-in-law addresses the daughter-in-law using the term *donnuccia* (from *donna*, "woman," and the diminutive suffix -*uccia*, that indicates something small and of little value). These insults multiply, as I show below, as the *Contrasto* proceeds.

Third, the women use pronouns that indicate control or possession of the environment or things inside it (Goodwin, calls these "character ties," 1990:88-90). In particular the mother-in-law recalls several times her ownership over the house. In octet #5 and #7, "my home" (B 4 and G 23), and in octet #9, "my roof" (B 34).

Depictions of the self as powerful, by making threats, are also

---

[163] In the first octets I presented, it may appear that "powerful language" is used much more often by the mother-in-law. This is due to the fact that I have not included in the analysis the octet #8, sung by the daughter-in-law. In general, though, both mother-in-law and daughter-in-law use "powerful language" to a similar degree. Please refer to Appendix F for a full transcription of this *Contrasto*.

common. For example in octet #5, the mother-in-law threatens to send away the daughter-in-law "with a kick" (B 6). In octet #7, she produces again a similar threat (G 24).

Finally, notice the repeated use of the subject pronoun *io*, "I," that we find in octets #5 (A 3), #6 (C 9), and #9 (A 33). This use underlines the power of the speaker as agents. This use is even more notable in consideration of the fact that in Italian (differently from English) the subject pronouns are usually not included in sentences (they are to be understood from the context of the sentence). The use of such "powerful language" increases as the verbal dueling escalates.

IV. c. Contesting "Appropriate" Female Behavior.

From octet #10 Realdo switches to a new argument. The *Contrasto* switches from a duel over the possibility (for the daughter-in-law) to go away or remain in the family, to reciprocal attacks centered around the attribution of personal behavior, or better, mis-behavior. To underline this shift, notice how Realdo here addresses the audience. Only in the last two verses (47-48) does he reverse to addressing Altamante:

(Octet 10) Realdo (daughter-in-law)
C 41 *sentite che ignorante le ragi\<ona\>*
   listen to his uneducated/ignorant way of talking[164]
D 42 *tutto il giorno le sta a pettegolare*
   all day she spends gossiping
C 43 *e di lavare un vestito o nun é bona*
   and she is not good at washing even a single garment
D 44 *o nun é mai andata a lavorare*
   and she has never gone to work
C 45 *oggi vorebbe fá la donna bona*
   today she would like to be the good woman
D 46 *una giovane un viene a sopportare*
   she cannot tolerate a young one
E 47 *se io un lavorassi da mattina a sera*
   if I did not work from morning to evening
E 48 *nun mangeresti nemmeno una pera*
   you would not even have a pear to eat

---

[164] Notice the uptake of the other person's speech in mocking fashion, as a way to show her inadequacy or inappropriateness. This can also be considered an example of use of "powerful speech."

49   AUD? = [ha ha ha ha ha
50   AUD = [((applause)) ((some people laughing))

Here Realdo, in his attack, indirectly reveals some expected activities connected to the gender role of being "mother-in-law," or more generally "woman-part of the family." Among these activities are washing garments (work inside the house – C 43), and working for a salary to help the family economically (D 44). The daughter-in-law accuses the mother-in-law of not doing either of these activities, but spending her time gossiping (D 42). On the basis of such statements, the daughter-in-law then doubts the attempts of the mother-in-law to pass as a "good woman" (C 45), namely somebody that, being morally better than others, can elevate herself to judge their behavior.

The daughter-in-law continues by accusing the mother-in-law of being intolerant in her attitude toward a "young woman" like herself (D 46). Notice that the daughter-in-law has stressed the difference in age between herself and the mother-in-law already in octet #6 (D 14). Below, this difference will become more and more relevant.

Finally, the daughter-in-law compares such behavior to her own, emphasizing that she works all day (E 47), and claiming for herself a role as bread-winner inside the family (E 48). In doing so, she claims for herself an economic power inside the family. She opposes it to the economic uselessness of the "lazy" mother-in-law. Thus she claims authority with respect to the mother-in-law (an authority which is also moral) on the basis of her labor, or her role as "producer" inside the family.[165] The mother-in-law, in turn (octet #11), attacks this "moral authority" of the daughter-in-law by accusing her of having been a prostitute:

(Octet 11) Altamante/Mother-in-law

E 51 *tu se' stata ni mmondo una battagliera*
    you have been in the world a trouble maker
F 52 *e t'hanno vista anche su i mmarciapi<edi>*
    and they have seen you even on the sidewalk (prostituting)
G 55 *se c'era sempre la legge Merlini*
    if there was still the Merlini law[166]

---

[165] It is interesting to reflect on the fact that Marxism attributes power and authority to the working class on the same base, namely that they are the "producers."

[166] Here the poet makes a mistake. He should have said: "if there was *not* the

G 56 *e t'eri sempre a spasso pe' asini*
   you would be still walking among the brothels
57   AUD? = [he he he he he he
58   AUD = [((applause)) ((some people laughing))

Here the mother-in-law, in insulting the daughter-in-law, refers not only to a particular gender(ed) occupation (being a prostitute), but the insult has to be understood with reference to what constitutes appropriate female behavior, namely the refraining from sexual promiscuity. In octet #16 and #18, Realdo will also accuse the mother-in-law of having had liaisons with many men. The poets thus attack each other's honor, by accusing each other of sexual promiscuity. Such behavior in turn is seen as endangering the honor of the whole family. In the following octet (#12) Realdo continues attacking the behavior of the mother-in-law, by accusing her of not having been a good mother or wife:

(Octet 12) Realdo/Daughter-in-Law
G 61 *non ha mai accudito ai tuoi bambini*
   you never took care of your children
H 62 *e la famiglia tu l'ha rovinata*
   and you ruined your family
I 63 *povero tuo marito lavoratore onesto*
   poor husband of yours! An honest worker
I 64 *da patimenti l'ha fatto morí presto*
   with grief you made him die early
65   AUD? = ha ha ha ha
66   AUD = ((applause))

Realdo accuses the mother-in-law of "failing" both as a mother (by not taking care of her children – G 61) and as a wife (leading her husband to a premature death – I 64), thereby ruining her family (H 62). Thus Realdo is claiming again that the mother-in-law has not been following the prescribed rules of "good" "woman-in-the-family" behavior. As such, not only he is indirectly indexing what those rules may be, but also showing that the behavior of a particular person (the mother-in-law in this case) can break those rules (and possibly be called to account for it).

Merlini law…" In fact it was the Merlini law that abolished the brothels after the end of the fascist regime.

In the next octets, the mother-in-law answers accusing the daughter-in-law to be a "frivolous" woman, too preoccupied with her physical appearance, which is seen as "immoral" in terms of a more conservative ideology that dictates that a woman should "play down" her physical appearance, and avoid showing her bodily attributes. This new attack starts in octet # 13. Here Altamante recalls attention on the fact that the daughter-in-law changes hair-color often (K 71):

(Octet 13) Altamante/Daughter-in-Law
K 71 *una vorta l'é mora una vorta l'é bionda*
    one time she is brunette and one time she is blonde
K 72 *cosa ne fa di bella vagab<onda>*
    what can you do with such a lazy one
73   AUD? = ( ) meglio
              better
74   AUD = ((laughing)) ((sparse applause))

Next Altamante associates such behavior with laziness (has she nothing better to do than spending time with the hairdresser?) (K 72). The underlying idea is that putting on make-up and changing hair color are activities restricted to immoral women (maybe prostitutes), thus shedding a negative light on the daughter-in-law. It is important to notice two things here. First, although this ideological stance was stronger in the past, and it may be present today among the most conservative minorities, or, in played down forms, among older people in Tuscany, it is by no means shared by everybody or even by a large group of people. Tuscan women use make-up as a normal activity and change hair color according to the fashion trends, as is generally true for Italian women. Altamante, thus, is depicting his personage as a more conservative (older) woman. In this way he also presents the mother-in-law as more "traditionalist." She is a person who abides by traditionalist female roles.

The second important element to keep in mind is that Altamante does not necessarily share the beliefs and opinions that he portrays. He is playing into the role which has been given to him, with all the artistic weapons available to him as an experienced poet.[167] His portrait of the mother-in-law is partially a parody of an old mother-in-law, excessively jealous of her power in the family, extremely

---

[167] He may also be adopting arguments which are common to this particular theme of *Contrasto*.

conservative and backward. After all, humor is the main goal of the poets, and entertainment is the main goal of the performance.

Finally, by claiming for the mother-in-law a more "traditionalist" ethic/morality, Altamante is also indicating to Realdo a possible direction in which the discussion may move at this point, namely a confrontation between "conservative" vs. "progressive" views of gender roles inside the family. This in turn, could be played as a confrontation between an older and a new generation of women, and thus be played along age lines. In fact, in the next octet, Realdo promptly picks up the suggested development:

(Octet 14) Realdo/Daughter-in-Law
K 75 *se una vorta so mmora una vorta bionda*
  if one time I am brunette and one time I am blonde
(75)   AUD? = ha ha ha ha
L 76 *io tutt'i ggiorno vó a lavorare*
  all the day I go to work
K 77 *o povera vecchia rubiconda*
  poor old ruddy woman
L 78 *che l'ignoranza un ti viene a mancare*
  that you never are at a loss for ignorance
M 79 *ma di quello che dici non mi stupisci*
  but with what you are saying you do not surprise me
M 80 *perché te la gioventú nun la capisci*
  because you do not understand young people
81   AUD = ((sparse applause))

The daughter-in-law presents herself as a working woman, of a more "modern" or "progressive" way of thinking. First of all, the daughter-in-law declares that since she works (she earns a salary – L 76) she can do as she pleases, including spending money for make-up or hairdressers (K 75). It is her economic power, then, that it is claimed as a warrant for her "liberation" from conservative[168] gender roles. This is a very important point, and I will come back to discuss it later on, in the next section.

Having defended her own actions, the daughter-in-law underlines

---

[168] There are specific reasons why I use the term "conservative" rather than "traditional:" 1) Tradition includes change; 2) Tradition is not necessarily synonymous with "lack of freedom for women;" 3) Tradition is continuously created.

the fact that the mother-in-law is an old woman (K 77) who cannot understand young people (like herself) (M 80). A fracture is presented between an older and a younger generation. This opposition between the "past times" and the "present times" is a quite common theme in the *Contrasto*, and takes several forms. For example, it can take the form of an opposition between an old person and a young one, between "nature" (associated with something primordial) and "science" (associated with present developments), or just between the "old ways" and "new ways." The fundamental idea is a comparison between a "pre-modern" state and a "modernity" seen as unavoidably advancing. I will come back to discuss this in the next section.

Altamante, for his part, in the next octet, continues to underline the connection between the outward appearance (make-up, movements of the body) and inner "lack of morality" of the daughter-in-law:

(Octet 19) AltamanteMother-in-Law

B 114 *la mattina ti trucca e la va via*
    in the morning she makes up and she leaves
A 115 *si tinge il labbro <e la si fá il capello>*
    she paints her lip and makes her hair
B 116 *<la fa la gongolante pe'lla via>*
    she smiles too much along the road
A 117 *sempre alla barba di mmi figlio grullarello*
    always fooling my little idiot of a son

The mother-in-law accuses the daughter-in-law of exposing herself too much by putting on make-up (B 114) and lipstick (A 115). She then accuses her of exposing herself provocatively to the eyes of other males (by smiling too much in the street - B 116 – thus endangering the honor of her son). Here, though, the mother-in-law concludes by insulting her own son, implying that he is a fool since he lets his wife behave so "immorally" (A 117). The implied idea is that the son is not controlling the wife (and that he should and could if he wanted).

These women are fighting for power inside the family, but the mother-in-law ostensibly adheres to an ideology that it is actually the son who should have the power. By offending the son for not keeping the daughter-in-law in place, she is paying lip service to an ideology that says that the husband should have the power to control the wife's behavior. Notice that the mother-in-law is veiling her belief that her son, by dealing himself with the daughter-in-law, is supposed to spare her from the task of having to deal with a possible antagonist to power. What we see is a powerful woman using males (and their supposed power) to keep subordinate women in their place.

The mother-in-law adopts a very conservative ideological stance vis-a-vis gender roles (conservative by Tuscan standards) to impose her authority over her daughter-in-law while at the same time excusing herself morally, by avoiding taking responsibility for the way she tries to impose her power in the family. According to Jane Collier, women are "political actors." Their "quarrels" inside a family play a role in the shaping and reshaping of both social relations and of the organization of power relations in the larger society (1974:94).[169] The mother-in-law shows herself to be an expert politician, exercising a power whose source she declares to be external from her self, namely located in her son. The daughter-in-law, though, attacks her husband herself:

(Octet 20) Realdo/Daughter-in-Law
C 121 *anche lui come te gli é uno stucco*
      even him, like you, is a *stucco* (never happy, always complaining)
D 122 *si vede bene che ti rasso[miglia*
      it is obvious that he is like you
123   AUD? =   [ha ha ha ha e ride anche lui
124   he is laughing too

In so doing, she refuses the supposed power of her husband in her life. She demeans him by calling him a *stucco*, an offensive Tuscan word, indicating "somebody who is never happy with anything." The word and the way it is used are very "dismissive" of the husband's possible claims. But it is in the 24th octet, later on, the one that closes the *Contrasto*, that the daughter-in-law concludes her attack of the power of the mother-in-law:

---

[169] This also means that we have to rethink kinship structures as political structures.

(Octet 24) Alternated[170]

Altamante/Mother-in-law

B 158 *ma la socera la nora mai nun teme*

    but the mother-in-law never fears the daughter-in-law

(158) AUD? = (   )

Realdo/Daughter-in-Law

C 159 *se non teme la nora la socera o quel che dico io*

    if the mother-in-law does not fear the daughter-in-law or what I say

C 160 *di casa ti porto via il marito mio*

    I will take away my husband from your house

The daughter-in-law's threats to leave the household with her husband (C 160), may be a glimpse of the break-down of the traditional family. Such break-downs happen when the daughters-in-law, no longer needing the family economically, become a centrifugal force inside it and thus push toward the creation of smaller family units, or neolocal residencies. This new economic independence is in turn connected to the passage from a peasant economy to an industrial one, and with the abandonment of the countryside and urbanism movements, both of which have been important phenomena in Tuscany in the post-war period.

V. A Female Poet's Voice in the *Contrasto*.

In the previous *Contrasto* "women" are portrayed by male poets. Therefore, I thought it important to present the voices of Tuscan women themselves. In my work on Tuscan Community Theater (Pagliai, 1999), a verbal art genre where women's voices are very strong,[171] I found similar representations of power struggles and hierarchies among them. Moreover, I found the portrayal of similar

---

[170] The last two octets of a *Contrasto* are done "alternated," namely sung by both poets together. Each poet produces one verse of the first six verses, then the poet who started the octet produces the 7th and 8th verses. The same is repeated in the next octet, but with the poets switching turns, so that the other poet now gets to sing the 7th and 8th verse. Sometimes, when the *Contrasto* is too "heated up," the poets may produce several of these alternated octets, in an attempt to "get the last word." Otherwise, the alternated octets may have a conciliatory mood.

[171] In Tuscan Community Theater, many of the performers are women. Women are involved in all the parts of the production, as actors, writers, directors, and also technician, prompters, sustainers and fans. They prepare costumes and scenery as well.

hierarchies in a *Contrasto* where one of the poets performing was actually a woman, Liliana Tamberi. This was again a *Contrasto* between "Mother-in-law and Daughter-in-Law," sung by Liliana together with Elidio Benelli (see figure #11).

The divergence in interests and agendas of different women inside the family is well shown in this *Contrasto*, of which I will present the first two octets.[172] It was sung as part of a performance in Migliana, a small town in the province of Prato (August 2, 1997). The setting was a local feast organized by the city council. Five poets were present at this performance,[173] and they took turns contrasting with each other.

Figure #11: Liliana Tamberi (left) and Elidio Benelli (right) in Migliana.

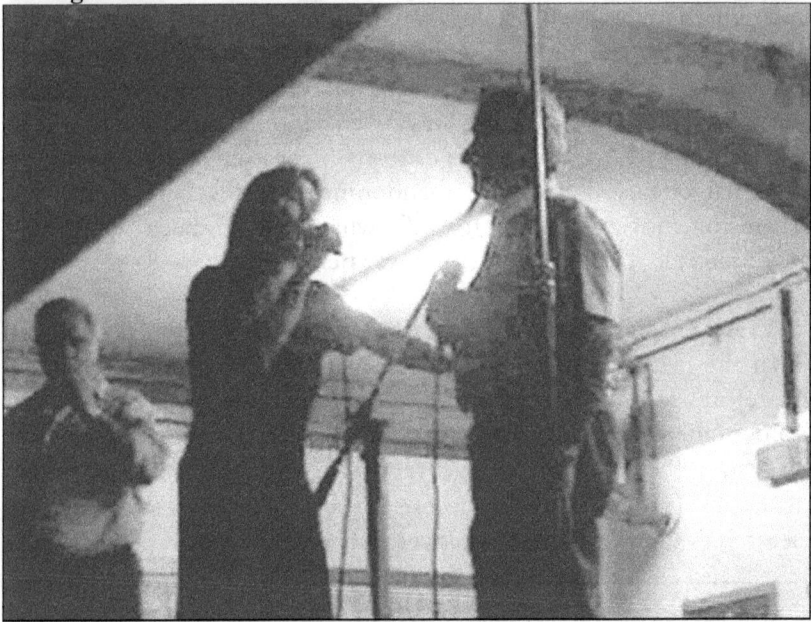

The performance was held in the large, paved area behind the local *circolo ricreativo*, "recreational club." This area must have been usually used as a restaurant as well. A basic wooden stage had been assembled next to the building, and behind the stage, a long table had been prepared where the poets and their friends – including me – dined

---

[172] Please refer to the Appendix F for a full transcription of this *Contrasto*.

[173] Elidio Benelli, Altamante Logli, Davide Riondino, Liliana Tamberi and Realdo Tonti.

before the performance. The area in front of the stage was covered with orderly rows of plastic chairs, where most of the audience sat. There was a large audience and people had to sit on the floor as well.[174] The place was surrounded by plants and trees, which made it very pleasant.

Since the setting was rather isolated behind a building, there were no passersby and the audience, composed of women and men at various ages and including many children, remained attentive throughout the performance. They also suggested a very high number of themes (the children in particular suggested many of them). In part because of this, and in part because of the relatively high number of poets present, the *Contrasti* were shortened to include only 9 to 16 octets each. The *Contrasto* between mother-in-law and daughter-in-law included only 9 octets. The poets chose their personage before starting to sing. In the first octet, Elidio/mother-in-law presents an initial harmonious situation:[175]

(Octet 1) Elidio/Mother-in-law

A 1 *vieni mia nora darmelo un bacetto*
  come, my daughter-in-law, give me a little kiss
B 2 *qual siei la regina in casa mia*
  since you are the queen in my house
A 3 *presto mi darai un pargoletto*
  soon you will give me a baby
B 4 *e che tutti in famiglia si desia*
  that everybody in the family desires
A 5 *col reciproco amor con tanto affetto*
  with the reciprocal love with so much affection
B 6 *ti prego farmi questa cortesia*
  I pray that you will grant me this courtesy
C 7 *e soddisfá dovrai i miei pensieri*
  and my hopes you will have to satisfy
C 8 *una cosa che s' aspetta volentieri*
  with something that is waited for gladly

The mother-in-law starts by showing great affection for her

---

[174] It is difficult to give an estimate, but I would say around three hundred people were in attendance.

[175] I believe it is traditional in this particular theme to start with the presentation of an harmonious relationship that then becomes progressively disrupted.

daughter-in-law (A 1), and seems to relinquish to her the power in the house (B 2). In the third verse, the mother-in-law starts unveiling what her desire is, namely to be given a grandchild (A 3). Notice that she states that the baby will be given to her – not the father (A 3). Then she adds that the same is the desire of the whole family (A 4). In the second part of the octet, she again uses affectionate words, to coax the daughter-in-law into satisfying her desire (C 7) by having a baby. In these verses the daughter-in-law is shown love and considered as part of the family in her role as "reproducer" of the family itself. No mention is made of a possible role as a "producer." The answer of the daughter-in-law, anyway, immediately hints at her role as "producer" in the household:

(Octet 2) Liliana/Daughter-in-Law

C 9 *pói aspetta so vvani desideri*
   you can wait, they are vain desires
D 10 *e mi ci manca pure che un figliolo*
   even a child! that's all we need!
C 11 *e non mi bastano tutti i pensieri*
   like if it wasn't enough all the worries
D 12 *che te le da- che me le dá il tu figlio giá da solo*
   that already your son alone gives me
C 13 *e te lo dice qui sí la Tamberi*
   Tamberi is going to tell you right here
D 14 *con questa cosa spero ti consolo*
   with this fact I hope to console you
E 15 *su questa cosa no non l'avra vinta*
   on this thing you will not win
E 16 *se speri di vedemmi presto incinta*
   if you hope to see me pregnant soon
17   AUD = ((applause))

The daughter-in-law refuses the suggestion of motherhood given by the mother-in-law (C 9). She refuses to be a mother (E 15-16). The mother-in-law had shown interest in the preservation of the family, but the daughter-in-law denies this interest, showing a different agenda. First, she doubts that a child is in her best interest (D 10), and then she considers the fact that having to look after her husband already gives her enough troubles to deal with (D 12). Then, in verse 15, she suggests that the mother-in-law's proffers of love may just be an indirect way to obtain things, to win the daughter-in-law to her desires (E 15).

In this *Contrasto*, thus, different women's agendas inside the family are portrayed. These agendas depend on the women's relative positionalities in respect to the other members of the family. Age, class and power may contribute to shape these different goals. As the daughter-in-law declares in her next octet, the reason why she does not want to have a child is that she already has enough family work, serving the other members:

(Octet 4) Liliana/Daughter in law
B 26 *e ci s'ha in questa casa un gran da ffare*
   in this house we have a lot to do
A 27 *ci mancherebbe pure della prole*
   that's all we need! children!
B 28 *non basta giá il pulire e il cucinare*
   like if it was not enough the cleaning and cooking

Sylvia Yanagisako (1991), in a study of Northern Italian entrepreneurial (high middle class) families, shows that males and females inside a family may have different goals and a different hierarchy of interests. She proposes to see "family members' goals and strategies as the culturally specific, gendered interests and strategies of real people living and acting within a particular history of social and economic transformation" (1991:323). Recognizing that women may have different interests means recognizing that the family can be a ground for the negotiation and struggle for power (Yanagisako, 1991:323). In the family, gender and social relationships can be reproduced, contested and transformed (1991:324). Similarly, the *Contrasto* itself is a locus where power relationships among women can be portrayed, contested and negotiated.

VI. Gendered Roles and Ideologies.

After reading the preceding *Contrasti* in terms of "female hierarchies" I want now to briefly rethink them in another key. We could in fact, as I have already started to point, see them as a "generational" *Contrasto*, which opposes the views of gender roles of an older generation of Tuscans with the view of the younger generation. This is an opposition, as I already noticed, that pits the "old ways" against the "new ways." This opposition could be read in turn as one between pre-modernity and modernity. As I will argue in this section, these views are in turn connected to a "Marxist" world view or matrix that (as I discussed in chapter 2) today is reflexively connected to the Tuscan culture.

Marxism is a strongly modernist philosophy. In Italy, Marxism as realized in the Italian Communist Party, is also a nationalist project.[176] Nationalism, in turn, is the offspring of modern times. Thus in Tuscany Marxism often mediates between images of modernity and pre-modernity. The poets, both as leftists and as Tuscans, are influenced by these political ideologies and, in the course of history, have contributed to shape and propagate them (see chapter 4). Thus they become the mediator between images of modernity, political ideologies, and local audiences.[177]

As I argued earlier, definitions of gender are always ideological (thus subjective, but belonging to a socially constructed objectivity). Gender divisions are ideological because they depend on the ideological views of those who define them. This in turn should make us reflect on the connection between images of gender and political ideologies, which shape those images. Ideas of gender and gender roles, then, must be seen as part of larger systems of ideologies. The answer to the question who/what is a woman is inevitably a politically bound answer.

This leads me to theorize that the poets conceptualize women according to a political-ideological plan, or according to the political ideologies that they are "defending." They present ideological images of womanhood. But isn't this what social scientists do as well? The *Contrasto* then, can be read as a confrontation between two images of womanhood and gender roles. The first upheld by the more conservative traditionalist imagery, the other proposed by Marxist ideals.

Interesting in this regard is the mention, which I discovered recently, of a *Contrasto* which is supposed to have been sung by the poets Idalberto Targioni and Fortunato Chiti in 1911. The theme of this *Contrasto* was "the woman according to the socialist morals vs. the woman according to the catholic morals." Here it is clear that

---

[176] Gramsci believed that only in a unified nation sharing a common language could the proletarian masses be organized to oppose capitalism. Thus nationalism came before internationalism. The Italian left eventually shifted, between the sixties and the seventies, to positions that admitted federalism (as I discussed in chapter 2), but remained opposed to ethnic separatist claims.

[177] As they were the mediator between national political stances and their local audiences in chapter 4.

"womanhood" is a political issue.[178]

VI. a. Contrasting Gender Roles: Housewife Vs. Employed Woman.

An interesting *Contrasto* in this regard is one on the theme *Casalinga e Impiegata* ("Housewife vs. Employed Woman – white collar employee). This *Contrasto* was recorded in Ribolla (a small town in province of Grosseto) on the 19th of April 1998. The occasion was the annual meeting of the *Poeti Bernescanti*.[179] The *Contrasto* was sung by Realdo Tonti with another poet that I could not identify,[180] and that I will indicate as "Poet 2."

In this particular occasion, the matching of the poets into pairs and with a theme and personage had been done randomly, by extracting a ticket from a bowl. So the poets did not have to agree on who was doing each part and they immediately started their duel. In his first octet (#2) Realdo affirmed his happiness as an employed woman. The housewife answered (octet #3) by underlining the importance of taking good care of her own family:

(Octet 3) Poet 2/Housewife
A 19 *in casa mia altra cosa avviene*
   in my house another thing happens
B 20 *per la famiglia io vivo che e' preziosa*
   I live for my family, which is precious
A 21 *guardero' sempre che ognuno stia bene*
   I will always take care that everybody is fine
B 22 *per vive per mangia' in frettolosa*
   You are in a haste: living, eating
C 23 *tu che vai null' ufficio e la (ser ede)*
   you that go in the office and (come out in the evening)
C 24 *a volte di un mangiar ti po succede*
   and sometimes you do not even eat
25   AUD = ((applause))

---

[178] After all feminism and Marxism were born in the same *milieu* and they are the result of the attempt of marginalized groups to claim a place as historical subjects.

[179] I have already discussed this particular context in chapter 3.

[180] This *Contrasto* was recorded by my parents, Raffaello Pagliai and Lelia Nesti, in my absence. Many poets come to this meeting from all over Tuscany and central Italy, so I did not know many of them personally, and their names are difficult to reconstruct from the recording.

The housewife declares that she lives for her family (B 20), whose welfare she considers as the most important thing (A 21). Then, she opposes such life to the "living and eating in haste" of the working woman (B 22). This also shows, in turn, a shared cultural assumption, namely that a working woman will have no time to be a "good mother" or even to take good care of herself and her own diet (C 24). Thus the housewife upholds her traditional gender role, as she notices the negative sides of working outside the house. In the octet #4,[181] Realdo argues that the housewife has no knowledge of the life of an employed woman, since she is always relegated in the house. Next, the Poet 2/Housewife recalls the discomforts of having to wake up early in the morning to go to work:

(Octet 5) Poet 2/Housewife
A 33 *Io chedo che di tanto un ti diverta*
    I believe that you are not really having that much fun
B 34 *alzarsi tanto presto la mattina*
    to wake up so early in the morning
A 35 *sai bell' onesta nella coperta*
    you know beautifully honest in the covers
B 36 *or che il maggio a noi ci si avvicina*
    now that May is getting closer
A 37 *io sai che sono una cuoca esperta*
    you know that I am an expert cook
B 38 *e per il pranzo e la mia meddicina*
    and for lunch (which is) my medicine
C 39 *il pronto sempre all'ora e 'lo facevo*
    ready always at the right time I would make
C 40 *e a mezzogiorno sempre mangio e bevo*
    and at noon always I feast
(40) AUD = ((applause))

The housewife states that she can stay (honestly) in bed (A 35), and then prepare good meals for herself (37-40). Thus Poet 2 presents an "idealized" image of what being an housewife is. Notice that this image also indexes a certain social class, an urban middle class. This image of being an housewife as a "relaxing" life also recalls the ideals

---

[181] Not presented here, see Appendix F.

and promises of economic abundance of the modern dream of capitalism. Thus Poet 2 bases his argument by invoking the privilege of the upper classes (applied to women) who do not have to work. This gender role thus indexes a class division.[182] In the next octet (#6) though the employed woman negates what the housewife stated so far:

(Octet 6) Realdo/Employee
C 41 *o quello che facevi lo vedevo*
   what you would do I did see
D 42 *indaffarata da mattina a sera*
   always busy from morning to evening
C 43 *ma anche io credi e mangio e bevo*
   but I too, believe me, eat and drink (well)
D 44 *e po n' ufficio tasto la tastiera*
   then in the office I write on the typewriter
C 45 *su una bella poltrona mi sedevo*
   I seat on a beautiful chair
D 46 *tanto sia d' inverno o primavera*
   in Winter like in Spring
E 47 *e poi quando comincia la giornata*
   and then when the day starts
E 48 *sempre prima di me ti trovo alzata*
   I always find you awoken before me
49   AUD = ((laughing and applause))

Realdo states that the work of the housewife is heavier and repetitive, never-ending (from morning to the evening – D 42). The employed woman instead can just sit at her chair and move her fingers on the keyboard (44-45). Moreover, the employed woman negates the image of not being able to take care of herself. On the contrary, she can eat and drink well (C 43). Finally, he notices that the housewife, far from being able to linger in bed, has to wake up earlier than anyone else (E 48). Thus Realdo proposes a different image of housewifery, one that in turn indexes a different social class at the same time: the lower, working class. Here the housewife has to labor

---

[182] Compare Adachi's (2000) account of upper class housewives in Japan as "symbols" of national womanhood.

hard all day.[183]

This image is also connected to an ideological stance. In fact this is the image of housewifery proposed by the left. While the communist party has always insisted that women and men, having equal rights and duties, should both be able to work outside the house,[184] at the same time they have often proposed that housewives, as laborers, should receive a salary for their work. Unpaid domestic work, in turn, is seen almost as a form of slavery. Similar views are found among Italian feminists. Indeed the feminist movement in Italy was originally and fundamentally a leftist movement. In this view the housewife becomes a symbol of oppression on women carried out by capitalism through the imposition of "differential" and "gender based" roles (like the housewife).[185]

This thinking is veiled in Realdo's first attack, but it will become clearer later. Here instead he presents the work of the employee as "relaxing" in opposition to the work of the housewife. In the next octet (#7) the housewife brings a different attack, namely she opposes her own power inside the family to the powerlessness of the employed woman in the workplace:

(Octet 7) Poet 2/Housewife
F 52 *se tu fai sbaglio la trovi i padroni*
    if you make a mistake the boss is right there
E 53 *io invece in casa mia so abbituata*
    instead in my home I am used
F 54 *ognuno accettera' le mie opinioni*
    everybody accepts my opinions
G 55 *ma se tu scrivi a volte e scrivi male*
    but if you write sometimes, if you write something wrong
G 56 *i conti poi te(i) fai col principale*
    then you have to deal with the boss

---

[183] Again, for a parallel with Japan, see Tamanoi's discussion of the idealization of Japanese country-women and of the *komori* versus the realities of their hard labor and exploitation (1998:75 & fol.).

[184] Work is a right of the person, as a base for economical independence and thus personal freedom. I will came back to this later on.

[185] Moreover, we should keep in mind that the two poets collaborate in developing the theme. Thus, in a sense, by proposing the image of the "happy housewife," the Poet 2 is opening the road for an attack presenting the image of the "hard laboring housewife."

57   AUD = ((applause))

Here Poet 2 switches to a new argument, producing an octet quite interesting in view of what I discussed before regarding women's power in the family. He notices that the housewife has a high degree of power inside the family. First, to be an employee equated with a loss of power: the employee is always under the direct control of a higher authority, her boss, who can establish what is done right or wrong (F 52). Notice that the word *padrone*, "boss" in Italian has also the meaning of "master" or "owner" thus giving much force to an image of the employee as a "slave of the office."

Then the housewife opposes this to her own situation. Notice the use of the possessive in *casa mia*, "my house," (E 53) – here she establishes herself as the owner of the house. In the next line, in fact, she states that everybody there accepts her opinions (F 54). Although played down by using "opinions" rather than "wishes" it is clear that she is referring to being in control, being able to impose her point of view over the rest of the family.

Finally, the Poet 2 goes back to underline that on the contrary, the employee has to account to her boss for any possible error (G 55-56). Notice the word *principale*, (lit. principal) used here to indicate the boss. This word evokes the existence of a hierarchy in the work place, in respect to which the employee is in a lower ranking position. Thus the Poet 2 opposes the power of the housewife in the family to the powerlessness of the employee in the workplace. Next Realdo states that the housewife also makes mistakes, although they remain hidden behind the walls of the house. The Poet 2 (octet #9) answers by inviting the employed woman to her house, so she can see for herself how her life is better. In octet # 10, Realdo goes back to the image of the housewife as "house slave:"

(Octet 10) Realdo/Employee
A 75 *sempre a lavare ti si rompe i reni*
    always washing until your kidneys are broken
B 76 *ma tu lo fai si con bramosia*
    but you do it indeed with desire
A 77 *se nel mio mondo poi tu ci vieni*
    then, if you come in my world
B 78 *e tu vivrai con piu' allegria*
    you will live with more joy

Realdo implies that the housewife is "mislead" since not only she works so much (until her back is broken – A 75), but she even likes it (B 76). On the other hand, the employee lives in another world (A 77), one that the housewife is ignorant of. Realdo implies that if the housewife should realize her "sad" situation, she would abandon the house and live "with more joy" herself (B 78). Here he hints at the idea that only the woman who becomes "self aware" of her oppression can liberate herself (and thus come to a full enjoyment of life).

To summarize, this *Contrasto* shows that political ideologies influence the way in which women (and their labor) are represented. Next, I want to discuss further the connection between economic independence and freedom of choice. As Ernestine Friedl (1986) argued, starting from a materialistic definition of power as economic power, the measure of power is given by the real decisional power that women have (in her case, in Greek society) to decide about the economic enterprise of the family. This includes their decision-making power with regard to issues connected with the welfare of the family, such as the decisions over the choice of the husband or bride for the sons and daughters. This authority, in turn, is based on the fact that women have economic power, both because they are producers, through their work, and because they bring to the family part of the inherited goods.

VI. b. Contesting Sexual Roles: Boy Vs. Girl.

In section IV, I already showed how the daughter-in-law may claim authority and power in the family on the basis of her ability to contribute economically to it. I will now proceed to analyze a new *Contrasto*, where I believe this power-claim becomes more generally applicable to contexts outside the family. This *Contrasto* between *un ragazzo e una ragazza*, "A Boy and a Girl,"[186] was sung by the poets Altamante Logli and Realdo Tonti during a performance in Malmantile, a small town in the province of Florence, on July 5, 1997

---

[186] I need to spend a few words here on the terms "boy" and "girl." The Italian terms *ragazzo/ragazza* mean both "boy" or "boyfriend," "girls" or "girlfriend." Moreover, in Italy this term is applied not only to teenagers, but to unmarried men and women in general. Thus it refers only partially to age, and it indexes the marital status of the person. To make a *Contrasto* between a boy and a girl implies that the two may have a sexual liaison between them, but no marital ties (or kinship obligations).

(see figure #12). The theme is part of a sub-set of themes that pit against each other a man and a woman; for example "Husband and Wife," "Husband, Wife and Lover" or similar ones.

Figure #12: *Sagra* of the Goose in Malmantile.

The context of the performance was a local *sagra del papero*, "feast of the goose." Although the *sagra* had been originally planned to happen in the local *campo sportivo* (extramural field), because of a sudden rainy and cold weather plans had been changed. Rain is quite unusual in July in Tuscany, thus the organizers had erected a temporary large tent attached to a small building used as a kitchen. Inside the tent were three long lines of tables bordered by benches. The place was quite overcrowded with people eating, and there was no stage.[187] The poets, who had been dining with their friends and "their" anthropologist, around 10pm stood up in the corner near the kitchen, and started singing. The audience was very warm and ready to participate, the poets were in full form, and I remember this as one their most comic and fun performances.

The *Contrasto* "boy vs. girl" takes place toward the middle of the

---

[187] Hence I could not set up the tripod and had to record the entire performance holding the video-camera in my hand.

performance. It immediately takes a "sexual turn." Namely what gets discussed are norms and ideas about the sexual behavior of men and women. After discussing, in the first four octets, who is doing each personage, Altamante/Boy starts by opposing the acceptable sexual behavior of women and men:

(Octet 5) Altamante/Boy

A 33 *A me tu m'ha a dire- a me tu mi devi dire chi ti piglia*
    you have got to tell me- you should tell me who is going to take you
B 34 *o ragazzina se' troppo pendente*
    o little girl you are too much bent
A 35 *l'omo gli é un cavallo a sciolte briglia*
    man is a horse with loose reins (galloping)
B 36 *e gira da i ssud e da i pponente*
    he goes around to the south and to the occident
A 37 *vá dalla madre, la socera e la figlia*
    he goes to the mother, the mother-in-law and the daughter
B 38 *e dappertutto ce l'arota i ddente*
    and everywhere he sharpens his tooth
C 39 *e te tu se una ragazza abbandonata*
    and you are an abandoned girl
C 40 *da tanti giovanotti rigirata*
    turned around by so many young men
(40) AUD? = ((smiling))

The boy starts by doubting if anybody would ever want (as a wife?) the girl (A 33), since she is *pendente*, "bent," namely imperfect, marred (B 34). Thus he is evoking the belief that women have to keep themselves "pure" by avoiding sexual contact with males. Notice that it would be wrong to consider such belief as "culturally shared" in Tuscany. Although the ideology (not the fact) of female purity (before marriage) was upheld, especially in the past, by Christian morality, today it is upheld only by a segment of the population, usually a conservative or religious minority. Still, the possibility to be stigmatized for an overt sexuality is much higher for women than for men today (not only in Tuscany, but throughout the Western countries at least).

On the basis of the same ideology, the situation for males is practically inverted. Sexually promiscuous behavior was traditionally culturally encouraged (or at least accepted), and connected (probably) to images of "strong" masculinity. In fact, Altamante in the next few lines proposes that the boy is "free" to have sexual liaisons with as many women as he pleases (A 37- B 38). Notice how the poet evokes manhood at the beginning of verse 35, associating "man" with the image of a "stud" (A 35). Namely he evokes a powerful sexuality for himself while at the same time he denies it to women – for whom an attempt to enjoy the same kind of sexuality would mean stigma and "refusals" (as unmarriageable) by men (C 39-40).

Figure #13: Logli (left) and Tonti (right) in Malmantile.

The boy thus hints that a sexually free woman becomes unmarriageable and she is thus "abandoned" (C 39), namely "condemned" to be a tainted woman. Altamante is thus taking an extremely conservative position, but also one that, since its rootedness in hegemonic conservative views of male/female sexuality, it is difficult to contrast/oppose. Indeed it seems to be rooted in "objective reality" itself (the objective reality, socially constructed, of the powerlessness and lack of freedom of choice of "women").

Having considered this, Realdo's strategy in the next octet is particularly interesting. The girl shifts the focus, in the first two verses, from sexual behavior to "economic behavior," by accusing the boy of living "day by day," namely not having a stable occupation (C 41). Then she opposes to that her own behavior as a girl who "earns her living," namely she immediately underlines her economic independence (D 42):

(Octet 6) Realdo/Girl

C 41 *Fó come te nun vivo alla giornata*
   I do not live day by day like you

D 42 *sono ragazza il mio lavor me lo guadagno*
   I am a girl that earns her work

C 43 *quando gli arriva poi la mia serata*
   then, when my evening comes

D 44 *io esco fori con il mio compagno*
   I go out with my partner

C 45 *te una vedi un te n'é capitata*
   you, see, you haven't gotten any

D 46 <*e io lo capisco il tuo lagno*>
   and I do understand why you are grumbling/whining

E 47 *ragazze nun ne trovi dappertutto*
   you will not find girls everywhere

E 48 *mi pare a me tu sia troppo brutto*
   it seems to me that you are too ugly

In the second two verses, the girl goes back to a discussion of sexual behavior. In doing so, though, she stresses not power, but egalitarianism. She says that when the evening comes (C 43), thus when she has finished her working day, she goes out with her partner (D 44). Having done her duty, she now has the right to enjoy herself as she pleases. The use of the word *compagno*, "partner," indexes an egalitarian relationship of reciprocal support (the word *compagno*, as we saw in chapter 4, also means "comrade"). This choice of words is even more important. The word *compagno* is rarely used in Italy to indicate a "significant other" (but it is quite common among feminists, or where politically correct talk is necessary).

Thus the girl has constructed her discourse in a way that bases her right to choose a companion, to be a peer to him, and to enjoy herself in her leisure time, on her ability to work, namely on her economic power. Notice that this is the same argument Realdo uses in defending the "employed woman" in the previous *Contrasto*. The idea that economic power can be an enfranchising solution to the plight of women's oppression is not new. The same thinking, as I previously showed, we find both in Marxism and feminism.

For example, in first wave feminism, activists like Olive Schreiner noticed the connection between paid labor and personal freedom. Schreiner wrote: "The woman should be absolutely and entirely independent of the man" (quoted in McClintock, 1995:286). Anne McClintock, in her analysis of Schreiner's ideas, writes: "Without economic independence, women had no power and no form of redress. Here Schreiner went beyond the emergent feminist critique of marriage, ... she was more aware than most that the real issue was 'the sex purchasing power of the male' " (1995:286).[188]

In the *Contrasto*, the acquired economic independence allows the girl to refuse the young man and deride him. In fact the girl concludes her attack by wondering if the boy's "sexual freedom" is not just a way to avoid facing the fact that he does not have a partner. Then (E 48) she gives her punch line: maybe the reason is that the boy is too ugly. Here she is also proposing the idea that women, far from being passively waiting to be chosen by males, may actually doing the choosing themselves, and impose their own "aesthetic" rules.

VI. c. Ideological Images of Womanhood: The Nun Vs. the Prostitute.

Before closing this section I would like to briefly discuss a third *Contrasto*, between a "Nun and a Prostitute." This theme is quite common, and it has some common features, to which I will refer. This one was recorded during the performance in Migliana, which I mentioned previously. It was sung by the poets Altamante Logli and Davide Riondino.[189]

In the *Contrasto* between "Nun and Prostitute," the personages may seem at first to represent the two faces of the bidimensional woman of western symbolism: the Madonna and the whore. Things though are quite more complicated in the *Contrasto*, as the prostitute ends up accusing the nun of fornication with priests and friars, thus showing that the side of the Madonna is just an hypocritical faked image. On

---

[188] It is indeed striking how several arguments that Realdo does in this *Contrasto* are similar to arguments proposed by Schreiner. Since the possibility that Realdo may know her writings is to be excluded, the connecting link must be found elsewhere. I believe it must be found in the socialist ideologies. Schreiner in fact also considered herself a socialist.

[189] Davide Riondino is a man in his forties, born in the province of Arezzo. He is a famous Italian pop singer and cabaret performer. He is known all over Italy for his music and his appearances in TV. Few, anyway, know that he also sings *Contrasti*, every once in a while. Although he is not an expert poet, he has a very personal style and is a very funny improviser.

the other side, both these personages share the characteristics of not being married, thus they are constructed outside of kinship ties. Both, in different ways and for different reasons, have renounced having a family. Because of this, both personages are often portrayed as incomplete, precisely because of the absence of kinship ties. Notice, for example, the way Altamante/prostitute addresses Davide/nun:

(Octet 3) Altamante/Prostitute

B 18 *il tuo avvenire credi é bell'e spento*
　　your future, believe me, it's already extinct
A 19 *non hai ne un marito e ne una prole*
　　you do not have an husband nor children
B 20 *te schiava tu rimani in un convento*
　　you, like a slave, remain in the convent

Here the prostitute tells the nun that she has no future (B 18), namely no possibility to leave a descendant, since she has no husband or children (A 19). She then calls her a "slave," prisoner in the convent. In octet #5, the prostitute again recalls the topic of slavery (C 39), adding to it a lyric depiction of the nun as a "withered flower" (C 40):

(Octet 5) Altamante/Prostitute

C 39 *troppo schiava tu sei te del cielo*
　　too much a slave you are of the sky
C 40 *resti un fiore appassito sullo stelo*
　you remain a flower withered on the stem
41　AUD = ((general applause))

Even in the attack, the prostitute seems to show a sympathetic emotion toward her adversary. In other developments of this same theme, the women accuse each other of being "slaves:" of male sexual desire the first, of religious fanaticism the other. The conclusion of the poets[190] is that they are both slaves to an economic-ideological system that on one hand buys and sells bodies, and on the other imposes its authority through obscurantism and fear of religious dogma.

The *Contrasti* between "Nun and Prostitute," then, are deeply

---

[190] I gathered this information in subsequent conversations with Altamante Logli, in which I asked him the meaning of this *Contrasto*.

political. They problematize traditional "monodimensional" views of women, by trying to depict what it means to be a "prostitute" or a "nun." One fulcrum of this story is often revolving around the idea that both have been deprived of something very important: namely the possibility to create affective ties and raise children, thus giving life to the next generation of humanity. Both are sterile figures in their monodimensionality, in their separation from kinship ties. They have become trees that give no fruit. The image of sterility, slavery and ultimate disappearance in the absence of offspring becomes symbolic, for the poets, of the operations of capitalism on the human bodies.

VII. Conclusion.

Harold Garfinkel as early as 1967 noticed that gender is an institution, socially produced and reproduced (1967). Gender is constructed in everyday interactions. The poets render this construction evident in their "doing being" men and women. If a male poet can become woman and speak with a woman's voice, what does this tell about what "being" a woman is? It can indeed show how "womanness" is constructed in everyday life. A person is a woman then (but not a generic woman, rather a mother-in-law, or a daughter-in-law, or a wife, etc.), because in being a woman she can fit inside a niche of society that allows her to exercise a certain amount of power with respect to men and to other women. When I position myself as a woman, I also position myself with respect to the universe of social relationship that are also relationships of power.

It may be worth considering at this point a possible objection: in representing gender roles are the poets not reifying them, reinforcing their authority right at the same moment when they seem to undermine it? Are they naturalizing gender roles, while they debate them? Similarly Kondo, in her essay on the theater play *M. Butterfly*, writes: "Must one reinscribe stereotypes in order to subvert them? … Though the issue is vexed, I have argued elsewhere (1990) that there can be no pristine space of resistance, and that subversion and contestation are never beyond discourse and power" (1997:53). As far as the *Contrasti* are doing a parody of gender roles, they refer to a common stereotypical knowledge of what the roles are. Does this means that they may reinforce those stereotypes, reaffirming them as real?

According to Judith Butler: "the refusal of the law might be produced in the form of the parodic inhabiting of conformity … a repetition of the law into hyperbole" (1997:382). She then wonders, if "parodying the dominant norms is enough to displace them – indeed, whether the denaturalization of gender cannot be the very vehicle for a reconsolidation of hegemonic norms. ... drag may well be used in the service of both the denaturalization and the reidealization of hyperbolic heterosexual gender norms" (1997:384). She underlines that the individual is always implicated in the regimes of power that s/he opposes (1997:384). Thus Butler theorizes a coexistence of resistance and acquiescence.

It seems to me that the *Contrasto* is not so much "naturalizing" or "deconstructing" gender. It is instead continuously presenting different views of it, each of which is portrayed as "natural." The *Contrasto* presents different ideological images of womanhood, and it presents them as antinomies. It opens up the conflict to scrutiny, but never tries to resolve it. The "truth" about womanhood does not lay in either side, and a synthesis of them is impossible: this conflict can never be resolved.

The poets do more than representing an ideology of womanhood that is possibly already naturalized in society. The humorous way in which the poets drive the evocation of "womanhood" to its extremes – never failing to obtain a response of roaring laughter from the audience – introduces an element of doubting, of deconstruction of perceived realities. They thus invite the audience to look into the complexity of being human, or the complexity of the construction of the social self, and the complexity of the social elements that make each person a unique individual. By laughing, the audience indirectly shows it recognizes the portrait/portraiture, but also that it recognizes such constructions of personhood as something to be laughed at, a mono-dimensional image of what, in everyday experience, is instead a unique construction of individual particular selves – selves that never correspond adequately to the ideology expressed in the portraiture.

7
ARS POETICA:
IDEOLOGIES OF STYLE AND PERFORMANCE

There's a blind man here with a brow
As white as a cloud.
And all we fiddlers, from highest to lowest,
Writers of music and tellers of stories,
Sit at his feet,
And hear him sing of the fall of Troy
(Edgar Lee Masters, 1992:34).

I. Introduction.

What is art? Where does the artistic inspiration come from? And who are the artists? It may be obvious to an anthropologist knowledgeable of cultural relativism, that these questions can have an infinite number of answers. In the western world, "high art" is distinguished from "popular art." The second may be "ethnic art," "folk art," "pop art" or simply "craft."

In chapter 2, I showed how the formation of the new Italian nation was connected to an attempt to create a "standard national language." This attempt conformed to the prevailing linguistic ideologies of the time, which saw a necessary and exclusive relationship between language and nationality. The "language question" in Italy went hand in hand with an attempt to create or define a national literature: a literature that could be representative of the new nation. Such "national art" excluded genres like the *Contrasto*, in the same way in which linguistic planning had excluded linguistic variation.

Part of being able to define themselves as artists, then, means for the poets to be able to define art in a way that will not exclude them. In doing so, they uphold a different and complex *Ars Poetica*. This is a system of beliefs about art, artists, and performance, that is continuously reinforced in conversations among poets. Its dictates and implications are continuously analyzed, revised, defended and argued upon. Such a system moves independently from official art and claims for itself a different sphere of taste. A sphere that, as I will show, is constructed as "precedent" to "high art" itself. This Poetic Art as defined by the poets is different (although with similarities) and at times in contraposition with the Poetic Art as defined by the "intellectuals" of the Italian nation state.

I will articulate the poetic art underlying the *Contrasto* in three parts. The first includes the beliefs regarding the provenance of art itself, and the connected origin of the authority of the poet. Here, by looking at the reasons why the poets became poets, I will show the existence of a common idea as to where the poetic art itself originates. The second part regards the ethos of the poets, their moral call, which is connected to their sense of self-importance in society. This includes their personal and political beliefs, their ethical stances, and their worldview. The third part regards the characteristics of the genre, namely the "aesthetic system" on whose basis the artistic production will be judged. This includes the elements that distinguish a "good" from a "bad" poet (or performance), namely the linguistic ideologies of style. These three parts define a complex ideology of language use in art performances. As such, they mediate between the actual performance of *Contrasti*, and the official (national) views of art.

Finally, I need to say a few words regarding the methodology. I will use in this chapter several excerpts from the interviews I conducted with Altamante Logli and Realdo Tonti, not just because I like to let the poets talk in their own voices, but especially because I could never express their ideas better than they do themselves. I want to underline though, that my knowledge about this Poetic Art is not based exclusively on the interviews, but rather on the whole fieldwork.

These ideas are shared by the poets and their public. I learned them by listening to the poets and their friends conversing about them, during dinners, walking in the streets, driving in the car, reflecting or commenting on a recent performance. I saw this poetic art enacted in the performances. I learned it by asking other Tuscans about it. At times I would interrogate the poets or their fans; at times I would propose my hypotheses to them as to "what they were really doing" and then listen to their "deconstruction" of those hypotheses. I learned it by having the poets patiently correct my mistaken assumptions, thinking about their words, and then thinking again.

II. National Poetic Art and the Place of Folklore. [191]

While language planners and intellectuals were trying to define the standard language, the intellectuals were also involved in an attempt to define a national literature and "culture." Indeed often the same scholars were active on these two fronts at the end of the nineteenth century. I will consider one case in particular, the poet Josué Carducci. I will then briefly discuss the development of folklore studies.

Carducci[192] contributed to the debate around the creation of the new Italian language, as we have seen already in chapter 2. But he also aimed at the definition of a "national figure of artist," namely at the definition of the characteristics that would identify art contributions as properly Italian. Carducci believed that a "really national" literature had to "get closer to the people again" (quoted in Franceschini 1989:100; my translation). Thus Carducci started, according to Franceschini: "a project of Italian literary history aiming at 'forming a civil Poet, citizen and purely national' " (Lett., I, 67; quoted in Franceschini, 1989:100; my translation). His attempt explains how he came to be seen as the *Poeta Vate* (prophet poet) of the new nation.

Carducci's ideas were interestingly similar to Herder's call for a poetry that must remain close to its origin among the *volk* (Bauman

---

[191] I decide to look at Folklore studies, instead of Anthropology, because the later is a relatively recent and limited enterprise in Italy. Still today, there is no independent department of Anthropology in Italy, and most Italian anthropologists receive their B.A. degree in other disciplines. Moreover, Folklore as a discipline developed in Italy concurrently with the formation of the nation, and it subsumed under itself aspects, like ethnographic methods, that in the United States are usually associated with Anthropology. In many respects, I believe, Cultural Anthropology in Italy can be seen as a product of an internal evolution in Folklore, and in fact it is often lumped and confused with it by the "lay" person.

[192] Considered one of the major Italian poets of the last century, Giosué Carducci was born in Tuscany in 1835 and died in 1907. He believed that an Italian language had to be shaped on the model of the language used by the literate class in the 1300.

and Briggs, 2000:177). This view of poetry had the consequence to "vest great responsibility in the poet. ... Poets are the culture makers" (Bauman and Briggs, 2000:182). In Herder's words: "A poet is the creator of a nation around him" (Bauman and Briggs, 2000:182).[193] This can be seen as a self-fulfilling prophecy in Italy, where poets like Manzoni[194] and Carducci are involved at every level in the making if the nation.

Carducci was also very interested in folklore and often used folk themes in his poetry. In consideration of this interest it may be surprising, at first, to discover that he gave a very negative judgment of the *Contrasto*. He wrote: "To sing, certainly they sing: but when the songs are not old things, they are nonsense and loud obscenities with certain strange verses that may God save us: and also save those who do not have a strong stomach from the folk improvisers" (quoted in Cirese, 1969:57; my translation).

Thus, while pursuing the spirit of the "people of the origins," Carducci refused as nonsensical the production of the "people of the present" that seemed to his eyes (and in general to the eyes of the folklorists in the same period) to have lost its original creativity (see Cirese, 1973:161). The Italian anthropologist Alberto Cirese very pointedly notices that this "people of the present" were the same claiming a place as political subjects. The *Contrasti* were indeed carriers of political demands, as we saw in chapter 4. The romanticized "people of the origins" instead were, as Cirese notices (1973:138), not the peasant masses, but the bourgeoisie (a middle class from which Carducci himself was coming). As Cirese writes:

> The limits of populism – that will become increasingly evident in the idyllic falling off that overshadowed much Italian demology after 1948 – reside in the fact that it conceived a *people-nation*, that had its own innovative significance in the first phase of the Risorgimento, but never got as far as to conceive a *people-social classes*, as vice-versa the historic developments were imposing (1973:130; italics in the original).

Thus, Carducci's nationalist project can be seen also, from the beginning, as a (conservative) political project. But why were Herder's

---

[193] Here, as Bauman and Briggs notice, Herder had the insight of recognizing a political dimension to poetry and to tradition itself (2000:183).

[194] I discussed Manzoni's involvement in the standardization of the Italian language in chapter 2.

ideas, which had shaped European romanticism at the beginning of the nineteenth century, still active in Italy fifty years later? The explanation must be found in the general lateness of the birth of folklore studies in Italy. This in turn must be seen in the context of the general lateness of the formation of the Italian nation in respect to others in Europe.

While Carducci was defining an official art, the folklorists were taken by the task of defining the (subordinate) place of "folk art" in respect to it. Niccoló Tommaseo, considered the founding father of Italian folklore, was deeply influenced by romanticism and the Germanic scholars (like the Grimm brothers). He set forth to find the Italian people, traveling through the Tuscan countryside, and in 1832 published his first book on folk poetry and song.

The first folklorists following Tommaseo, gathered *stornelli*, *rispetti*, *strambotti*, ballads, prayers, and proverbs in the hundreds,[195] but practically completely disregarded the *Contrasto*. These first scholars privileged the gathering of lyric texts. They at times even edited out more "scatological" arguments, and freely "corrected" the texts. Cirese refers to this first period of Italian folklore studies in the following terms:

> The aesthetic interest dominates everything, generating continuous comparisons between the traditional songs and the works of great authors. The ethical component is very strong as well, leading to exaltations of the purported moral purity of the folk poetry. The interventions of the editors on the texts, to eliminate linguistic or moral 'impurities,' are not rare (1973:137).

The successive "positivist" period in Folklore, at the end of the nineteenth century, led to a more systematic gathering of texts, with a privileging of the adherence to the originals, and to the first attempt at distinguishing cultural areas in the peninsula. The theoretical premises, anyway, changed little.[196] It was during the parenthesis of fascism, in which folklore was bent to mainly celebrative purposes, that Gramsci wrote his "Observations on Folklore" which, unpublished until 1950, assumed more and more importance after the Second World War.

---

[195] *Stornelli*, *rispetti* and *strambotti* are idyllic kinds of songs, talking about love (or about hate). Ballads are narrative songs.

[196] Important works in this period are those of D'Ancona, Nigra, Rubieri and Pitré.

Gramsci's formulation was indeed a notable breakthrough. For Gramsci, folklore must be seen as an expression of the life of the masses, which he identified as the subaltern. As such, the view of the world expressed in folk art opposes itself to the hegemonic conception of the world (1975:27, c.1). But, Gramsci also believed that the masses did not produce art, but only adopted and re-adapted art forms originated elsewhere, namely in the intellectuals' world of "high art." This conviction is indeed in tune with Gramsci's vision of the intellectuals as "guides" for the masses.

For Gramsci the folk songs are: "written not by the people nor for the people, but by them adopted in as far as they [the songs] conform to their [the people's] own manner of thinking and feeling" (1975:1, c.60; note written between 1930 and 1931; my translation). The implications of this argument were already noticed by Ernesto De Martino (one of the recognized founding fathers of Italian Anthropology) who, in 1952, noticed that such a conception is the equivalent of considering folk art: "the rubbish damp of cultural history" (De Martino, 1986:118-119).

Another problem with Gramsci is that he tends to see the "subaltern" as a social class (the "non-intellectuals," the peasants, or the proletarian class). But I believe, on the contrary, that subalternity is a condition that cuts across social classes, and belongs to a whole society or culture. Gramsci's formulation did not question the nostalgic romanticizations of subalternity (for example, the myth of the "great communist soul of the peasant"). This romanticization and identification of subalternity with the peasant lifestyle, always seen as archaic and on the brink of disappearance, has a long tradition in Italian Anthropology and in Folklore.

Thus in Italy a dichotomy between "high art" and "folk art" is present since the moment of formation of the nation. On one side the "national poet," on the model of Carducci, on the other the "folk production," studied by the folklorists. The genre of the *Contrasto* finds itself in an awkward position among them. On one side, it has a history of interrelations and exchanges of themes and ideas with the literary tradition. Still, it is shunned by the literary critics. On the other side, it is continuously created to express the needs of the "people of today" rather than the "people of the origins." As such, it was for a long time dismissed by the folklorists. But what do the artists themselves (and their followers) think of what art is, and their place in it? I will try to answer these questions in the remainder of this chapter.

III. Sing Through Me, O Muse!

From where does the authority to speak on art come? This is a question that literary and art critics and exponents of "high art" rarely ask themselves. Views of artistry are part of social reality, and thus lived, not discussed. For the intellectuals and their scholars, I can see it as emanating from the institutions of the nation-state (e.g. the academies and the educational system). But from where does the authority of the Poeti Bernescanti come? Namely, what is the ideological understanding that the poets have regarding the origins of their art and of their authority as artists?

Their authority cannot come from the academy or the educational system. Accepting the definitions of "official art" would mean, for the poets, accepting being confined at the lower end of the art hierarchy. Refusing such definitions, on the other hand, is not completely possible, as they are part of the hegemony, and thus imposed as "non-arguable" realities.

The Poets as artists are constituted and see themselves as figures that have authority in matters of "art." After all, it is because of this authority that people go to see the performance. The anthropologists themselves, by seeking out these artists, reinforce such an authority. They demonstrate to the people that their artists command respect and interest even from outsiders.[197] How is this authority constructed and negotiated vis-a-vis the hegemonic discourse regarding "high art" and "folk art"? To answer this question, I have to start where they started, as children. Poetry and the life of these artists cannot be separated, so I will look at two narratives, in which the poets Tonti and Logli recount how they came to be poets. The first narrative is from Realdo Tonti:

> It is a voice that I always heard, this one, since I was a boy, this thing of singing. (I have been) always attracted by these historical songs, that's it. First as a Storysinger. When I was young, in this town, or in the nearby towns in the province, there were many very good improvising poets, much better than I was, many more. And I would feel very attracted to them, to the point oftentimes of leaving my games as a boy, and going to

---

[197] My affiliation with UCLA was seen at times by the poets as a sign of my allegiance to a foreign power. This was generally a positive thing, as I was not associated with local institutions that the poets may have distrusted.

listen to them in the plaza, in the market. They would sing on Sunday. They would be in the market, in the plaza. At that time, there were many *poeti a Braccio*. Among them, we can mention Andreini, Piccardi, Ceccherini, and (Pescini). ... And I naturally was- I was taken. I was really- I could not resist, that's it, I had to go listen to them and oftentimes the idea would come to me, to say something. But, you know, [I had] a panicky fear, right? In front of such poets.

I want to notice a few important points in this account. First, Realdo depicts himself as being "called" to poetry, since his childhood. So the call to sing is seen as innate. Second, notice the words he uses. He "heard a voice," to which he was "attracted." Thus, poetry is almost an entity, although undefined, something outside of him that speaks to him. Where did the voice come from? Who gives the "gift" of poetry? Often the poets refer to the Muses. I heard several times a poet acknowledging another poet by saying: "He too drank from the spring of Helicon" (the mountain where the Muses live). This should not be taken to mean that the poets actually believe in the existence of the Muses. It seems though that the call is perceived as having a semi-divine origin. As such, it comes from a power much higher than any human power.

Third, notice how Realdo does not depict himself as choosing, but as "being chosen," as the attraction is so strong that he, as a boy, would leave his games to go listen to the poets. Thus, in a sense, the "listening to other poets" is seen as successive and dependent on the call itself. The poet insists that he could "not resist" such a call. This implies that the voice of poetry is stronger than the individual will. It also implies that the person is not responsible for following it. To renounce responsibility, though, can be seen as a strategy to acquire agency.

This sheds further light on what we saw in chapter 4, namely the poet calling on the genre itself to answer the questioning of the policeman. Even in this case, the poet renounces putting the authority on himself, but shifts the authority to something external and more powerful than himself. In doing so, he also protects himself from any possible judgment on his artistry that may come from other sources of authority, like academia. In both cases, the poet seems to deny agency as an individual, while at the same time empowering himself as an artist.

The fourth point to notice is that his call leads Realdo to the other poets. Namely, he starts to identify them as the group to which he would like to belong. These poets, at the same time, inspire him with awe (and a bit of fear). Having realized, already as a boy, his difference from the other children (who would not leave their games to go to the market), he now looks forward to a community of other artists, to whom he would like to "say" something, namely in whose interactions he would like to participate. Before discussing Realdo's words any further, I now pass to Altamante's description[198] of the events that led to his call:

I would leave with the sheep in the morning; I would come back at night.[199] It was exactly in contact with nature, you know, that I started to improvise a few rhymed verses. I received the gift of poetry. In the pasture, when I had no sadness, I would singsong these simple verses. As I sang, a young man heard me. He was a road maker from Vaiano. Now he has been dead maybe for seven or eight years. He was my friend; I was very affectionate to him. [He was] maybe fifteen years [older than me]. Well if I was, twelve years old, he must have been twenty-three. He had been in the draft already and he was working at making the road that from Vaiano goes up on the mountains of the Calvana. So, this road maker was listening to me- in that *mulattiera* [road used by mules]. He was making the road in the *mulattiere* of those mountains. His name was Nello Paranti. ... He was a poet. After getting acquainted with him, when we would meet it was with him indeed that I acquired the knowledge of poetry. We need to say that it was my *estro* [inspiration, gift]. My coming out was, practically, it was at the feast of grapes in Vaiano, about 1934 I

---

[198] I have to say that Altamante's narrative, quite articulated, was partially told to me and partially read to me from a notebook, where he had sketched a brief autobiography. When I asked him about his life, he took this old notebook and started to read. While the points in which he is reading are quite recognizable in the recorded tape, because of the shift in paralanguage, the difference is partially lost in the transcription and in the translation.

[199] He worked as a shepherd since he was 7 years old.

believe, in a local (feast). They were singing poetry. My friend Nello invited me. There were other poets. I too took part to that evening. But I was too small, they could not see me: "come little poet, courage! Help us, do accept," one said. So it was that I accepted. They put me on the table, otherwise I would have remained hidden among the people, who were standing, and [the poets] were also standing. I took courage and I sung some poetry. What I said I cannot remember. For me, a boy, it was a great satisfaction. I was applauded by everybody and hugged by the poets.

Here we can start noticing some of the same themes of Realdo's narration. In both cases the poet, still a child, feels the call of poetry. This can be seen as a gift, or an inexplicable urge. In this case, though, the child, isolated in the woods, almost does not know what he is doing until he is discovered by another poet, Nello Paranti. From Nello, Altamante acquires "the knowledge of poetry." Namely in some way the meaning of his "singing" is explained, or revealed, to him. Notice that Altamante never mentions "learning." The boy-poet already knew how to make verses. In fact, Altamante underlines: it was my *estro*," namely his natural attitude. But it is through the encounter with the other poets that his singing becomes meaningful. Notice also how, at the beginning, he underlines that it was "in contact with nature" that he started to make verses. Did "nature" then teach him? Again, we find a personification of a semi-divine entity.

In the last part of the narrative, Altamante talks about his "coming out," namely the first time he sung with other poets in front of a public. The choice of words is interesting; "coming out" implies a revelation. And this happens in fact through an "elevation," also literally, since he is put on a table, so that he is no longer "hidden" among the standing audience. Even here, as for Realdo, we have a reference to the awe that the boy-poet feels: he has to take courage.

A new and important element is the invitation of the older poets to join them: "Come, little poet, courage! Help us, do accept." [200] The boy is called to join their singing as a peer, whose help is needed, not as a beginner. Since poetry is not learned, it is already present in full

---

[200] In general anybody who dares to step on a stage and challenge a poet is respected and acknowledged by the poets themselves, and is engaged in verbal duel.

inside the boy. It only needs to "come out," to be expressed. In both cases, this expression is mediated by the presence of the community of poets, who make it possible by allowing the boy to join them. If the first source of art is a semi-divine call, the authority also rests on this community of poets. Notice the closure: the boy is applauded by the audience (his poetry has touched them) and embraced by the poets. From that moment, Altamante will be one of them.

In Altamante's narrative there is a further element: the depiction of the idyllic context of the shepherd with his herd is at the same time life and myth. It is the pastoral myth of "Arcadia," the happy land where every peasant is a poet. It is the same romantic myth that pushed Tommaseo to look for songs among the Tuscan mountain people. The myth becomes reality in Tuscany, in Altamante's life. And in turn, Altamante's life, his birth, is rooted in the myth. I believe that this myth of Arcadia, shared by the poets and many of their students, is a source of power and authority. The life of the poet, from its beginning, revolves in a different reality, on a different ground, one where the Goddesses still rule.

To summarize: poetry is a gift, innate in the poet. It comes from an external, semi-divine force that calls the poet irresistibly. This gift gives the poet his authority, and allows him to become part of a community of peers. The poet does not choose, does not create the verses, but they seem to come to him. To my question (tendentious) concerning why he liked to do poetry as a child, Altamante answers:

> Do you think I know it? He! He! I don't know it. I don't know how to account to myself for it, you see? Ho! I don't know how to account to myself for it indeed- I don't know how to account for it. These verses would come to me, like this, you see? These verses would come to me (Interview 11/9/97, side B, 183 and fol.).

So the poet cannot "account" for what he is singing. Again, we see how in renouncing authorship, he renounces responsibility at the same time. Considering how "dangerous" this genre is, how it can easily offend people (not only the powers that be, but also practically anybody), I believe that this offers a protection to the poets, who can be, after all, an easy target to retaliations. But in doing so, he is also renouncing agency as an individual. The poet declares himself to be not an agent, but an instrument through which the agency of an external power is expressed.

From what I have shown so far, an idea of art emerges, which is quite different from the one upheld by folklore or by literary criticism. First of all, it gives the authority to "reveal" the poet only to the other poets and their audience. Any external institution or "art critic" is excluded from it. But there is a second point, in which this view of art opposes itself to the institutional view, and that is around the question of "learning." Poetry cannot be "learned" but it is innate. In various occasions, when Altamante would comment on a young poet's (Ettore Del Bene) interest in poetry, he would recall and justify it by saying that Ettore's father used to sing some poetry himself. Because of the way poetic ability is seen, as innate, poets do not feel they need to explain anything to their disciples. In fact, they recognize no disciples. Realdo expresses well the idea that poetry cannot be learned:

> Realdo: You cannot buy it and you cannot study it.
> Anthropologist: I see
> Realdo: It is hh hh he he he! If you have it you have it; otherwise, you are not going to make it, that's it. Not even if you study at the university for fifty years. You can take the pen and write it, but to improvise (you cannot). This is why this thing, this singing is a natural art.

Realdo's statement comes at the end of a narrative in which he had been telling me of his encounter with the students at the University of Rome, where he had been called to perform. Education can be bought, art cannot. Because of it, any poor, uneducated person can have it. In a society in which status is given on the base of money or education, Realdo is turning the world upside down.

Realdo goes on to state that poetry cannot be studied, it must be "had," innately possessed. In the schools, people can study metric and music, Folklore and Anthropology, but cannot "improvise" even one verse. Without inspiration (from the Muses?) words are empty shells. Notice the way Realdo opposes writing to improvising. To "write" a verse can be learned, but the "improvising" cannot be learned. What is so special, then, about "improvising" (which also means performing)? The oral word that passes through the poet's mouth and dissolves in this air comes from elsewhere, it is "true" inspiration. Here in some way Realdo defines two alternative views of art, two different canons for poetry. The art of the *Contrasto* he defines as "natural," not learned or bought. Realdo concludes:

Naturally you express what you feel inside and thus, that is what is carrying you. Because I found myself oftentimes singing ... with professionals, who do it as their job, right? They have studied music all of their life so they have a voice and an orchestra. But they look like plaster casts. But of course if you do not have it inside- ... But then what is it? It is what you transmit more than what- more than the framing. ... Sometimes I ask myself, why is it that they like us? I do not know. But, you know, it is something that enters [inside you] because- that's why it has been defined a natural art (side A, 096 and fol.)

So Realdo opposes the "technical perfection" to the "inspiration," in art. The second seems to be able to talk to the heart of the audience, thus obtaining a response from them even in absence of the first.[201]

This is an important point of contrast between the poets and the "intellectuals" which are those that, having received a high level of schooling, in a sense "know how to write" and get their authority from their knowledge. In opposition to that, the poets describe their authority as coming directly from "nature," from a power then that is superior to any earthly powers. Here the poets ideologically oppose themselves to the hegemonic thinking imbued in the educational system and in society, that puts authority and knowledge in the hands of the educational institutions and of the intellectuals.

The poet in the moment of creating, becomes the *Vate* (prophet, oracle, seer); the Muse speaks through his mouth. The poet then becomes the untouchable, his/her voice being the voice of divinity or the voice of tradition. The virtuosity of the poets is a sign of some kind of a call, which makes them sing often in spite of themselves. This kind of poetry cannot be learned; the ability must be in innate or inherited.

---

[201] It is interesting here to recall Tedlock's discussion of Cushing as a Hopi Bow Priest (1983:329). While the other priests created their prayers in their hearts, Cushing would have them written on a piece of paper. The writing empowered Cushing and made him able to participate to the ritual. But at the same time, it made him deaf to the real call, to the real understanding of the meaning of the prayer, which could only come from his heart. The professional singers described by Realdo, similarly, are deaf to the call of the muse.

IV. The Ethos of the Poets.

Two opposing views of the relationship between art and the political sphere were expressed in the thought of two important Italian scholars: Antonio Gramsci and Benedetto Croce. Gramsci subsumed the artists under the category of the intellectuals, which he saw as an active part of society. He wrote: "The mode of being of the new intellectual can no longer consist in eloquence..., but in active participation in practical life, as constructor, organizer, 'permanent persuader' and not just as simple orator" (in Showstack Sassoon, 1987:276).[202] In his view, art is always connected to the political sphere, and can be used as an instrument of hegemony or resistance. Apolitical art is hegemonic, because it implicitly legitimizes the present hegemonic power. This legitimization is fundamental to the maintenance of the status quo.

Gramsci was opposing himself to Croce and his followers of the historic-idealistic school, who upheld a view of art as "not-ideological," of "true" art as abstracted from the conditions of social living (in Showstack Sassoon, 1987:249). Croce wrote that intellectuals' "sole duty is to raise to a higher spiritual level through scholarship" (in Showstack Sassoon, 1987:249).

As many scholars have noticed, the definition of art, and the role of the artists in front of political power, is different in different cultures. Caton, for example, discusses how Yemenite poets can move people to battle (1990). Felipe Ehrenberg, a Mexican painter and writer, affirms that: "Mexicans have always known that artists are the spokespeople of society" (1994:132). In contrast, Carol Becker (1994) notices that in America, art has often been defined as entertainment, as appropriate to leisure, and thus separated from the political domain. Art is produced continually in large quantities as a commodified good, as part of the entertainment industry (see Rosler, 1994:57). It obeys the logic of the capitalist market. To define art as political or apolitical, then, is only to scratch the surface of the problem. Any definition of art is connected to a particular discourse.

Part of the discourse about poetic art that revolves around the *Contrasto* is also an understanding of the place of the poet in society. As I showed in chapter 4, the poets have traditionally been fervent political activists, most often affiliated with the parties of the left. As

---

[202] Gramsci re-elaborated Lenin's position that saw the only function of the intellectuals (including the artists) as upholding the cause of the dictatorship of the proletariat.

such the poets' ethos tends to rest on Gramsci's view, that is the view of the Italian left. In the following excerpt from an interview, for example, Altamante's views are clearly connected to Marxist ideals of internationalism and equality among human beings. Notice how he fuses them with Christian ideals of brotherhood:

> I have no borders. Because – even from a Christian point of view – God is one. You wouldn't think that he created first America and then Russia and then us. ... I believe [Jesus] did not even exist. But anyway, ((laughing)). ... The love for the country- ok! But we need to have love for the world. The love for the country! (There shouldn't) be borders created. There should not be any frontiers in the world. There should be a universal world, where you could travel, (without considering) (race) and similar things. Because the country is to the advantage of certain gentlemen that capitalize on it. It does not need martyrs or heroes. It would need honest people, people that would know how to do their duty and would give to everybody something to eat. This is what the country needs, not heroes and not martyrs and to think- so if someone is dead – poor one – I can feel sorry indeed. Yes, but on the other side, when at the same time they killed two hundred and fifty people there in Algeria. They killed them. They cut the throats of eighty children. How long have we talked about it? One day only. Of [Princess Diana], all the newspapers of the world are still talking. We always make the history of the rich. And this I do not accept (interview 11/9/97, tape 1, side B, 452 and fol.).

Here Altamante presents a theme quite common among the poets, namely that the artist has no country. So, instead of the image of "national poet" proposed by Carducci, Altamante proposes an international poet. But Altamante's attack on nationalism becomes even more direct when he states that the nation "is to the advantage of certain gentlemen." Thus, Altamante seems to see nationalism as an ideology at the service of capitalism.

Altamante also recognizes another face of nationalism, namely racism. His statement that there should be no border, then, is more than a mere adherence to internationalism. It must be understood on the background of the situation in Italy today, in which immigration from other countries is quite strong, and racism against the immigrants is growing. Altamante's words are an indictment of the mass media as well, who measure with different scales the worth of the life of the poor and of the rich.

The poet cannot accept this, and indeed these views are at the base of much of his poetic production. They often emerge in the way he articulates his arguments in the *Contrasti*, especially in those of political argument. Thus, I believe the understanding the poets have of art is closer to the Gramscian view of art as political. For them, being a poet means at the same time to be a spokesperson. They perceive part of their responsibility as poets to express the voice of the people. For example, Realdo, in the following excerpt from an interview, depicts poetry almost as a counter-language, born from the situation of oppression of the Tuscan peasant masses:[203]

> The poetry *a braccio* you know- you understood a bit of the way it is. It was born in the threshing-floor of the peasants, you know. Because they could not really express themselves, then they would always talk implicitly. Maybe us Tuscans, this [usage of] throwing things out through allusion in our language, we took it from those traditions indeed. Because us Tuscans, we do not have a straight talk.

Here Realdo hypothesizes an origin of poetry as a veiled form of expression for the peasant masses. Notice that a similar linguistic ideology, as Marcyliena Morgan has shown, is today uphold by many African Americans in the US, who feel that AAVE was a language of resistance created by the slaves to exchange information without being heard by their overseers (Morgan, 1994:129).[204]

If there are similarities between the views of the poets and those of Gramsci, at the same time there are also important differences. Gramsci privileged the intellectuals, who had to be "organic," namely coming from the classes whose voices s/he had to express. The poets, instead, as we saw, negate the importance of "education" in their art. The inspiration for them comes not from the social, but from elsewhere.

Finally, an important thing to notice is that art, for the poets, cannot be separated from life and in turn, from militancy. The best example of this I had during an interview with Altamante. I had been trying to construct a classification of the *Contrasti*, and I was questioning Altamante to obtain a definition of the "historic,"

---

[203] See Appendix G (Side A, 096 and fol.).

[204] It is interesting also that another genre of improvised sung poetry, Rap, that shares many similarities with the *Contrasto* (similarities recognized by the poets themselves and by their audiences), has also been seen as a form of anti-language (Halliday, 1978).

"social" and "ideal"[205] *Contrasto*, according to a subdivision he had previously suggested. Asking Altamante for a definition of a "social" *Contrasto*, I got this answer:[206]

> You always have to hammer home this [idea]: if we are born equal, and if the world belongs to God, it was created by God, then why should one have 30,000 hectares of land, and another one have not even a hovel where to live? This is the social problem. They give you a theme, let's say between the capital and the labor. You are going to be a worker or a capitalist. You must ask [the capitalist]: to arrive where you are- ... some may advance with their own intelligence. But those who hoard everything, I mean, and exploit always and always, they are a class of exploiters. Then you must throw [this question] there: why are we doing these things? The social injustice exists, and we fight it, even without being a communist or anything. We fight for social justice and equality, and to create order in the world. In the world, there should be bread for everybody, right? Someone has bread to throw away, you see, and someone else does not have (anything). This is (about social justice).

Rather than a definition, Altamante explains to me the kind of ideas that should be expressed. These ideas have a Marxist matrix. Altamante here is giving me a lesson. His perception of art does not seem to be separable from social action, or a moral view of existence. Doing a theme on social issues is already having a certain point of view (moral and political) over those social issues. In this sense my request to keep the various topics separated from a comment over them was futile and wrong. I was looking in some way for a taxonomy that could then be made alive in everyday political actions. But for Altamante the taxonomy is already embedded inside his moral and political thinking.

---

[205] Altamante includes a *Contrasto* between Bertinotti and D'Alema in this category *a sfondo ideale* (with ideal/ideological frame). Probably because in this case what is discussed are different approaches to the solution of the same perceived "social problem." The different position of the opposite sides is thus seen as an "ideological distinction," or as a discussion over the "ideals," namely the bases of Marxism.

[206] See Appendix G (8/24/98, tape 1, side A, 000 and fol.).

V. Aesthetic Systems and Linguistic Ideologies.

An important part of a poetic art is a set of rules as to how an "art work" should be created and/or performed. These rules are part of an aesthetic system and from them depends the definition of what is "real" or "good" art versus what is not, and who is a real artist versus who is not. An aesthetic system is also connected and interrelated with assumptions regarding language and language use, namely to linguistic ideologies. Following, I will discuss some of the ideologies of language in the *Contrasti*, as they emerged from my conversations with the poets.

I have to say, first, that the poets share the same knowledge of the metric structure (octet, verse, and hendecasyllables) with the scholars. The metric system, thus, can be included in the poet's perception of his "ars poetica." Among these metrical elements the one that emerges as most important, both in describing the characteristics of the *Contrasto* and in judging a performance, is the rhyme. Therefore, I will use it as a point of departure in analyzing the third and last part of the *Contrasto*'s poetic art.

The poet who cannot "find the rhyme" will loose face. For a beginner, finding the rhyme seems to be the most difficult element, and often a novice poet will interrupt his/her performance because of it. In this case, the older poet or even the people in the audience will start suggesting rhymes. The rhyme is, thus, one of the characteristics of the *Contrasto* that most impresses the audience and scares the novices. The importance of the rhyme lies not only in its difficulty, but also, as Alessandro Fornari[207] made me notice:

> The rhyme is not only an artifice to remember things, it is also a way to find Truth. The one who finds the rhyme, finds it, and does not create it. You see, the found rhyme confirms the concepts. Therefore when there is a rhyming couplet, when they coincide, and the rhyme is found, it means that what we are saying is true. We use it also in everyday language. ... From this is derived, as you know, also the expression 'to answer by rhymes,' which means, in fact, to give a definitive answer (Interview 1, Florence, 7/10/97, B 316; my translation).

From my fieldwork, several linguistic ideologies emerge regarding

[207] Fornari is a professor at the University of Florence. He studies folk songs in Tuscany, especially in the province of Pistoia, and collaborates as editor of the review "Toscana Folk."

the use of the rhyme. All of them are metalinguistic,[208] namely they are not unconscious beliefs, but on the contrary, they are part of an ongoing discourse regarding art and the performance of the *Contrasto*. They are continuously discussed, negotiated and elaborated upon by the poets and their fans. As such, I consider them as commonly held knowledge of the genre.,[209] shared by the poets and their followers.[210]

In chapter 3, I discussed the metric of the octet, with rhymes that follow the scheme ABABABCC. The rhyming part of a verse starts from the syllable on which the last stress of the of the verse falls. The rhyme, thus, considers not only the sounds, but also the stress: *cánto*, "song," rhymes with *vánto*, "boast," but not with *cantó*, "sung." Having said this, I like to start from a dichotomy: the poets distinguish the rhyme in *chiusa*, "closed," or *aperta*, "open." A closed rhyme, is one that is found in very few words. It is "difficult" in the sense that it can create a problem for the poet who has to use it. An open rhyme, instead, is easier, since there are many words with the same ending. Here is how Altamante describes them:[211]

---

[208] My thanks to Jennifer F. Reynolds who pointed out this fact.

[209] You will notice that most of the examples I give are taken from an interview with Altamante Logli. The reason for this is that, after more than one year of fieldwork, I set up this interview exactly to gather and record, from the voice of one poet, these "rules" of poetic art. This should not be taken by any means to indicate that what is said here are Altamante's personal beliefs. When I went into this interview, I had already learned the linguistic ideologies discussed. My questions to him were geared to obtain from him a repetition of what I already knew.

[210] It is important to remember that although shared, these are not the dominant ideologies regarding poetry and poetic art. They are instead created and elaborated by the poets in continuous confrontation and in opposition to the dominant ideologies regarding art (that are probably better represented by the writing of Italian academicians). It could be exactly because of this, namely that the poets have to continuously confront themselves with dominant ideologies of art, that their "poetic art" is pushed to the level of consciousness. There, as metalanguage, it is made available for discussion, elaboration and reflection among the poets themselves and their public. For further discussion of the naturalization of dominant ideologies of language, see also Kroskrity, 1998; and Briggs, 1998:248.

[211] See Appendix G (8/24/98, tape 1, side A, 386 and fol.).

Altamante: If I leave you a closed rhyme I throw you head over heals, you are not going to pick it up again, you know?

Anthropologist: A closed rhyme is a difficult rhyme?

Altamante: A difficult one because there isn't another one, you understand? Once at Sant'Angelo dalle Ore, they gave me this octet ...:

"You have come to sing at Sant'Angelo *dallé Ore* [of Ore]

I would send you to look after goats and *péore* [sheep]"

péore [sheep] right? I said:

  "I explode like *una metéore* [a meteor<u>s</u>]"

Ha! Ha! Ha!

Anthropologist: Is it more difficult with a proparoxytone[212] rhyme?

Altamante: A proparoxytone is like '*cávolo*' [cabbage], '*diávolo*' [devil], '*trógolo*' [trough].

Anthropologist: Yes, yes

Altamante: '*núvolo*' [cloudy], hh you know, these are impossible to pick up again, they are (proparoxytone) words, you see. ... After *metéore* [meteor] I (said) *técore* [with you] and *mécore* [with me]. ... In the end, I was able to broach it again. But there are certain rhymes that you cannot pick up, no (way)!

Thus, the difficulty of the rhyme depends on the position of the stress as well. Words with accent on the penultimate syllable are more common in Italian. Proparoxytone rhymes or those with the accent on the last syllable are more often closed, and difficult.

It appears from Altamante's words that the difficulty of the rhyme must be understood in performance. Altamante is teaching me a fighting art, something that can throw somebody "head over heels." Of course, the cunning knowledge of leaving a proparoxytone accent, to throw the other off balance, is not difficult to teach. What is difficult is to know how to defend yourself, to answer to the attack. This is where the wit and fantasy of the poet, as well as his linguistic knowledge, plays a role. This is also where the "poetic license," the ability of the poet to create new words or change them, becomes relevant. For example in this case, the use of the archaic poetic words *tecore* and *mecore* (which in Tuscan with the dropping of the /k/ sound would be *teore* and *meore*[213]) creates a perfect rhyming. Notice also the grammatical creativity in "*una meteore*" (a meteor<u>s</u>), with the lack of

---

[212] Accent on the third from the last syllable.

[213] See Appendix C.

agreement between the singular article and the plural noun. The correct expression would have been "*delle meteore*" (plural) or "*una meteora*" (singular).

To leave closed rhymes is not seen as a good thing and the expert poet should avoid it, for two very important reasons. The first is that it can create *imbarazzo* (loss of face, embarrassment) in the other poet. The *Contrasto* is generally a cooperative achievement. Embarrassing the other poet may disrupt the performance, and it may bring the singing to an end, thus reflecting negatively on both poets.

Beginners, who may not have an "awareness" of the difficulty of the rhyme they are producing, often leave closed rhymes. For an expert poet to leave a closed rhyme to a beginner, on the opposite side, it may be seen as a mean action.[214] For an expert poet to produce a closed rhyme, then, is a "fault" that can be judged negatively, unless the context justifies such usage, namely if the *Contrasto* is not moving along cooperative lines anymore, but it has become "competitive." Then creating a difficult situation for the other poet is what one wants to achieve.[215]

In this case, a second layer of dueling happens in the *Contrasto*: a "rhyme duel." Usually only very expert poets can risk to escalate difficult rhymes in rhyme duels. As such they are rare, but when they happen they settle deep in the memory of the poets and their fans. They may be recalled and narrated again and again even after many years. Some of them may become "legendary." In conclusion, an open rhyme is not always the preferred option. Much depends on the context, the participants, and the effects that they want to achieve.

A second important reason why a closed rhyme should be avoided is that they "close" the development of the argument.[216] Here, we see a link between rhyming and the construction of meaning. A closed rhyme may force the other poet to use any similar rhyme he can find, sacrificing the meaning of his discourse. This, in turn, will hinder and diminish the beauty of the octet, and of the *Contrasto* itself. A poetic sense starts to emerge regarding the rhyme, which is more complex than simply seeing them as "easy" or "difficult." The rhyme must

---

[214] But it can also be, more subtly, a means of exclusion.

[215] Altamante doubts that a poet should strive for competitiveness. He says: (8/24/98, tape 1, side B, 027 and fol.): "You want to make a poet look good, you should not embarrass him with difficult rhymes."

[216] I believe, in fact, that the name "open" and "closed" may actually refer to the rhyme's capacity to open, enlarge an argument or close it.

allow, not stop the development of the argument. A closed rhyme may also lead the other poet to re-use a certain word more than once in the same octet, to find the rhyme. But a poet should avoid repeating himself, since this repetition creates a closure in the topic. Here in Altamante's words:[217]

> There, we do not get out of the circle anymore. Because we do not enlarge, right? We do not get larger, you understand?

Such repetition is seen as a "fault" or as a sign of an inferior performance. Although, as Altamante clarifies, such repetition may be justified as an exception if there is no other known word with the same ending. He states:[218]

> Altamante: We can use [a rhyme] again, maybe if there is only one of them. Even Dante in one place, I believe he repeats the same word. Dante Alighieri. In a certain point, I believe that-
> Anthropologist: Is that so?
> Altamante: Hu:::::m he repeats because there is no other rhyme. What can we do? We put that one.
> Anthropologist: Sometime, that's it, I see.
> Altamante: Because if I say "the piston of the *pompa* [pump], I do not want that by chugging it *rompa* [may break down]. How would you do to repeat three rhymes in an octet with *rompa* [may break down]?

Notice how in this case he also reinforces his statement, by recalling Dante's usage. Dante is thus seen as an ultimate authority. This choice is highly ideological in itself, not only because it underscores the connection to a written literary tradition, but also because it connects the *Contrasto* directly to the "highest" recognized form of poetry. That Altamante is invoking Dante as authority is underlined by the way he repeats his name. He first says "Dante." Then a sentence later he repeats "Dante Alighieri." Here he is not clarifying which Dante is he talking about. Any Italian would have immediately understood the first time. I believe he repeats the full name almost to honor him, and thus establish Dante's authority.

---

[217] See Appendix G (From Altamante 8/24/98, coding: tape 1, side A, 494 and fol.).

[218] See Appendix G (8/24/98, tape 1, side A, 386 and fol.).

A closed rhyme may also lead a poet to "invent" a word that could rhyme with it. In this case, the danger is of losing the meaning of the sentence. In this case, it is better to re-use a "difficult" rhyme than to invent a word that would have no sense. In Altamante's words:[219]

> If you say rhymes that have no meaning, how are you going to do? With the rhyme there has to be also a meaning for the discourse [*discorso*].

Thus Altamante is explicitly pointing to the fact that metric and meaning should both be considered. Both must be preserved, to obtain a perfect verse. The "poetic license" to change words or accents on words, can be used up to a certain point. A balance has to be kept. The rhyme should highlight the meaning, not hinder it. It should be the precious pearl seal on the necklace of the octets. Without an understanding of this, poetry and beauty are lost.

This leads to another important layer in understanding the poetic art of the *Contrasto*: rhymes also have a beauty in themselves. This beauty is only partially connected to the meaning of the word, and in part is internal to the rhyme itself. Altamante tries to communicate this complex idea to me in the following excerpt:[220]

> [In some cases] there are the [correct] rhymes. But the discourse won't come out beautiful. <u>The rhymes are beautiful on-</u>[221] ('*andare*' [to go] there are too many: '*andare*,' '*arare*' [to go, to sow]. Or also like '*agli*' [to him], '*a seminagli*' [to sow to him], '*a zappagli*' [to hoe to him], '*a rincalzagli*' [to tuck in to him]. That way anything can rhyme. He! He! Indeed! Then the discourse turns out fine.) <u>You see, the discourse [should be]</u> on a '*cuore*' [heart], '*amore*' [love], '*splendore*' [splendor]. Or '*sole*' [sun] '*parole*' [words] '*scuole*' [schools], (..........), '*viole*' [violets], you see? '*Crea*' [s/he creates], '*orchidea*' [orchid], '*assemblea*' [assembly], '*idea*' [idea], '*Giudea*' [Judaea/Judaean], '*dea*' [goddess].

Altamante here refers explicitly to aesthetic ideals, rather than to a mechanical use of a "rhyming rule." He starts by noticing that the

---

[219] See Appendix G (8/24/98, tape 1, side A, 386 and fol.).

[220] See Appendix G (8/24/98, tape 1, side A, 386 and fol.).

[221] I use underlining to highlight Altamante's switch among two separate arguments, a switch that in speech he underlines with a change in paralanguage. He starts from an argument, then passes to a second argument, then goes back to finish the first argument.

correct rhyme in itself may not make a "discourse" beautiful. After starting to say what a beautiful rhyme is, he stops and starts to give examples of rhymes that are very "easy." His judgment on them is not positive: "there are too many." But he recognizes that with them the "discourse turns out fine." Thus the meaning is satisfied, but the aesthetic sense is not. If difficult rhymes should be avoided, rhymes that are common, too easy, should also be avoided. Indeed easy rhymes are those that the poets "leave" to the beginners.

Which rhymes then, should be used? Altamante continues by giving a list of them. In doing so, notice that he says that "the discourse should be" on them. So, there is not just rhyme, but a kind of discourse which goes with them, and that is considered not just meaningful, but beautiful. This discourse appears to be built on rhymes whose meaning evokes images and feelings that are seen as beautiful.

Distinctions like "poetic" and "referential" language here loose meaning, as both seem to converge in the rhymes. In a sense, the rhyme *-ore*, for example, is beautiful because it includes words like "love," "splendor," or "heart." In turn the rhyme *-ore* will, when used, beautify the verse. In chapter 4 I argued that the metric structure of the octet must take precedence over meaning, because it protects the poets from the eventual consequences of their words. Here, though, it appears that in the view of the poets, structure and meaning cannot be separated if art is to be achieved.

Still, I need to add another element: interaction. This emerged as I was still trying to obtain from Altamante a hierarchical order (anthropological blindness!) between rhyme and meaning. So I posed a question to Altamante, and I got quite a revealing answer:[222]

> Anthropologist: When you hear a rhyme, which is the final one, you have very little time, right? To think the next verse. ... Is the verse the first thing that you think? ... Or do you think about the rhyme first?
> Altamante: No, I need to think about what he is saying! Like, if he tells me let's say ... that I am good for nothing, ... I need to answer to what he told me to defend [myself], right?

Interaction in performance is the point, around which meaning and form rotate.

---

[222] See Appendix G (8/24/98, tape 1, side B, 027 and fol.).

VI. Conclusion.

In conclusion, I have tried to show in this chapter that while official ideas of poetic art and of the place of "folk art" in respect to "high art" developed over more than 100 years in the Italian nation state, the poets also have their own poetic art. Both of these systems entail and are connected to sets of linguistic ideologies. Here, I have looked in particular at the ideologies that the poets share, and that accompany their performances as part of a continuous metalinguistic commentary.

What the Poets and the "folks" thought of art was disregarded by all the theorists who tried to decide what art was. Neither Gramsci's followers nor their opponents thought of asking the poets what "art" is. I have tried to show, instead, that by asking that question much can be learned.

In creating an opposition between a "learned" vs. a "natural" art, the poets are subtracting their art from the institutionalized hierarchies of art. They instead reconstruct a different paradigm for judging their art. This is a paradigm of which they and their fans are the undisputed judges.

I said before that the *Contrasto* acts as a centrifugal force in respect to common views of reality. But, it cannot be forgotten that centrifugal and centripetal forces always act together. In this chapter, then, I have shown some of the "centripetal forces" that define the genre of the *Contrasto* and in a sense, have allowed it to maintain a structure practically unchanged for hundreds of years.

8
CONCLUSIONS

In this dissertation, it was my goal to furnish a multilayered approach to the study of verbal art performance. By highlighting the linguistic and political ideologies involved in the production of art, I showed the relevance of the study of performance as a key to understanding social action. From the analysis emerged the potentiality of verbal art as a means of reflection on social events and expression of people's voices. This in turn points to a critique of the academic definitions of what constitutes art and its "goals." Such definitions imply inclusions and exclusions that index particular ideologies. Art and aesthetic systems, therefore, need to be seen from a political-economic perspective.

Looking at linguistic ideologies made it necessary to pay attention to the formation of dominant linguistic ideologies regarding art in Italy. In chapter 2, I explored the historical formation of the Italian nation-state and the consequent creation of an Italian standard language. In fact, as Voloshinov argued, the creation of standard rules and a standard language is a way of enforcing or re-enforcing a particular authority (Dentith, 1995:26), in this case the authority of the new ruling class. Looking at the Italian nation-state, in turn, required me to look at the linguistic ideologies and visions of art that contributed to its formation. In chapter 7, I discussed the ways in which the poets construct a "poetic art" which is alternative to the one proposed by the Italian intellectuals and institutionalized by the Italian nation-state.

Verbal art performances are also a ground on which centrifugal forces (Bakhtin, 1981) – forces that in any society tends toward the creation of multiple possibilities – may express themselves. In the specific case of the *Contrasto*, which is a form of verbal duel, these centrifugal forces take shape in the presentation of contrasting views of social reality. I have explored three areas in which the poets make "socially constructed realities" more complex, namely the areas of politics (chapter 4), ethnic identity (chapter 5) and gender (chapter 6).

According to Garfinkel (1967), everyday reality is connected to a moral sense of things being "right" or "wrong." The members of a society treat social facts as factual, regular, natural. This "moral" view of reality comes under attack in the *Contrasto*. The "rightfulness" or "wrongness" of what Garfinkel calls "the natural facts of life" (quoted in Heritage, 1984:192) are contested in the verbal duel. Political beliefs, gender and identity are contested as well. The sense of "moral" facts is lost in the continuous contraposition of one to other possible moralities (see for example the *Contrasto* "The Nun vs. the Prostitute," in chapter 6). There are no more "natural" beings in the *Contrasto*: no natural females or males, no natural communists, no natural Tuscans. Each of these categories instead is proposed as scrutinizable, contestable, and reinterpretable.

This study has important implications for the understanding of identity. In chapter 5, I demonstrated how ethnic identity is connected to place, thus construed situationally. Moreover, identities can be negotiated and contexted in the *Contrasto*. These findings fully support Kroskrity's argument regarding the situationality of ethnic and other social identities. As in the case of the Arizona Tewa studied by Kroskrity, "by highlighting the active and creative role that speakers take in symbolizing their relevant social identity, these data encourage us to abandon an inappropriate emphasis on the immutability and coercive nature of particular social identities" (1993:205).

I wrote at the beginning of chapter 1, that verbal duels offered a privileged point of view in the study of social realities. It has become apparent, throughout the chapters that the power of the *Contrasto* to question established views seems to lie in the "antinomic structure" of the duel itself. Future research should look in these terms to other traditional forms of verbal dueling present in other cultures and societies.

If we follow Berger and Luckmann's formulation of reality as socially constructed (1966) through language,[223] then in the *Contrasti* the contrary happens, and language works at destroying reality. In the performances reality is presented as unstable, as subjective, and especially, as the result of the ability of the poet to impose his reality over the reality of the other poet[224] (see chapters 3 and 4). The *Contrasti* are exercises in complexity. They tackle the most fundamental tenets of the society, and what is most important, they do so in the public sphere.

It was then fundamental to understand how the artists justify and legitimize their attack to social realities. I have looked at the way the complex formal structure of the *Contrasto* may offer a way for the poets to "protect" their ability to propose alternative visions (chapters 3 and 4). The call for an "external authority" that the poets do allows them to decline responsibility for their words, protecting themselves from possible retaliation of offended parties, while at the same time empowering their agency as artists (see chapter 7). Invoking an external authority is also diametrically opposed to the idea of an "absolute truth." It is equivalent to doubt that truth can be found in the correct univocal analysis of the "facts."

The *Contrasto* is first of all poetry, and as such deeply intertextual. It is the intertextuality in poetry, its continuous referring to another voice, to another source of authority, that led Locke to see poetry and rhetoric as dangerous arts, arts of fallacy (see the discussion of Locke's thought in Bauman and Briggs, 2000:159). In rhetoric there is always more than one truth; truth is dialogical. But in the verbal duel, the dialogs stops and turns in the antinomy, it can never be resolved. So the regime of truth becomes forever unattainable.

My discussion of the *Contrasto* opens many questions, some of them requiring further study. Much still needs to be said about this complex genre. I will examine a few of the directions in which my inquiry can move next. First of all, only a few of the topics commonly discussed in the *Contrasti* have been included here. There is a corpus of *Contrasti*, for example, of historical argument. Their analysis promises to furnish alternative ways to look at Tuscan history.

Second, while I have discussed views of womanhood, many topics

---

[223] Communicative exchanges are seen by Berger and Luckmann (1966) as a collaborative effort at the construction and maintenance of a common reality.

[224] We can see this in the continuous disputing of reality, the continuous presentation of at least two points of view about it.

center on male figures. Images of masculinity and male identities are continuously performed and contested in the *Contrasti*. A study of masculinity in the *Contrasto* thus could shed further light on the construction of gendered identities.

Third, while humor is extremely important in the performance, it has received very small space in this dissertation. It is clear though, that a lot of the artistic value and of the political relevance of these verbal duels depends on the ability of the poets to obtain from their audience a laughing response. A future study of irony and laughing in the *Contrasto* will add further layering to our understanding of verbal art.

Finally, the changes in the *Contrasto* as it passes to a new generation of young poets, should be analyzed. During my fieldwork, I recorded several performances in which young poets would sing. These are interesting on one hand, as they can show eventual pedagogical models deployed by the older poets in teaching to their young disciples. On the other hand, the poetical production of the disciples themselves allows to see eventual differences in the performing style of the *Contrasti* across generations of poets, thus possibly shedding light on the future of this genre.

In terms of future research, three important areas emerge. First, there is the need for an understanding of the linguistic ideologies present among the Tuscan population and how they may differ both from the national linguistic ideologies and from the ideologies of the poets. Second, it becomes important to look at other genres of verbal art – especially those in which the presence of female artists becomes more relevant – as well as other forms of verbal duels performed in Italy. An example of the latter could be Rap, which has become common as a performative genre in the last two decades. Finally, there is a need to look at the most recent changes in Tuscan history, namely the beginning of mass-immigration from other countries, and how this, in turn, influences local images of "self" and "other." This could be reflected in changing perception of Tuscan "identities" and find in turn expression in the *Contrasto*.

APPENDIX A

I. Transcription Notation.

There is no established system of notations for the transcription of Tuscan Italian. I have used the conventions used in the writing of standard Italian, but adhered to the Tuscan pronunciation as much as it was possible without the use of a phonetic notation. In particular, I have followed the following rules:

1) I transcribed the *gorgia* using the "h" symbol. Where sounds were dropped (usually /k/, /t/ and /v/) I did not included them in the transcription of the word.
2) In written standard Italian, elision is usually represented by the apostrophe - ' -. I applied this convention to the spoken Tuscan Italian, were elisions are much more frequent.

There is an established tradition for the transcription of the *Contrasti*. This tradition follows written poetry and represents the singing turn of a poet as an octet, namely a stanza of eight verses. I have used this same form of transcription in this text. In Addition, the following transcription conventions (generally used in Conversation Analysis) apply:

1) (Words in parenthesis) = words are unclear.
2) (.......) = words I cannot hear.
3) ((Double parentheses)) = indicate production of specified sound by the speaker or audience, including applause and laughing.
4) [   ] or [= square brackets indicate overlapping between two

different speakers.

5) <   > = laugher from the audience overlapping the speaker's words or singing.

6) AUD = audience

7) AUD? = unknown person in the audience

8) Ha! He! hhhhh = laughing

9) I transcribe sentences spoken by other than the singer by indenting them and indicating the name of the speaker, followed by a colon. These sentences are also numbered, although they are not part of the octet.

In translating, I have opted to use idiomatic English, to make it easier for the reader to follow the meaning. The drawback of this decision is that much of the linguistic creativity of the octets (as discussed especially in chapter 3 and 4) is lost in the translation.

APPENDIX B

I. Performances, Poets and *Contrasti*.

The following list includes all the *Contrasti* and series of octets I have recorded. It does not include other genres that were performed on the same occasions.

I. a. 1994.

1) Interview with the poet Pirazza in Monghidoro (province of Bologna). During the interview, Pirazza does solo performances of several traditional *Contrasti* and other songs in octets.

- Pia dei Tolomei.
- Peasant vs. Urbanite.
- Priest vs. Peasant.
- Peasant vs. Landowner.
- The Departure of the Americans.
- The Modern Woman.

I. b. 1997.

2) 5/23/97 - *Festa Pensionati*, "feast of the retired people," in Grosseto. Performance of the poets Elidio and Francesco Benelli with the *Cantastorie*, "Story-singer," Eugenio Bargagli.

- Opening Octets (all poets).
- Open Theme: about the Maremma area, then about aging (Benelli brothers).
- The Blond (E. Benelli) and the Brunette (F. Benelli).
- Closing Octets (all poets).

3) 6/16/97 - *Festa dei Carbonai*, "feast of the coal-makers," in Tobbiana (province of Pistoia). Performance of the poets Nello Casati and Realdo Tonti.
- Opening Octets (both poets).
- Open theme: about the coal-makers (Tonti and Casati).
- The Blond (Casati) and the Brunette (Tonti).
- Open Theme: reciprocal praises (Casati and Gabriele Ara from the audience).

4) 6/21/97 - Music Festival in the plaza of Santa Croce, "Holy Cross," in Florence. Performance of the poets Realdo Tonti, Altamante Logli and Liliana Tamberi.
- Opening Octets (all poets)
- The Water (Tonti) and the Wine (Logli)
- Wife (Tamberi) and Husband (Logli)
- Closing octets (all poets)

5) 7/5/97 - "*Sagra* of the Goose" in Malmantile (province of Florence). Performance of the poets Realdo Tonti and Altamante Logli.
- Opening Octets
- Open Theme (reciprocal insults)
- The Boy (Logli) and the Girl (Tonti)
- The Landowner (Logli) and the Peasant (Tonti)
- Closing Octets

6) 7/6/97 - Festival "PDS for the young people" in Legri (province of Prato). Performance of the poets Altamante Logli, De Sanctis, Mauro Chechi, Ettore Del Bene and Gianni Ciolli.
- The Doctor (Logli), the Priest (De Sanctis) and the Gravedigger (Chechi).
- Open Theme: reciprocal praises (De Sanctis, Ciolli, Del Bene and Logli).
- Closing Octets (all poets).
- Octets between Logli and someone in the audience.

7) 7/9/97 - Festival "PDS for the young people" in Legri (province of Prato). Performance of the artist Carlo Monni.
- Octets (memorized) between father and son.

8) 7/10/97 - Festival of the parish in Santomato (province of Pistoia). Performance of the poets Altamante Logli and Nello Casati.

- The Blond (Logli) and the Brunette (Casati).
- Logli sings octets in honor of Pistoia.
- Argument in octets among the poets, which brings the performance to an alt.

9) 7/17/97 - Summer performance series at the park of Isolotto, in Florence. Performance of the artist Carlo Monni with a brief intervention of the poet Altamante Logli.

- Octets against the Women (Logli)
- The Nun and the Prostitute (Logli, memorized).
- Closing Octets (Logli).

10) 8/2/97 - Summer festival in Migliana (province of Prato). Performance of the poets Elidio Benelli, Altamante Logli, Davide Riondino, Liliana Tamberi and Realdo Tonti.

- Opening Octets (all poets)
- The Smart (Logli) and the Stupid (Tonti)
- The Mother-in-Law (Benelli) and the Daughter-in-Law (Tamberi)
- The Nun (Riondino) and the Prostitute (Logli)
- Prato (Riondino) vs. Pistoia (Tonti)
- The Priest (Benelli) and the Priest's Housekeeper (Tonti)
- Closing Octets (all poets)

11) 8/7/97 - Festival of Liberation in Papone (province of Pistoia). Performance of the poets Realdo Tonti and Altamante Logli.

- Opening Octets of political argument
- The Mother-in-Law (Logli) and the Daughter-in-Law (Tonti)
- Octets addressing a person in the audience
- Closing Octets
- New Closing Octets –> Mountains (Logli) vs. Plains (Tonti)
- Octets addressing a person in the audience
- Octets by Fabrizio Ferroni addressed to the anthropologist

12) 8/29/97 - Festival of Unity in Florence. Performance of the poets Realdo Tonti and Altamante Logli, with interventions of the poets Ettore Del Bene, Gianni Ciolli and Gabriele Ara.

- The Fox (Tonti) vs. the Hunter (Logli).
- Prodi (Tonti) vs. Berlusconi (Logli).
- Open Theme: praises, then insults (Logli and Del Bene).

- Open Theme: praises (Tonti and Ciolli).
- Open Theme: insults, then praises (Logli and Del Bene).
- Open Theme: insults (Tonti and Logli).
- Octets against the Women (Logli).
- Opening octets (Ara).
- Open Theme (Ciolli, Tonti, Ara and Del Bene).
- The Bachelor (Del Bene), the Married Man (Ara) and the Lover (Ciolli).

13) 8/30/97 - Festival of Liberation in Tavernuzze (province of Florence). Performance of the poets Altamante Logli and Ettore Del Bene.
- Opening Octets (both poets).
- Open Theme: insults (Logli and Del Bene).
- Octets on the Sport-fans (Logli).
- The Bachelor (Del Bene) and the Married Man (Logli).
- Open Theme: praises (Logli and Del Bene).
- Octets on the Death of Poetry (Logli).
- Octets on the Fearful War (Logli).
- Closing Octets (both poets).

14) 9/6/97 - Feast of the wine at the Rufina Wineries in Pontassieve (province of Florence). Performance of the poets Realdo Tonti, Altamante Logli and the group of folk songs and dances *Maggiaioli del Mugello*.
- Octets between Logli and the singer of the *Maggiaioli*.
- Open Theme: about wine, then insults (Logli and Tonti).
- Pistoia (Tonti) vs. Florence (Logli).

15) 9/7/97 - Local town feast in Quarrata (province of Pistoia). Performance of the poets Realdo Tonti, Altamante Logli and Nello Casati, with various interventions from other artists.
- Opening Octets (all poets).
- The Member of the Green Party (Logli) and the Hunter (Tonti).
- The Blond (Tonti) and the Brunette (Casati).
- Berlusconi (Casati), D'Alema (Logli) and Prodi (Realdo).
- Closing Octets (all poets).

16) 9/14/97 - Festival of the parish in S. Niccoló Agliana (province of Pistoia). Performance of the poets Realdo Tonti, Nello Casati, Ettore Del Bene and Gianni Ciolli.

- Opening Octets (all poets).
- Mother-in-Law (Tonti) vs. Daughter-in-Law (Casati).
- The Idiot (Del Bene) and the Smart (Ciolli).
- Open Theme: about food and wine, then about young people and old people or Past vs. Present (all poets).
- Closing Octets (all poets).
- Octets exchanged between Ciolli and someone in the audience.

17) 11/25/97 - Festival of the A.R.C.I. in Florence. Performances of several artists, including the poets Realdo Tonti, Altamante Logli, Liliana Tamberi and Davide Riondino.
- Opening octets (all poets).
- The Churchgoer (Logli) and the Atheist (Tonti).
- The Wife (Logli), the Husband (Riondino), and the Lover (Tonti).

I. c. 1998.
18) 4/19/98 - VI meeting of *Poeti Bernescanti* in Ribolla (province of Grosseto). Performance of the poets: Altamante Logli (Firenze), Mastacchini (Suvereto, Livorno), Luigi Staccioli (Riparbella, Pisa), Realdo Tonti (Pistoia), Lio Bianchi (Massa Marittima, Grosseto), Azerio Lupini (Arezzo), Ivo Marcucci (Arezzo), Antonio Mariani (Viterbo), Gianni Ciolli (Prato)
- Opening Octets
- Octets on the meeting itself (Logli and Mastacchini)
- Housewife (Arezzo??2?) and Employed Woman (Tonti)
- Present Times (Ciolli) and Past Times (Bianchi)
- Marriage for Love (??3?) and Marriage for Money (Mariani)

19) 7/20/98 - Festival of Liberation in Spedalino (province of Pistoia). Performance of the poets Realdo Tonti, Gianni Ciolli and Gabriele Ara.
- Open Theme (offences)
- The Wife (Ciolli), the Lover (Ara) and the Husband (Tonti).
- Open Theme (about wine) then City vs. Countryside (Tonti and Ciolli).
- The Priest (Ara) and the City Major (Tonti).
- Closing Octets

20) 7/26/98 - Local feast at Lido di Pandoiano (province of Pisa). Performance of the poets Realdo Tonti and Altamante Logli, with the

folk singer Eugenio Bargagli.
- Opening Octets (Tonti and Logli).
- Water (Logli) and Wine (Tonti).
- The Husband (Tonti) and the Lover (Logli).
- Exchange of octets between Bargagli and Tonti.

21) 8/30/98 - Festival of Unity in Florence. Performance of the poets Altamante Logli and Gianni Ciolli.
- Opening Octets (both poets).
- Octets against the Women (Logli).
- The Bachelor (Ciolli) vs. the Married Man (Logli).
- The Peasant (Logli) vs. the Landowner (Ciolli).
- Mother-in-Law (Ciolli) vs. Daughter-in-Law (Logli).
- D'Alema (Ciolli) vs. Berlusconi (Logli).

22) 9/5/98 - Festival of Liberation in Viaccia (province of Prato). Performance of the poets Realdo Tonti and Gabriele Ara.
- Opening Octets (both poets).
- Open Theme: about the food, the wine, then against young people (both poets).
- D'Alema (Tonti) vs. Bertinotti (Ara).
- The Pope (Tonti) vs. the Berlin Wall (Ara).
- The Mother-in-Law (Ara) vs. the Daughter-in-Law (Tonti).
- Closing Octets (both poets).

I. d. 1999.
23) 9/3/99 - Festival of Unity in Florence. Performance of the poets Gianni Ciolli and Altamante Logli, during a performance of the artist Carlo Monni.
- Opening Octets (Logli and Ciolli).
- The Peasant (Ciolli) and the Landowner (Logli).
- Octets against the Sport Fans (Logli).
- The Bachelor (Ciolli) and the Married Man (Logli).

24) 9/18/99 - Feast of the wine and beer at a Barberino Colle Val D'Elsa (province of Florence). Performance of the poets Realdo Tonti and Gianni Ciolli, with intervention of Umberto Puntura.
- Opening Octets (Puntura, Tonti).
- Open Theme: praises (Tonti and Puntura).
- Closing Octets (Puntura).
- Open Theme: about food (Tonti and Ciolli).

- Open Theme: praises (Tonti and Puntura).
- The Beer (Ciolli) vs. the Wine (Tonti).
- Closing Octets (Ciolli and Tonti).

APPENDIX C

I. Languages Spoken in Italy and Their Varieties.

Italian citizens today speak more than thirty different languages (Grimes, 1988). Unfortunately, there are no systematic surveys done on the languages spoken by the 1,500,000 non-Italian immigrants who live in Italy today. In the following list of the languages spoken in Italy, I give the English version of the name of each language first (if available), followed by the Italian version in parentheses.

Albanian, Tosk (Albanese)
Bavarian (Bavarese)
Bergamasco
Catalan (Catalano)
Cimbrian (Cimbro)
Corsican (Corso)
Emiliano
Franco-Provençal (Franco-Provenzale)
French (Francese)
Friulian (Friulano)
German, Standard (Tedesco)
Greek (Greco)
Italian (Italiano) – Includes Tuscan as a dialect.
Italian Sign Language
Judeo-Italian (Giudeo-Italiano)
Ladin (Ladino)
Ligurian (Ligure)
Lombard (Lombardo)

Neapolitan-Calabrian (Napoletano-Calabrese)
Piedmontese (Piemontese)
Provençal (Provenzale)
Romani, Balkan (Romancio)
Romani, Sinte (Romancio)
Romani, Vlach (Romancio)
Sardinian (Southern)
Sardinian (North-Eastern)
Sardinian (Central)
Sardinian (North-Western)
Serbo-Croatian (Serbo-Croato)
Sicilian (Siciliano)
Slovenian (Sloveno)
Venetian (Veneto)

II. Characteristics of the Tuscan Variety of the Italian Language.

The following characteristics I have extracted from the published researches and comparative studies on Tuscan.[225] For each example, I give the Standard Italian word followed by the Tuscan word, then the English translation in parentheses:

II. a. Sets of Vowels.

The Italian languages have different sets of vowels. Tuscan (like Italian) has a 7 vowels system: i, e, ɛ, a, ɔ, o, u.

II. b. Phonological Characteristics.

Phonological characteristics of Tuscan include:

1) The distinction between /e ɛ/ and /ɔ o/

2) The diphthong /wɔ/ is often reduced to /ɔ/ : fuoco –> foco (fire).

3) The Tuscan vowels are different from the standard, the point of

---

[225] In particular Canepari, 1979:213-216, and Rohlfs, 1966. For further information on the Tuscan variety of the Italian language see also Agostiniani, 1989; Agostiniani and Giannelli, 1990; Brodin, 1970; Canepari, 1985; Giacomelli, 1984/85; Grassi, Sobrero and Telmon, 1997; Tolomei, 1992. For further information on the Occidental variety of Tuscan see also Giacomelli, 1975; Giacomelli, Gori and Lucarelli, 1984; Nerucci, 1901.

articulation is more advanced.

4) Elongation of the last vowel of the utterance, usually manifested as [e]:
piú → piúe (more)
bus → busse (bus)

5) Gorgia:
– /p t k/ → /φ θ h/ when preceded by vowel (also if the vowel is the preceding word).
– /h/ in some parts of the region becomes /H/ or even /Ø/.
– /p t/ can also become /Ø/ in Pistoiese, Pratese (occidental Tuscan).
– /p t k/ preceded by consonant become aspirate.

6) Between vowels, /b d g/ may be realized as [β δ γ].

7) /cˇ gˇ/ between vowels are pronounced as [ʃ ʒ]:
cacio → [ka:ʃo] (cheese)
agile → [a:ʒile] (limber)

8) /s/ preceded by /n/ or /l, r/ may become affricated [(t)s]:
penso → [pɛn:(t)so] ([I] think)

9) Frequent assimilation of consonantal groups and of nasals and liquids:
tecnico → tenniho (technician)
un ragno → ur ragno (a spider)

10) /ts/ and /dz/ are usually reinforced (long = geminate) when between vowels. So are /ŋ, l, ʃ/.

II. c. Syntactic Characteristics.
Syntactic reinforcement: The preposition "a" derive from the Latin "ad" by assimilation to the consonant that follows it. Thus, although not graphically shown, groups of this kind have a reinforcement/elongation of the consonant following the "a" in the spoken language. This pronunciation is kept in Tuscany (and Southern Italy) but lost in Northern Italy:
a casa → [ak'ka:sa] (at home)
The same syntactic reinforcement is produced by other prepositions, pronouns, auxiliary forms, conjunctions, adverbs (da, su, tra, fra, ho, ha, do, fa, fu, va, che, chi, qui, qua, se (conj.), ma, o, e, dá,

dí, lá, giá, giú, sé, ció, piú, come, dove, sopra, qualche) and all the polysyllables with the accent on the last syllable.

III. Characteristics of the Occidental Tuscan Variety.

The following list I have gathered partially from the studies on the subject, and partially from my own fieldwork in Tuscany. For each example, I give the Tuscan word followed by the Standard Italian and English translations in parentheses.

III. a. Phonological Changes.
1) Changes in the vowels:

a → e	e.g. andea (andava, was going)
a → i	e.g. andíano (andavano, [if] they would go)
	vadino (vadano, may they go)
	comprino (comprano, [they] buy)
e → a	e.g. dua (due, two)
e → i	e.g. rimiscolare from rimescolare (mescolare,
	to mix) corrire (correre, to run)
e → ia	e.g. giangiva (gengiva, gum)
i → o	e.g. doventare (diventare, to become)
o → u	e.g. uliva or ulia (oliva, olive)
o → a	e.g. ramaiolo, from romaiolo (mestolo,
	dipper)
u → a	e.g. grembiale (grembiule, apron)
u → i	e.g. imbria'arsi (ubriacarsi, to get drunk)

2) Changes in Consonants:

c → g	e.g. gosta (costa, [it] is priced)
	sagrificio (sacrificio, sacrifice)
ch → st	fistiare (fischiare, to whistle)
	stiaffo (schiaffo, slap)
d → g	veggo (vedo, [I] see)
d → n	lampana (lampada, lamp)
d → z	penzolare (pendolare, to pendulate)
g → d	diacere (giacere, to lie)
gh → d	diaccio (ghiaccio, ice)
l → n	antro (altro, other)
l → r	cardo (caldo, warm)
n → r	smarimettere (manomettere/aprire, to open)
ni → gn	gnente (niente, nothing)
r → n	zanzana (zanzara, mosquito)

r → s	bruciassi (bruciarsi, to burn oneself)
	vedessi (vedersi, to see oneself)
	lasciassi (lasciarsi, to break up)
s → c	verciare (versare, to pour)
zz → cc	tôcco (tozzo, piece)

3) Changes Due to Prothesis:

a	arritornare (ritornare, to come back)
g	granocchio (ranocchio, frog)
s	sbrendolo (brindello, tatter)

4) Changes due to Paragoge:

| e | noe (no, no) |

sie (sí, yes)

mee (me, me)

5) Changes due to Apheresis:

e	du' (due, two)
u	'bria'o (ubriaco, drunk)
c	'redere (credere, to believe)
	'resta (cresta, crest)
n	'un (non, not)
q	'uello (quello, that)

6) Changes due to Metathesis:

dreto (dietro, behind)

7) Modifications due to Syncope:

o →	furno (furono, [they] were)
	levorno (levarono, [they] took off)
	andorno (andarono, [they] went)
	mangiorno (mangiarono, [they] ate)
/k/ →	amío (amico, friend)
	larimare (lacrimare, to shed tears)
	dio (dico, [I] say)
	bao (baco, bug)

Note: "c" falls between two vowels, but also in front of an "r."
Notice how the *syncope* of the "c" substitutes the Florentine *gorgia*. The *gorgia* appears again, as an aspiration, in the slower pace of talk.

| g → | spiolo (spigolo, corner) |
| l → | utimo (ultimo, last) |

q →	a'uila (aquila, eagle)
r →	tera (terra, earth)
	pore (porre, to put)
	córe (correre, to run)
t →	anda'o (andato, gone)
	rispecchia'o (rispecchiato, mirrored)
v →	'ndo'e (dove, where)
	gio'anotto (giovanotto, young man)
	po'ero (povero, poor)
	era'amo (eravamo, [we] were)

8) Changes by epenthesis:

b	cambera (camera, bedroom)
d	tutt' e ddue (tutti e due, both)
	all' addiaccio (al freddo, in the cold)
l	tullo, from tu un lo (tu non lo, you do not ... it)
m	stommao (stomaco, stomach)
n	hane> hae> ha (ha, [s/he] has)
r	tronare (tonare, to thunder)

9) Other Changes:
l = palatalizes the /l/ in front of "i"cavagliere (cavaliere, knight)
eramo (eravamo, [we] were)

III. b. Morphological Differences.
1) Irregular plurals:
mano (s.), mane (pl.) (Italian: mano, mani; hand, hands)

2) Qualo? (m.) Quala? (f.) (Italian: Quale? (neuter); which one?)

3) Constant elimination of the final "-re" of the Infinite Mood of the verbs:
andá (andare, to go)
vedé (vedere, to see)
sentí (sentire, to hear)

4) In the plains variety of the Pistoiese Occidental Tuscan (and probably toward Agliana and Prato) we also find a contracted form of the Past Participle (with retraction of the accent on the preceding syllable):
ándo (andato, gone)

cásco (cascato, fallen)
trónco (troncato, cut)
cómpro (comprato, bought)

5) Also notice the archaic form for the past participle of the verb "to go:"

ito, Latin = itum (andato, gone)

APPENDIX D

I have included here the full transcription and translation of the *Contrasto* "D'Alema vs. Bertinotti" which was analyzed in chapter 4. I have also included the original excerpts, from the interview to Altamante Logli, that are analyzed in the same chapter.

I. *Contrasto* between D'Alema and Bertinotti.

This *Contrasto* was sung by Realdo Tonti e Gabriele Ara in Viaccia (province of Prato), on the 5th of September 1998. During the previous half-hour, the poets had been singing free octets, having received no topic from the public. Now, as Gabriele is singing an octet, Realdo moves toward the public to receive a piece of paper from somebody (out of the visual space of the camera). Such pieces of paper usually suggest a topic (the topic can otherwise be requested orally). Realdo shows the piece of paper to Gabriele, who just finished his octet:

Gabriele: *Bertinotti e D'Alema, he he he*
           Bertinotti and D'alema, he he he

(Octet 1) Realdo
Ed ora s'entra in un altro tereno
And now we enter in another terrain
lo vedi gli é arrivato vo dire il tema
I mean, you see, the theme has arrived
e di cantarlo un si po' fare a meno
and to sing it we cannot do without

vo di tra Bertinotti co' D'Alema
I mean, between Bertinotti with D'Alema
e qui si mescola la pa-hh-glia e i' ffieno
and here the straw and the hay get mixed
a questo punti sa' la terra e trema
and at this point, you know, the earth trembles
ma per un trovassi in un pelago di guai
but, not to find ourselves in a sea of troubles
o dimmi te la pa-h-rte e tu farai.
o tell me, which part will you do

(Octet 2) Gabriele
Io ti rispondo come tu lo sai
I will answer you as you know
come poeta non fai- nun fui mai inerte
as a poet I was- I was never inert
m' ha' parlato di pelaghi e di guai
you spoke to me about seas and troubles
ti rispondo come i' ffiglio di Laerte
I will answer you like the son of Laertes[226]
io del mar mai mi spaventai
I was never afraid of the sea
e l'Odissea fu nel- per Odissea andai in terre deserte
and the Odyssey was in- for the Odyssey I went to desert land
o sceglila la parte dico il vero
o choose the part, I tell the truth
come fece il cantore ceco Omero.
as it did the blind singer Homer

(Octet 3) Realdo
Vo di tu mi vo mette' ne' mmistero
I mean, you want to keep me in a mystery
sento la scelta ancora nun l'hai fatta
I hear that still you haven't made your choice
dimmi 'al'é quello falso e quello vero
tell me which one is the false one and the true one
senno la testa mia diventa matta
otherwise this head of mine will become crazy

---

[226] Laertes was the father of Odysseus.

guarda d'esse' piú chiaro e piu sincero
try to be clearer and more sincere
perché la cosa qui nun si baratta
or the thing here is not being swapped[227]
te lo ripeto ancora vo' di' per Dio
I repeat to you again, I mean, by God!
il che tu nun pigli te lo piglio io.
what you don't take I will take.

(Octet 4) Gabriele/Bertinotti
E allora o benedetto Iddio
And then, blessed God!
voglio smette' di darti gianduiotti
I want to stop giving you *gianduiotti*[228]
vol dire che la scelta la fo io
this means that I will do the choosing
vol dire che mi piglio Bertinotti
this means that I will take Bertinotti for myself
e che D'Alema ve lo dico anch'io
and I tell you[229] too that D'Alema
non é tra i meglio che in terra e furon cotti
is not among the best that on earth were cooked
se me lo servissero per mangiare
if they would serve him to me as food
mi toccherebbe andare a vomitare
I would have to go vomit

(Octet 5) Realdo/D'Alema
Suvvia collega nun esagerare
Colleague, let's not exaggerate
mi sembra he tu pigli una brutta strada
it seems to me you are taking an ugly road
di tutto tu mi vieni a contestare
you contest me for everything

---

[227] Namely: otherwise we cannot exchange our ideas.

[228] The *gianduiotto* is a kind of chocolate candy. Namely, Gabriele is not going to make things easy for the other poet anymore.

[229] Addressing the audience.

o qui un si mangia ne fieno e ne biada

here we are not going to eat neither straw or hay[230]

tu sai con chi si deve ancor lottare ....

you know with whom we still have to fight[231]

[four verses are missing here due to changing the video-tape]

(Octet 6) Gabriele/Bertinotti

  ... boni

        good

t'hai agito si da intelligente

you acted indeed as an intelligent one

ogni tanto sentire e non ragioni

every now and then you do not listen to reason

e a noi tu non ci tratti bellamente

and you do not treat us nicely

pensa un pochino delle pensioni

think a bit about the pensions[232]

si volea fa e un s'é fatto niente

we wanted to do, and we have done nothing

tu ti se messo con que' cervelli fini

you sided with those thin brains

e chi d'ha' dato retta se no a Dini

and to who did you listen? to Dini[233]

(Octet 7) Realdo/D'Alema

La politica ha subito i suoi destini

Politics were subjected to their destinies

---

[230] I am not sure about the meaning of this sentence, but it may refer to the fact that no decisions can be made if Bertinotti keeps contesting everything D'Alema does.

[231] Namely against capitalism, or the conservative parties.

[232] He is referring to a debate in the government regarding a financial law that also affected the retirement pensions that, in Italy, come from the state. In establishing an alliance with Bertinotti in order to create a government together, D'Alema had promised to follow Bertinotti's program regarding the retirement pensions. After the formation of the governmental coalition, though, the PDS had instead supported the program of the center-right.

[233] Italian politician in the center-right.

se oggi come ieri non é uguale
if today it is not like yesterday
che sia Prodi o che sia Dini
it may be Prodi[234] or it may be Dini
chi comanda gli é sempre i' ccapitale
the capitalism is always in command
colle idee si varcano i confini
with the ideas wecan move past the boundaries
vo di c'é chi fa bene e chi fa male
I mean, there is who does good and who does evil
nun letichiamo tra noi e damoci ragione
let's not argue and let's admit that we are both right
e facciamo della rivoluzione
and let's do the revolution

(Octet 8) Gabriele/Bertinotti
Le parole le sarebben bone
The words would be good
ma' fatti un corrispondan' abbastanza
but the facts do not correspond enough
perché tu nun ci hai dato il guiderdone
because you did not give us the guerdon
con la bicamerale all'alleanza
with the bicameral[235] to the alliance
con lui che gli é servo de' ppadrone
with him[236] that is a servant of the master[237]
e di televisioni e n'ha abbastanza
and has enough TV channels

---

[234] Romano Prodi was then the Italian First Minister. He was put in charge by an alliance of parties that included both the parties of the left.

[235] He is referring again to the fact that the PDS used its alliance to PRC to get to the government, but then did not "reward" the PRC by listening to its requests. The "bicameral" is the senate plus deputy chambers.

[236] As it will become clear in the next sentences, here Gabriele is referring to Berlusconi, then an ex-First Minister. A businessman that owns the major private TV channels, Berlusconi is the richest man in Italy. In the beginning of the 90s, he created his own party, *Forza Italia*, through which he was able to go to the government, although for just a few months.

[237] Namely the capitalists.

canale quattro, canale cinque e anche sei

channel four, five and even six

fosse per me io l'imprigionerei

if it was up to me I would put him in prison

(Octet 9) Realdo/D'Alema

Lo sento che sincero e che tu sei

I hear that you are sincere

ma facile no non é la battaglia

but the battle, no, it is not easy

siamo mille partiti e cinque o sei

we are one thousand parties and five and six

tutti puntati ci s'ha la metraglia

we all have a machine gun pointed toward us

quello che dici é vero eppur dovei

what you say is true, still I had to [do it]

o se l'idea tua le nun isbaglia

o your idea is not wrong

ma questi son tempi dimorto patiti

but these are very suffered times

quand'a i' ggoverno c'é mille partiti

when in the government there are one thousand parties

(Octet 10) Gabriele/Bertinotti

Parli di Cofferati e di Minniti

You talk about Cofferati and Minniti[238]

parli di un sacco di cervelli

you talk about a bunch of brains

falce e martello nascosti e rifiniti

The sickle and the hammer are hidden and finished off

sulla bandiera mettete i piselli

on the flag you put dicks

SCUSA!

Sorry! (toward the audience)

le rose volevo dir so- i rosi volevo dir sono fioriti

the roses, I mean, ar- the rose trees, I mean, are blossomed[239]

---

[238] Other Italian politicians.

[239] Namely, he can see a lot of pink around (instead of the red of Communism).

ma secondo me rimettete le pelli
I believe that you are growing your skins again[240]
perché la sola incontestabil cosa
because the only uncontestable thing
che il vostro rosso é diventato rosa
is that your red has become pink[241]

(Octet 11) Realdo/D'Alema
Nun so se vera l'é codesta cosa
I don't know if that thing is true
lo vedi ancor c'é la bandiera rossa
you see, still there is the red flag[242]
tu sse' daltonico io un la vedo rosa
you are color-blind, I do not see it pink
mi sembra sia sempre alla riscossa
to me, it seems to be always bound to reconquering
vedi che sventola la nun riposa
see how it waves, it does not rest[243]
tutte le vorte te la fa la mossa
every time it moves for you
e co' una quercia accanto che fiorisce in cima
and with an oak next blossoming on top[244]
e la farce e mmartello in fondo e lla concima
and the sickle and the hammer at the bottom to fertilize it

(Octet 12) Gabriele/Bertinotti
Per questi versi ci vorria la rima
For these verses we would need a rhyme
che la quercia- la farce e martel ne' PDS
that the oak- the sickle and the hammer in the PDS

---

[240] Changing skins, like snakes. The metaphor here means that they are no more what they were, namely that they are not communists anymore.

[241] Gabriele is referring to the fact that the PDS changed their flag from the traditional communist one to a new one (with very little red on it).

[242] In the PDS new flag, under the center, there is a small communist flag shown.

[243] The small communist flag is represented waving.

[244] The center of the PDS's flag shows an oak tree, with a large green foliage, under which there is the small Communist flag with the symbols of the crossed hammer and sickle on it.

la c'era una volta c'era prima
there was once, there was before
ma l'a un esiste piú ne' PS
but it does not exist anymore in the PS
niente piú la quercia la concima
nothing more fertilizes the oak
la rosa e' un leggero (telo d'esse)
the rose is a light (??)
che a me mi sa che in tutt'i ttu partito
to me, all of your party looks like that
anche i ttu baffo gli e' un po' scolorito
even your mustache is a bit discolored

(Octet 13) Realdo/D'Alema
Glié il tempo che passa tu l'hai sentito
It's the time that goes, you have felt it
la natura le va in evoluzione
nature goes in evolution
se un po' gli ha cambiato i' mio partito
if my party has changed a bit
e te la voglio dire la ragione
indeed I want to tell you the reason
gli é cinquant'anni che nun s'é capito
we haven't understood it in fifty years
eppure s'era anche all'opposizione
although we even were in the opposition[245]
per vede' se si trovava la meglio via
to see if we could find a better way
e s'é cambiato la diplomazia
we changed our diplomacy

(Octet 14) Gabriele/Bertinotti
Ma de' hompagni che per la via
But the comrades that along the way
il questa storia ormai infinita
in this history, now infinite
vissero una sorte amara e ria
lived a bitter and evil sort

---

[245] In Italy the parties who are not represented in the executive council of ministers, are called "the opposition."

molti se la persero la vita
many lost their lives
e quell'idea mi par che sia
and it seems to me that idea[246] is
ancora viva e ancora riverita
still alive and still cherished
ma son fra pochi e per questo mi lamento
but I am among few and because of this I moan
or siamo però quattro e domani cento
now we are four, though tomorrow we will be one hundred

(Octet 15) Realdo/D'Alema
O quando si cantava Fischia il Vento
O when we were singing "Blows the Wind"[247]
ormai gli é un tempo giá passato
but now that time has gone
e a ricordallo e che n'ho un tormento
and it's a torment for me to remember
di quel partito che gli era [dannato
of that party that was damned

        Ara: [((shakes head affirmatively))

camicie nere lá spiegate al vento
black shirts[248] there, unfurled in the wind
e il popolo veniva [ingannato
and the people were being conned

        Ara: [((shakes head affirmatively))

quando i Partigiani morivano sugli Appennini
when the Partisans[249] were dying on the Apennine[250]

---

[246] The Communist ideals.

[247] I believe this was originally a Russian folk song, then adopted by the Soviet party. Translated and rearranged in Italian, became a symbol of the resistance against fascism.

[248] The name given to the fascist militia organized by Mussolini.

[249] Name given to the civilians who fought against the fascists and nazis in Second World War.

[250] Chain of mountain going from Tuscany to Sicily.

gli stessi ladroni pigliavano '[kattrini
the same big thieves were taking the money

Ara: [(((shakes head affirmatively))

(Octet 16) Gabriele/Bertinotti
E ora fa i patti con quegli assassini
and now you make accords with those assassins
o meglio é quello che tu senti
or better, this is what you feel
ti fai i patti e trovi i confini
you make accords and set the boundaries
insieme a loro compagno o disc- camerati o discendenti
together with them comrade- camerati[251] or their descendants
dissi compagni e sbagliai i rini
I said "comrade" and I erred the rhymes
volevo dire porci e malfidenti
I wanted to say pigs and untrustworthy
che se tratti con Prodi o Berlusconi
that if you negotiate with Prodi and Berlusconi
di certo nun le trovi tue ragioni
for sure, you are not going to find your reasons

(Octet 17) Realdo/D'Alema
Cerco di non fa' troppe confusioni
I try not to bring too much confusion
o di cercarla la diretta via
and to find the direct path
come vedi ancor lotto-o contro i padroni
as you can see I still fight against the owners/masters
voglio dir per la democrazia
I mean to say for democracy

---

[251] The Italian word *compagno* does not properly translate in English. The English word "comrade" includes both Italian words *compagno* and *camerata*, although in Italian they are dramatically distinguished. *Camerata* is used to indicate a person sharing the same dormitory among soldiers. Otherwise, more generally, it applies only to fascists. *Compagno* situated the person as part of the left or as an anarchist. To call a person *camerata* is to call him a fascist, which in this context is a very strong insult.

io nun so' dalla parte dei ladroni
I am not on the side of the big thieves
l'ho mantenuta quell'idea mia
I kept that idea of mine
se dell'idee e che ce n'ho la scorta
if of ideas, indeed, I have a surplus
al mondo gliela vo' dare una svorta
I am going to give a turn to the world

(Octet 18) Gabriele/Bertinotti
Ma sa alla gente cosa gliene importa
But you know, people do not care
tu sai gli é come dare l'acqua ai somari
you know, it is like giving water to donkeys
i mass media ti danno questa vorta
this time the mass media gives you
l'opportunitá d'esser quello che appari
the opportunity to be what you appear
ad un poeta poco gliene importa
to a poet this matters little
te lo dicevo ora e un é guari
I was telling you now, it is not (a trouble)
che la sorte é sempre quella
but the destiny is always the same
al governo ci hai messo la morta[della
you put a mortadella²⁵² in the government

    Tonti: [((laughing))

    AUDIENCE: ((general laughing))

(Octet 19) Realdo/D'Alema
Quella di Bologna é la piu' bona e la piú bella [smiling]
The one from Bologna is the best and the most beautiful
vo dire sul mercato che ci sia
I mean to say, that there is on the market

---

²⁵² The *mortadella* is a kind of processed meat, of pink color. The statement implies that the PDS has substituted the red color of communism for a faded color, namely that they are no more true to the communist ideals.

Io vedi l'amo come una sorella
you see I love it like a sister
anche lui lotta la democrazia
even he fights for democracy
se la politica un é tanto bella
if politics are not too beautiful
pecché d'intorno c'é brutta razzia
because around there is ugly plundering
se noi ci si trova in questo stato
if we find ourselves in this situation
guarda di un da' la colpa all'affettato.
try not to blame it on the processed meat.

(Octet 20) Gabriele/Bertinotti
hh hh
Ci mancherebbe fosse anche al senato
That's all we need, to have it even in the senate
a tenere alto questo lume
to keep high this light
                                        ha ha ha
un altro -ha ha ha- come lui disperato
another ha! ha! ha! despaired like him
vorrei dire un altro salume
I mean to say another salami
solo un salame li depositato
only a salami there, deposited
attaccato e pieno di cacchiume
hung and full of crap
che le mosche gli hanno —h- fatto intorno
that the flies have done around it
potrebbe essere uguale alla luce del giorno
could be the same in the daylight

(Octet 21) Realdo/D'Alema
Via gli é sera un gli e' mezzogiorno
Come on it's evening it's not noon
anche te tanto sereno tu un istai
even if you don't seem too serene

pe' l'accozzaglie che tu hai d'intorno

because of the hodgepodge that you have around[253]
dimmelo ora come tu farai
tell me now what are you going to do
vo' di domani prima di mezzogiorno
I mean to say tomorrow before noon
o domall'altro quando t'incontrerai
or the day after when you will meet[254]
ora nun mi fa' ddire una cosa brutta
now don't make me say an ugly thing
tu se' in collutazione con Cossutta
you are in a scuffle with Cossutta

(Octet 22) Gabriele/Bertinotti
E per dirtela allora proprio tutta
And to tell you then the whole of it
io mi dibatto fra le pene dell'inferno
I struggle among hellish pains
perché sto a leticare con Cossutta
because I am quarreling with Cossutta
per volerci stare o no a i' governo
about remaining or not in the government
e questa situazione sai l' é brutta
and this situation, you know, is ugly
preferirei tentare a i' llotto interno
I would prefer to try at the internal lottot[255]
ma non parliamo di complihazioni
but let's not talk about complications
che queste son le nostre divisioni
that these are our divisions

---

[253] Referring to the divisions inside the PRC.

[254] He is referring to a meeting that Bertinotti was going to have with other leaders of the PRC. Among them in particular Cossutta. At the time, there was a split in the PRC. The faction headed by Bertinotti wanted to leave the government, to return to the opposition. The faction leaded by Cossutta wanted to remain in the government. Eventually this led, a few months later, to a split in the PRC, as Cossutta and his followers created another party, the *Partito dei Comunisti Italiani*, "Party of Italian Communists." The PRC left the government, while the PIC remained in the government.

[255] The meaning of this phrase is obscure to me.

(Octet 23) Alternated
Realdo/D'Alema
Allora amico portiamo le ragioni
Then, friend, we present our reasons

Gabriele/Bertinotti
E diciamo ognuno la sua meglio
And let's each say his best ones

Realdo/D'Alema
Per me son giusti i nostri paragoni
For me our confrontations are just

Gabriele/Bertinotti
Sta attento che sopra di te io veglio
Be careful because I watch over you

Realdo/D'Alema
Io lotto c- contro chi ci sfrutta e coi padroni
I fight against those who exploit us and against the masters

Gabriele/Bertinotti
Ma secondo me ci lotto meglio
But according to me I fight them better

Realdo/D'Alema
Te lo vo di' fin-fin da quando ero bambino
I want to tell you, since I was a child
ho lottato per gl'operai e i' ccontadino
I fought for the workers and the peasant

II. Excerpts from Interviews with Altamante Logli.
Scandicci (Firenze), 11/9/97.
1) Code: I 1-A-222:

Coi capi squadra gerarchi e balilli
With the chiefs of the action squads[256], the hierarchs[257] and the *balilli*[258]

---

[256] The fascist death squads.
[257] The local leaders chosen by the fascist regime.

co capi, centurioni capizona
with the chiefs, centurions and local chiefs[259]
e alla bocca ci s'avea i sigilli
our mouths had seals
per via di ella razza poo bona
because of that bad sort of people
almeno oggi si vive piú tranquilli
at least today we live more peacefully
perché un c'é piú nessun che ci bastona
because there is no one cudgelling us anymore
il Tiburzi, Mastrillo e il Passatore
Tiburzi, Mastrillo and Passatore[260]
di quella gente avete piú onore
had more honor than those people [the fascists]

2) Code: I 1-B-302:

Altamante: A San Vincenzo, s'andó a Campole, quando ci fanno smette di canta i carabinieri perché, si cantaa De Gasperi e Togliatti. Il carabiniere dice: "perché dici male di De Gasperi?" "Perché lui dice male di me" gli dissi io, no? Si fa il *Contrasto* in poesia (Madonna vá!). [...] allora gli era, dopo la guerra subito apito. [...] Passó la guerra fredda, capito, ci fu- ci fu un periodo che e Comunisti gli eran- gli erano a pe- pedinati, insomma esta gente di sinistra, vero? [...] Sí ecco, si passó una quindicina d'anni un só, la re- la democrazia fu un regime é? s'era sull'orlo Dio bono, apito, s'era sull'orlo quasi del tempo de colonnelli, in Spagna, come- come successe in- i colonnelli in Grecia, come al tempo che c'era- Dio bono ni mmondo c'era dei colpi di stato, gli hanno attentá di fallo anche guá. Perché la storia io sá, la memoria l'ho bona. [...] Si passó de momenti brutti, capito. E allora, anche la poesia, bisognaa fallo il conto. E come ti dio una volta qui a Badia, si cantava i Bbecchino, i Pprete, il Dottore e il Farmacista, quattro poeti. T'apparisce il maresciallo, e disse- il Becchino un se ero io o se era il Ceccherini, e gua- "e fo delle bue- faró delle bue fonde per sot- fondi- degli scavi profondi per sotterrare questi vagabondi" a il Prete gli disse, esto, quel poeta. Il Maresciallo ( ) "vie qua" mi dice a me "perché" dice "dicete male di

---

258 A *balilla* was a child or teenager member of the fascist youth organizations.
259 The poet is referring to the organization of the fascist militia and its divisions.
260 Three legendary brigands active in Italy at the end of the XIX century.

(lui) fate este ose osí. Sento avete rammenta il pprete gli é vagabondo e (io lavoro di piú), perché vu fate este cose ui?" dio "Ma! un son- ma son Contrasti di poesia, un si fa mia per letiare é?" "Ma" dice "voi un ci potei mettere un altro" e mi disse uno un gli (....) e gli avvió a dire "Maresciallo ci s'ha a mette lei ni' pposto di pprete?"

Anthropologist: Hhhh hu hu hu

Altamante: Ma gli andao a finí in galera! Un si potea dí cosí!

Anthropologist: Ha ha ha! Ma allora vi controllavano, la polizia veniva proprio alle rappresentazioni?

Altamante: A tutte le feste dell'Unitá c'era i carabinieri, tre o quattro carabinieri ritti a guardatti. E io mi daano ombra. [...] E il Cai di Pisa duró ancora dimolto tempo a nun vo- a nun volere nelle sale i registratori. Un li volea perché diceva "Noi, quando si va via di qui, un si sá il che vien detto".

Translation:

Altamante: At San Vincenzo, we went to Campole, when the police make us stop singing because we were singing 'De Gasperi versus Togliatti.' The policeman says: 'why are you saying bad things about De Gasperi?' 'Because he says bad things about me!' I told him, right? We are doing the *Contrasto* in poetry, by the Virgin! (Of course)! [...] This happened immediately after the war. The cold war came to pass, you understand, there was a period when the Communists were tailed, I mean, these leftist people, right? [...] Yes, that's it, we went through maybe fifteen years, I don't know, democracy was really a regime, right? We were on the brink, by God! You know? We were almost on the brink of the time of the colonels, like in Spain, like it happened in Greece, like at the time there was- Good Lord! In the world there were coups d'etat. They tried to do it here too. Because for history, you know, I have good memory. [...] We went through some bad moments, you know. So, even in poetry, we had to keep it into account, as I was telling you. Once, here in Badia, we were singing 'The Undertaker, the Priest, the Physician, and the Pharmacist.' We were four poets. Suddenly the marshal appeared, and he said- the Undertaker [had been saying] 'I am going to do deep excavations to bury these loafers.' That poet said [this] referring to the Priest. The marshal (then) tells me 'come here!' He tells me 'Why are you telling bad thing about (him), and [why] do you do things this way? I hear you have mentioned that the priest is a loafer and [you say]: I work more.

Why are you doing these things?' I say 'But they are not- but they are *Contrasti* in poetry! We are not doing it to really fight, you know?' He says 'But can't you put someone else in that place?' This is what he told me. And someone was about to tell him 'marshal, would you like us to put you in the place of the priest?'

Anthropologist: hh hhhhhh hu hu

Altamante: But I would have ended up in jail! We could not say like that!

Anthropologist: Ha! Ha! Ha! But then they were controlling you. Did the police come to the performances?

Altamante: At every Festival of Unity there were policemen, three or four policemen standing there looking at you. And that really bothered me. [...] The [poet Vasco] Cai of Pisa went on for a long time to refuse- he did not want tape recorders in the rooms. He did not want them because, as he used to say, "When we go away from here, no one knows what has been said."

APPENDIX E

I included here the full transcription and translation of the *Contrasto* analyzed in chapter 5. I also include an excerpt from an interview with Realdo Tonti, which I also included in chapter 5.

I. Closing Octets (*Contrasto* between Pistoia and the Mountain).

This *Contrasto* was sung at the end of a performance in Papone (Firenze), on August 7, 1997. After negotiating with the public, who wanted that the poet would continue their performance, Altamante said a few jokes. Then he started his closing octets:

(Octet 1) Altamante
Allora amici miei si fa partenza
Thus, my friends, we are departing
vedete gli é quasi mezzanotte
you see, it is almost midnight
io vi ringrazio della vostra accoglienza
I thank you for your warm welcome
e le corde vocali si so rotte
but my vocals cord have broken
ma io ritorno alla mia residenza
I go back to my residence
pian piano scenderó sopra alle grotte
very slowly I will descend over the caves[261]

---

[261] I am not sure to which caves Altamante is referring.

torno a Scandicci in mezzo alla pianura
I go back to Scandicci in the middle of the plain
vi dó la bonanotte e fò chiusura
I tell you goodnight and I close

AUD?: *Bravo! ((shouted))*

(Octet 2) Realdo
Vedete la poesia come l' é pura
see how poetry is pure
vo dire l' é gentile, genuina
I mean to say, it is gentle, genuine
anch'io me ne ritorno alla mia pastura
I too go back to my pasture
alla mia casa che nun é vicina
to my home that is not close
di lá da monti dall'altra pianura
over the mountains in that other plain
dove la cittá piú s'avvicina
where the city nears more
me ne ritorno con santa ragione
I go back with good reason
ma un iscordo la gente di Papone
but I do not forget the people of Papone.

(Octet 3) Altamante
Torna a s- Pistoia lá in quell'accquazione
Go back to Pistoia, there, in that stormy downpour

Realdo: <*He! Ho! Ora comincia (vai)!*>[262]
        He! Ho! Now you start (go on)!

torna lá nel mezzo ai <gineprai>[263]
go back there, in the middle of those tangles of troubles

---

[262] Note the audience's laughing answer to Altamante's first verse. It underlines the passage from the closing octets to a new *Contrasto*, at the same time recognizing and encouraging it.
[263] Literally, *gineprai* means "bushes of juniper," but it is generally used in its idiomatic sense of "troubles from which it is difficult to extricate oneself."

io ritorno alla mia abitazione
I go back to my abode
<che a Pistoia un ci> tornerei mai
since I would never go back to Pistoia

    AUD?: (   )

c'é la paura po' dell'infezione
there is also the fear of the infection
e poi ci sono tanti paretai
and then there are so many tangles of walls
ci son delle giornate tant' amare
there are some days so bitter
a forza sí di mosche e di zanzare.
by force, indeed, of flies and of mosquitoes

    AUD: ((laughing))

    AUD?: *[(e infatti) ce l'ho*
            (and in fact) I have them[264]

    AUD?: [Ha! Ha! Ha ha ha ha!

(Octet 4) Realdo
C'é le bellezze vedi le piú rare
There are the beauties, you see, the most rare
o quella l' é la tera degli amori
o, that is the land of loves
doe si coltivano cose-e molto rare
where the rarest things are cultivated
o specialmente delle rose e fiori
and especially roses and flowers
o lí non avrai delusioni amare
o there you will not have bitter delusions
o dove che si incontrano gli amori
where loves are encountered
invece te che abiti a Scandicci
instead you, living in Scandicci

---

[264] Referring to the presence of flies and mosquitoes, very common in summer.

e tu ti trovi sempre ne pasticci
you always find yourself in a mess.

    AUD: [((scattered applause))

    AUD: [((laughing)

    AUD?: (..........)

(Octet 5) Altamante
Ma -o son- ((coughing)) son venuto da le castagne e ricci
But I came from the chestnuts and the husks[265]
dove nasce i Bbisenzio sopra l'Appennino
where the Bisenzio River is born over the Appenine

    AUD: ((laughing))

l'acqua colava giú da que' renicci
the water was dripping down from those sliding sand deposits
e ti bagnó i' ssolo poverino
and soaked your soil poor one[266]
voglio vedere ome ti tu spicci
I want to see how you can unstick yourself
son nato fra la ch- fra i ccastagno e i' biancospino
I was born between the chestnut tree and the hawthorn
a Pistoia tu fa' di' mmormorio
in Pistoia you have to grumble
tu bevi l'acqua dove piscio io
you drink the water where I piss

    AUD: ((laughing))

    AUD: ((scattered applause))

---

[265] The Chestnut trees that cover the Apennine Mountains, are important symbols for the people living in them. They also furnished an important staple food. The chestnuts are gathered and cooked in various ways or ground to make flour, from which a sweet bread is done.

[266] The swampy plains receive their waters from the Apennine Mountains.

(Octet 6) Realdo
Tu sse nato lassú ni que ppendio
you were born there in that slope
ni ccomune laggiú di Cantagallo
in the commune of Cantagallo down there
di certo un ci starei vo dire io
I want to say, for sure I would not stay there
io sono rosso e te t'ha i mmuso giallo
I am red and you have a yellow face[267]
laggiú si dove vola i bbeccafio
down there where the fig-eater flies
e dove i mmerlo vedi casca in fallo
and where the blackbird, you see, falls in a mistake[268]
dove ci son tumurti e le macagne
where there are turmoils and blemishes
tu vivi solo a ghiande e a castagne
you live only on acorns[269] and chestnuts

(Octet 7) Altamante
Io sempre ameró le mie montagne
I will always love my mountains
la tra que faggi castagni e abeti
there among those beeches, chestnut trees and firs

Realdo: *bellina esta ui (ragazzi)*
         this one is pretty![270] (guys)

doe si mangia i maiali e si fa le lasagne
where we eat the pigs and we do the lasagne

---

[267] A reddish color of the skin is traditionally considered a sign of good health, while a yellowish color it is considered a negative sign.

[268] The word *merlo* means "blackbird" but also "fool." The first meaning is consistent with the mention of another bird, the fig-eater, in the previous verse, while the second meaning is more consistent with the idea of "falling into a mistake."

[269] Tuscans do not consider acorns edible by humans, but they usually give acorns to pigs. Thus, saying that somebody is eating acorns is an indirect insult.

[270] Here "to be pretty" is used in an ironic sense, meaning something that is funny and/or goes against one's expectations.

doe la natura mostra i su segreti
where nature shows her secrets
su i mmontanaro nun ci son macagne
up on the mountain there are no blemishes
e a quella sorgente ti diseti
and you quench your thirst to that spring
se tu va sulla Rasa e sul poggio di Buzzana
if you go on the Rasa or on the knoll of Buzzana
costa piú di Pistoia e tutt' Agliana
it is worth more than Pistoia and all of Agliana

Altamante: *Lui vié da Agliana*
        He comes from Agliana

(Octet 8) Realdo
La storia un l'ha studiata la piú lontana
you did not study the distant history
ti voi confrontar colla pianura
you want to compare yourself with the plain
della tua valle sperduta o si montana
of your lost and mountainous valley
che anche a lupi le gli li fa paura
that it scares even the wolves
tu ha ancora addosso i ppuzzo della lana
you still have on yourself the stink of the wool
delle pecore 'e porti alla pastura
of the sheep that you bring to the pasture
e allora i lletame ancora e tu strebbiacci
and then you still thresh the dung
t'ha mangiato polenda e castagnacci.
you have eaten polenda and chestnut cakes.

(Octet 9) Altamante
Io son felice di sta ddove i diacci
I am happy to stay where the ice is
dove cade la neve e la gragnola
where the snow and the hail fall
codesti son discorsi da pagliacci
those are discourses for clowns
proprio si vede e tu un c' hai la parola
we can really see that you have no words

sulle montagne no si tende i lacci
on the mountains we lay the snares
e po di tutto noi ti si fa scuola
and then on everything we are better than you[271]
laggiú nin quella perfida pianura
down there in that wicked plain
tu ma a di chi ci viene a te in villeggiatura
you should tell me who is going to come there for the holidays[272]

(Octet 10) Realdo
Quest' un é cosa che ci fa paura
this is not something that we fear
o ma la vita vedi é rigogliosa
o but life, you see, [in the plains] is luxuriant
ndove sfoggia l'odor della natura
where nature flaunts her smells
senti l'odor di ggelsomino, della rosa
you feel the smell of the jasmine, of the rose
invece te la ncima a quella frescura
instead you up on top in that coolness
dove n'infverno per i ffreddo non si riposa
where in the winter you cannot rest for the cold
dove di star l'umana specie e non é degno
where the human species is suited to stay
a dormi su pancacci fatti di legno
and you sleep on bunks made of wood

(Octet 11) Altamante
A rammentá i mmio paese non sei degno
you are not worthy no recall my town
ma sentite un pistoiese i che mi dice
but listen what this Pistoiese is saying
forse lu un ha virtú e ne contegno
maybe he has no virtue nor dignity

---

[271] Literally *ti si fa scuola* means "we make you school," namely: we can teach you because we are so much better than you are.

[272] The Apennine Mountains have traditionally been a location for summer tourism. In summer, their climate is sunny but cool while the plains are extremely hot and humid.

e lo ompiango povero infelice
and I feel sorry for him, poor misshapen wretch[273]

Realdo: *( ) ma va piano va via ( )*
                              (....) but slow down, come on (.....)

te de la vita n'hai disegno
you do not have the design of life
que be monti lo sai e le sue pan- pendici
those beautiful mountains, you know, and their slopes
quande quarche ragazza lasú ci porto
when I bring some girl up there
se ero vivo
if I was alive ((stops singing))
No! ero- ora sono vivo e nun ((sings again)) risorto morto
No! I was- now I am alive and I don't ((singing again)) come back dead
((stops singing))
torno vivo anche se ero morto
I came back alive even if I was dead
scusate! o sbagliao
sorry! I made a mistake[274]

(Octet 12) Realdo
Suvvia della carenza te ne sei accorto
come on, you should have realized your carency
nun fa tanta boria montanaro
don't show so much arrogance, mountai man
se no la storia vedi ti riporto
otherwise I will report you about history
se accanto alla pecora a i ssomaro
if next to the sheep and the ass
come studioso te lo fo conforto
I compare you as a scholar
che io da te vedi niente non imparo
since I learn nothing from you

---

[273] The word *infelice*, literally "unhappy one," is also a euphemism to indicate somebody who is mentally deficient.
[274] Talking to the audience.

della pianura mia ne fui la gloria
of my plain I was the glory[275]
perché del mondo feci l'arte e anche la storia
because in the world I did the art and the history as well

(Octet 13) Altamante
Codesta l'é tutta baldanza e tutta boria
yours is all rashness, all arrogance
andiamo via si andiamo a letto
let's go away indeed, let's go to bed
quest'omo mi perde la memoria
this man is loosing the memory
perde le rime l'arte e i cconcetto
he is loosing the rhymes and even the concept
ora gli e' tardi e un voglio fa bardoria
now it is late and I do not want to do revelry
e lo rispetteró pe que gl' ha detto
and I will respect him for what he said
conta più un somaro del mio paese
an ass of my town is worth more
che mezzo popolo sa di ppistoiese
than half the people of the Pistoia area

(Octet 14) Realdo
<Si vede l'ignorante [come é scortese>
It can be seen how the ignorant is impolite

    AUD: [((laughing))

    Altamante: *[ndiamo si va via (......). Ora un vó via più*
    come on, let's go away (.....). Now I won't go away anymore

tu l'ha messa la firma di mmontanaro
you put your signature as hillbilly
<guardatevi intorno> nel nostro paese
look around in our country[276]

---

[275] Realdo is speaking for the city of Pistoia, who was the glory of its plain.
[276] Addressing the audience.

ndove gli é un'arte di ppiú raro
where there is an art of the most rare
voglio dí di Firenze, i ppistoiese
I mean Florence, the area of Pistoia

> Altamante: *(che c'entra) Firenze (......)*
> (what does) Florence (have to do with it) (......)

e ora tu lo ngolli [boccone[277] amaro
and now you will swallow a bitter pill

> Altamante: *[(parlá di Firenze) (.......)*
> (to talk about Florence) (.......)

dimmi te i piazza di ddomo e i Bbargello
tell me, the plaza of the cathedral and the Bargello[278]
un tu gl' ha visti ncima a Diavello
you did not see them on top of Diavello[279]

> AUD: ((laughing))

> AUD?: *(bravo)*

> AUD: ((scattered applauses))

AUD: [((still laughing after previous octet))

(Octet 15) Altamante
[Ma sentite i cche dice sto zimbello[280]
But listen what he is saying, this laughing stock

> AUD: ((laughing))

---

[277] *Boccone* literally means "mouthful of food" or "bite of food."

[278] The museum of Bargello, one of the most important in Florence.

[279] This reference to Diavello is only partially clear to me. It seems clear that he is referring to a mountaintop with that name. Unfortunately, I do not know its exact location.

[280] *Zimbello* is literally a "decoy," often a bird or in the shape of a bird.

<vo mettere> Pistoia con Fiorenza
he wants to compare Pistoia with Florence
io dio gli é malato ni ccervello
I say that he is sick in the brain
oppure gli ha poca <intelligenza>
or he has little intelligence

    AUD: ((laughing))

io parlavo d'i mmonte morto bello
I was talking of the mountain very beautiful
indoe gli é nato la mia residenza
where my residence was born
se porto un pistoiese in piazza Signoria
if I bring a pistoiese in the Signoria Plaza[281]
l'acchiappahani se lo porta via.
the dog-catcher would carry him away.

    AUD?: *[Nooo! ((laughing))*

    AUD: [((lots of laughing))

    AUD: ((applause))

    AUD?: *(tu sta' in filo) (gli attacca) Pistoia, é?*
        (you are in trouble) (he is attacking) Pistoia, right?

(Octet 16) Realdo
Ecco nun tu dimostri la fantasia
There, you are not showing any fantasy
si vede propio e tu se di montagna
it is so obvious that you are from the mountain
io parlavo della pianura mia
I was talking of my plain
indove l'arte vedi un s'accompagna
where the art, you see, has no match

---

[281] Florence's central plaza, where are the Museum of *Palazzo Vecchio*, "Old Palace," the connected Uffizzi Museum, the Loggia of Orcagna, and the Marzocco Fountain.

gnerebbe e tu venissi a casa mia
you should come to my home
tu c' hai una scuola che l' é una cuccagna
where you can learn plenty[282]
invece lassú n montagna indoe se nato o ndoe tu stai
instead up there in the mountain, where you were born or where you live
o certe cose un le conosci mai
you will never know certain things

(Octet 17) Altamante
Ma vedi te entri di palo in frasca in tanti gineprai
but you see, [jumping] from a topic to another you enter in so many
tangles of troubles
gli é entrato ni ssolo fiorentino
you entered in the soil of Florence
ma te lo vedi un tu ti spicci mai
but you see, you never unstick yourself
allo perché hai lasciato l'Appennino
then why did you leave the Apennine?
se te a Firenze te tu ci verai
if you should come to Florence
ti insegnano i vvolgare e i' latino
they would teach you the Vulgar and the Latin
Firenze sai fu la cittá dell'arte
Florence, you know, was the city of art
é rammentata da tutte le parte
it is renown everywhere

> AUD?: *Ovvia!*
> That's it!

(Octet 18) Realdo
Ecco tu l'ha scoperte[   ] <le tue carte>
There! You have discovered your cards

> Altamante: [*ndiamo si va via per Dio*]
> let's go away, by God!

---

[282] Literally "you have a school that is a plenty" referring to the mythical *paese della cuccagna*, the "Land of Plenty."

se se' nato laggiú sull'Appennino
if you were born far there on the Apennine
io nacqui lo sai da un'antra parte
I was born you know in another place
vicino a i ssolo quello fiorentino
near to the soil, the Florentine one
e gli é lí che gli é nata tutta l'arte
and it is there that all art is born
ma te non lo sapevi [   ] pove[rino
but you did not know it, poor one

     Altamante: *[(c'era Cino)]   [Cino (......)*
          (there was Cino[283]) Cino (.....)

finché un venivi ni ssolo di Pistoia [e Ferenza
before you came in the soil of Pistoia and Florence

     AUD?:   [(.......)

anlon- ancor nun lla sapei la differenza.
you did not know the difference yet

(Octet 19) Altamante
Dove la germolió la mia semenza
there, where my seed germinated
io dico a Cantagallo fra que monti
I say in Cantagallo, on those mountains

Realdo: *bellino gli é peró (   )*
     nice he is indeed (   )

dove i ggenere umano gettó la sua semenza
where the human kind threw its seed
d'una bellezza che nun c'é confronti
of a beauty that there is no comparison

---

[283] Probably referring to the medieval poet Cino Da Pistoia, who lived in the 13th century; Cino was part of the *Stil Novo*, "New Style," and friend of Dante Alighieri. Here Altamante seems to be suggesting to Realdo a possible ending of the verse, and a possible defense of Pistoia.

spero e nun ti fischi questa udienza
I hope this audience does not boo you
pecché le baggianate t' aracconti
because you talk nonsenses
sento e tu vo fare tanta boria
I hear you want to show much arrogance
ma nun é roba a parlare di storia
but it is not for you to talk about history

Altamante: *via, l'ottava di saluto (va)*
      come on, the farewell octet, (go)

(Octet 20) Alternated
Realdo
Certo un vo la medaglia della gloria
for sure I do not want the medal of glory

Altamante
Vor di che io ti rifaró gli onori
it means that I will honor you again

Realdo
Tra tutte e due non c'é stata boria
among us both there was no arrogance

Altamante
Io nacqui tra le peore e pastori
I was born among the sheep and the sheperds

Realdo
Nel mondo ntero un si sa dov'é la gloria
in the whole world we do not know where glory lays

Altamante
Ormai gli é presciutti i miglior sapori
now the best flavors is the cured ham

Realdo
fin da i' momento che siamo nelle fasce
since the moment we are swaddled

l'artista un si sa mai ndove nasce
no one knows where the artist is born

(Octet 20) Alternated
Altamante
All'ombra de cipressi, alberi e casce
in the shadow of the cypresses, trees and acacias

Realdo
Oppure all' ombra de monti e le pianura
or in the shadow of the mountains in the plain

Altamante
Ma se a ( ) lo dipinse nelle fasce
but is to (.....) he painted him while swaddled

Realdo
Gli é sempre un dono e ti da la natura
it is always a gift that nature gives you

Altamante
o nun fa i pecor- nun fa i mmontone he fra l'erba pasce
do not do the sheper- do not do like the ram that grazes among the grass

Realdo
Se tu se naturale un c'é paura
if you are natural there is no fear

Altamante
E allora di chiudere é opportuno
and then it is opportune to close
sa a pigliá la ragione un po' per uno
let's take the reason a bit each

II. Excerpt from an Interview with Realdo Tonti.
1) Code: 5/23/99, I, side A, 328 and fol.

Realdo: Il campanilismo e' questo. Una volta tra paesi e paesi, un so, qui-qui a tempi che ero ragazzo io un giovanotto se passava il limite di andare a San Niccolo', se passava un certo limite si ritrovava o co sassi addosso, o con- sa l'ignoranza- magari se era innamorato di una ragazza di uel paese lì allora sì che- la sera uando andava in quel paese gliene facevano di quelle nere, ecco che i campanilismi, ne paesi eran cosi', capito. Te ti sembra una osa quasi inverosimile ma- ... sei molto giovane sei ... si, all'inizi di ssecolo brava, all'inizi di ssecolo, oe::::. Ma anche fino a avanti guera. Anche fino verso i trenta i trentacinque. ... C'era il campanilismo tra San Piero e San Niccolo', San Michele, quello era meglio. Magari un c'era i ppallone a- capito come ora pero' c'era la banda, la banda di San Niccolo' era meglio di ella di San Piero poi addio, venia i ontrasti, venia- insomma queste ose. ... Anzi i poeti a braccio ci trovavano proprio il pane

Realdo: Campanilismo *is like this. In the past, among towns and towns, for example; here, when I was a boy, if a young man would pass the limit to go to San Niccoló, if he would pass a certain limit he would find himself hit with stones. You know, the ignorance [of the people]. If he was in love with a girl of that town, it was even worse. The evening when he would go in that town, they would do him the worst tricks. It is the same with* campanilismo. *It was like this in the towns. To you it may sound something difficult to believe. ... You are young. ... Yes, [this was] at the beginning of this century, but even until the war, even until the 1930, 1935. ... There was* campanilismo *between San Piero and San Niccoló, San Michele*[284]. *This [would say that] they were better, because they had the soccer team, you see. The other one had the music band. The music band of San Niccoló was better than the one of San Pietro, and so on. This is how it was. Then there were* Contrasti. ... *Better, the poets would win their bread with it.*

---

[284] Villages that today are part of the town of Agliana.

APPENDIX F

I have included here the transcription and translation of the *Contrasti* analyzed in chapter 6.

I. Mother-in-Law Vs. Daughter-in-Law (Papone).

This *Contrasto* was sung during a performance in Papone (Pistoia) on August 7, 1997. The audience suggested the theme, "Mother-in-Law vs. Daughter-in-Law." After acknowledging the suggestion, for four octets the poets discussed who was going to take each of the roles. Finally, at the fifth octet Altamante started the duel.

(Octet 5) Altamante/Mother-in-law
sento che un sentimento bello e li raffiora
I feel a beautiful sentiment surfacing again
si vede che gli ha tanta sempatia
we see that she has so much sympathy
io son contenta d'avella una nora
I am happy to have a daughter-in-law
e che presto la venga in casa mia
and that soon she may come to my home
ma se la si intendesse fa camora
but if she should intend to make trouble
co una pedata te la mando via
with a kick I would send her away
se l'avesse un sistema un po' balordo
if she had a system a bit foolish

speriamo e si vada poi d'accordo
let's hope then, that we may get along

(Octet 6) Realdo/Daughter-in-Law
non voglio dí che la lingua io mi mordo
I won't say that I am biting my tongue[285]
o socera ti sei pronunciata
o mother-in-law, you made your statement
l'intenzione ce l'ho d'anda' d'accordo
I have the intention of getting along
anche se in casa tua sono arivata
even if I have arrived in your house
peró una cosa vedi ti ricordo
but, you see, I remind you of one thing
ormai um pohino é che ne sei invecchiata
by now you have become a bit old
e ora te lo dó un pensiero ardito
and now I am going to give you a daring thought [286]
tra moglie- tra la nora- tra il mmarito e la nora un ci mettere i ddito
don't put your finger between the husband and the wife[287]

(Octet 7) Altamante/Mother-in-law
ma perché il mio figliolo che ebbi partorito
but why my son, to whom I gave birth
ma se un l'avevo messo io nel mondo
it would have been better if I had given him life[288]
e gli era meglio se aveo abbortito
it would have been better if I had aborted him
guarda e donna mai porta' intorno
look what kind of a woman you bring around here
si vede nelle macchie e gli é finito
you see, he has ended up in the stains/woods

---

[285] The expression "biting one's tongue" means trying hard to refrain from saying something (that the speaker would like to say).

[286] Namely, something daring to think about.

[287] Italian proverb exhorting people to keep out of the personal business of married couples.

[288] Literally: "but if I had not put him in the world."

ma (badaa) son io e nun mi confondo
but look! I do not get confused
cerca di avé rispetto in casa mia
try to show respect in my house
sennó dopo tre ore tu va' via
otherwise after three hours you will go away

(Octet 8) Realdo/Daughter-in-Law
senti e donna trovai per la via
hear what kind of woman I found on my road
e gli é du' ore che sono arrivata
that I have arrived two hours ago
e giá le mi dimostra antipatia
and already she is showing me antipathy
povera donna come sei cascata
poor woman, how have I fallen!
subito dicce che mi manda via
immediately she says that she is going to send me away
quale scuola che sei educata
to which school have you been educated?
di quello che tu dici mi meraviglio
I marvel to what you are saying
nun ha rispetto neanche pe' i pproprio figlio
she has no respect not even for her own son

(Octet 9) Altamante/Mother-in-law
guarda donnuccia io te lo do un consiglio
look silly woman! I give you a counsel
quando tu sse' venuta sotto i mmio tetto
when you have come under my roof
m'araccomando un allungá l'artiglio
I recommend you, do not extend your claws
e guarda se tu porti di rispetto
and see to show respect
di donne ome te un mi meraviglio
I do not take marvel of women like you
e tra le gente veniva detto
They were saying it even among the people
si sentiva parlare in ogni zona
you could hear people talking in every place

il tu figlio t'ha sposato una cialtrona
your son has married a rascal

(Octet 10) Realdo/Daughter-in-Law
sentite che ignorante le ragiona
listen her uneducated/ignorant way of talking
tutto il giorno le sta a pettegolare
she spends all day gossiping
e di lavare un vestito o nun é bona
and she is not good at washing even a single garment
o nun é mai andata a lavorare
and she has never gone to work
oggi vorebbe fá la donna bona
today she would like to be the good woman
una giovane un viene a sopportare
she cannot tolerate a young one
se io un lavorassi da mattina a sera
if I didn' t work from morning to evening
nun mangeresti nemmeno una pera
you would not eat even a pear

(Octet 11) Altamante/Mother-in-law
una donna cosí cosa si spera
with a woman like this, what can we hope?
senti nuoruccia se tu mi concedi
listen little daughter-in-law, if you allow me
tu se' stata ni mmondo una battagliera
you have been in the world a trouble maker
e t'hanno vista anche su i mmarciapiedi
and they have seen you even on the sidewalk[289]
te- te t'anderesti messa in una galera
you should be sent to jail
perché questi discorsi e mi concedi
because of these discourses, if you allow me
se c'era sempre la legge Merlini
if there was still the Merlini law[290]

---

[289] Namely prostituting.

[290] Here Altamante gets confused. The logic statement would have been: "if there was not the Merlini law." The Merlini law, passed after the end of the Second World War, closed and prohibited the brothels (which had been legal

e t'eri sempre a spasso pe' asini
you would be still walking among the brothels

(Octet 12) Realdo/Daughter-in-Law
te non ha mai varcato i tuoi confini
you never went past your boundaries
una vagabonda tu se' sempre stata
you have always been lazy
degli altri a criticare i suoi destini
always critiquing the fates of other people
oggi con me tu sei un po' arrabbiata
today you are a bit angry with me
non ha mai accudito ai tuoi bambini
you never took care of your children
e la famiglia tu l'ha rovinata
and you ruined your family
povero tuo marito lavoratore onesto
poor husband of yours! A honest worker
da patimenti l'ha fatto morí presto
with grief you made him die early

(Octet 13) Altamante/Mother-in-law
ma sentite che modo di parlare é questo
but listen what way of talking!
prima che tu venissi in casa mia
before you came to my home
c'era l'unitá un c'era protesto
there wa unity, there was no protest
c'era l'amore e c'era l'armonia
there was love and there was harmony
ma te donna mondana io ti detesto
but you, mundane woman, I detest you
speriamo il vento che ti porti via
let's hope the wind may carry you away
una vorta l'é mora una vorta l'é bionda
one time she is brunette and one time she is blonde
cosa ne fa di hella vagabonda
what can you do with such a lazy one?

under fascism).

(Octet 14) Realdo/Daughter-in-Law
se la barca le va in balia dell'onda
if the boat is at the mercy of the wave
o dimmi che tu vieni a criticare
tell me what are you critiquing
se una vorta so mmora una vorta bionda
if one time I am brunette and one time I am blonde

io tutt'i ggiorno vó a lavorare
all the day I go to work
o povera vecchia rubiconda
poor old ruddy woman
che l'ignoranza un ti viene a mancare
you never are at a loss for ignorance
ma di quello che dici non mi stupisci
but what you say does not surprise me
perché te la gioventú nun la capisci
because you do not understand young people

(Octet 15) Altamante/Mother-in-law
come un serpente velenoso e che tu strisci
you crawl like a poisonous snake
lascia sta i cche ti dice questa vecchia antica
leave alone what this ancient elder is telling you
anche per te sa' il figlio tu s- tradisci
even for your own sake, you know, you are unfaithful to my son
l'é ben di fronte a un pubblico lo dica
it is good that I say this in front of the public
io ti dico le hose che un obbedisci
I am going to tell that you do not obey
e a fá le faccende gli par fatica
and she is too bothered to do the chores
se un gli metto una toppa alla sottana
if I did not put a patch on her gown
gli si vedeva la porta romana
you could see the Roman door[291]

---

[291] The door of a city that closes the access to the road that leads to Rome.

(Octet 16) Realdo/Daughter-in-Law
a vederti tu sembri una Befana
to see you, you look like a Befana[292]
come gli é triste vedi il tuo parlare
how sad it is, you see, your speech
la tua nomea ne viene lontana
your bad reputation gets far
in paese a me mi vennero a raccontare
in the town, people came to tell me [about it]
e poi riguardo a quella sottana
and then in regard to that gown
di questo te tu nun ne poi parlare
of that you should not talk
sembravi una moralista se cosí cortese
you looked like a moralist and so courteous
me l'han detto gli omini di tutt' i ppaese
all the men of the town told me [about it]

(Octet 17) Altamante/Mother-in-law
ma accidenta a i mmi figliolo e quando ti prese
be cursed my son and when he took you
e i mmio marito ando mi messe incinta
and my husband when he made me pregrant
ma perché le fece este brutte imprese
but why did he do these ugly actions
di portarmi vicino brutta pinta
of bringing near to me such an ugly painted woman[293]
la un aveva una camicia e ne un arnese
she did not have a shirt nor a utensile[294]
io uarche volta glielo do una spinta
some time I am going to give her a push
delle mutande le n'avea du paia
she had two pairs of panties
nun le volle nemmen la lavandaia
not even the washerwoman wanted them

---

[292] The Befana is the Italian traditional correspondent of Santa Claus. Represented as an old hag, queen of fairies, that brings presents to children at Epiphany. The word is also used to indicate an old ugly woman.

[293] Namely wearing too much make-up.

[294] Referring probably to the absence of a dowry.

(Octet 18) Realdo/Daughter-in-Law
senti ki cane come gli abbaia
listen how she barks like a dog
o speciarmente ando un ha piu difesa
especially when she has no more defence
che sempre a scorazza ni mmezzo all'aia
[a dog] that always runs about in the threshing-floor
e a parola mia e nun l'ha intesa
and did not understand my words
e oggi sembreresti cosí gaia
and today you would look so joyful
te lo vo' dire che nun é un offesa
I want to tell you, since this is not an offence
te lo dico e te lo batto cosí a martello
I tell you and I beat on it like with a hammer
in fronte tu ci hai il marchio di bbordello
on the forehead you have the brand of the brothel

(Octet 19) Altamante/Mother-in-law
te t'hanno visto sai- te t'hanno visto con tizio e con quello
they have seen you with this fellow and that other
la mattina ti trucca e la va via
in the morning she makes up and she leaves
si tinge il labbro e la si fá il capello
she paints her lip and makes her hair
la fa la gongolante pe'lla via
she smiles too much along the road
sempre alla barba di mmi figlio grullarello
always fooling my little idiot of a son
gli é il frutto della mia genia
this is the fruit of my descendance
tra le moine questi (tetti) e i ttrucco
between the blandishes, these (.....)[295] and the make up
sempre alla barba di i mmammalucco
always fooling that idiot[296]

---

[295] The word *tetti* means "roofs" but the meaning in this context is unclear.

[296] The word *mammalucco* literally translates as "Mameluke," namely a member of the military class that ruled Egypt between 1250 and 1517. In the Muslim countries the word then came to refer to a slave. In Tuscany the original

(Octet 20) Realdo/Daughter-in-Law
anche lui come te gli é uno stucco
even him, like you, is a whiner[297]
si vede bene che ti rassomiglia
it is obvious that he is like you
un s'accorge ando mi lavo quand'e mi trucco
he does not realize when I wash myslef and when I put on make up
o stanne certo che nessun lo piglia
and you can be sure that no one wants him
degli zimbelli vedi gli é i ccucco
you see, he is the laughing stock of the butts
perché fa parte della tua famiglia
because he is part of your family
tu ti credi sí bella e forte e arguta
you believe to be beautiful and strong and smart
'cidenta a me e quande ci son venuta
damn myself and when I came here!

(Octet 21) Altamante/Mother-in-law
gli e stavi bene nella notte muta
you would have been better in the silent night
sui marciapiedi lá a girovagare
there on the sidewalk, erring
non só da quala parte sei venuta
I do not know from which place you came
e chi ti venne a i mmondo a ingenerare
and who generated you in this world
ora vo' fa' una donna astuta
now you want to look smart
tante disgrazie la venne a portare
you came carrying so much grief
e quando e in casa c'é entrata lei
and when she entered in this house
siamo ridotti al miserere mei
we are reduced to God's mercy[298]

---

meaning of the word is lost and it is used as an insult.

[297] Literally: someone never happy or always complaining.

[298] The words *miserere mei* mean "have mercy of me" in Latin. They are part of a catholic prayer, the *miserere*, usually sung for the dying. To be at the *miserere mei*

(Octet 22) Realdo/Daughter-in-Law
tutt'i ggiorno lo vedi tu mangi e bei
you see, all day you eat and drink
e gli é perché io vo a lavorare
and it is because I go to work
d'avere una uccagna osí nun lo credei
you would not have believed to have an easy living[299] like this
prima de i ttempo che venni arriare
before the time I came
t'eri abituata davvero a i mmiserere mei
indeed you were used to the *miserere mei*
colla corona in mano sempre a pregare
always praying with the rosary in your hand
se ti volei levare la fame e ssete
if you did not want to go hungry and thirsty
devi andare in canoniha da i pprete
you had to go to the presbytery, to the priest[300]

(Octet 23) Altamante/Mother-in-law
povere pescio svanito dentro una rete
poor fish! disappeared inside a net
alla vecchietta un gli fa un richiamo
do not make a reproach to the elder woman
ma co i ssale io ti levo la sete
but I will take away your thirst with salt
ditti la veritá io sempre bramo
I always desire ardently to tell you the truth
che dice lei vu lo sentirete
what she says you will hear
io li porto rispetto e nun recramo
I bring respect to her and do not complain
ormai venuta l'é su da i ffango
since she has come out of the mud

---

then means to be almost hopeless.

[299] The word *cuccagna*, that I translated as "easy living" refers to the *paese della cuccagna*, the legendary "Land of Plenty." It also refers to the *albero della cuccagna*, "greasy pole" on top of which prizes were hanging for those who were able to reach them.

[300] Namely, she had to live on charity.

il male l'ha addosso la compiango
I feel sorry for the evil she has inside

(Octet 24) Alternated
Realdo/Daughter-in-Law
lo vedi che stupita ne rimango
you see how surprised I remain

Altamante/Mother-in-law
se ti dissi cosi dillo un mi preme
if I told you like this it is because I had too

Realdo/Daughter-in-Law
di quello e dici te io nun piango
I do not cry for what you tell

Altamante/Mother-in-law
siamo somari dello stesso seme
we are asses of the same seed

Realdo/Daughter-in-Law
sulla mia posizione io rimango
I remain of my idea

Altamante/Mother-in-law
ma la socera la nora mai nun teme
but the mother-in-law never fears the daughter-in-law

Realdo/Daughter-in-Law
se non teme la nora la socera o quel che dico io
if the mother-in-law does not fear the daughter-in-law or what I say
di casa ti porto via il marito mio
I will take away my husband from your house

(Octet 25) Alternated
Altamante/Mother-in-law
prendilo te tanto gli é un be fiho
you can take him, why, he is so ugly

Realdo/Daughter-in-Law
che dal tu corpo vedi é generato
that from your body was generated

Altamante/Mother-in-law
nun si sa ci s'ha qualcosa o c'é il belliho
you don't know if he has something[301] or it is the navel[302]

Realdo/Daughter-in-Law
se sempre te ni mmondo che ha sbagliato
it is still you, in thew world, that made the mistake

Altamante/Mother-in-law
per questo te di notte cambi rio
that's why in the night you change river[303]

Realdo/Daughter-in-Law
e gli era meglio se lui un era nato
it would have been better if he wasn't born

Altamante/Mother-in-law
e gli era meglio se un era venuto
it would have been better if he had not come [to life]
in casa mia ci aveo in meno un cornuto
there would have been one cuckhold less in my house

II. Mother-in-Law Vs. Daughter-in-Law (Migliana).

This *Contrasto* was requested by the audience during a performance in Migliana (Prato) on August 2, 1997. It was sung by the poet Elidio Benelli and his young disciple Liliana Tamberi. The poets chose their personage before starting to sing.

(Octet 1) Elidio/Mother-in-law
vieni mia nora darmelo un bacetto
come, my daughter-in-law, give me a little kiss

---

[301] Namely the male genitals.

[302] She implies that her son's genital are not properly developed, so that they can be confused with the navel.

[303] Referring to the daughter-in-law supposed unfaithfulness.

qual siei la regina in casa mia
since you are the queen in my house
presto mi darai un pargoletto
soon you will give me a baby
e che tutti in famiglia si desia
that everybody in the family desires
col reciproco amor con tanto affetto
with the reciprocal love with so much affection
ti prego farmi questa cortesia
I pray you to grant me this courtesy
e soddisfá dovrai i miei pensieri
and my thoughts you will have to satisfy
una cosa che s' aspetta volentieri
something that is waited for gladly

(Octet 2) Liliana/Daughter-in-Law
pói aspetta so vvani desideri
you can wait, they are vain desires
e mi ci manca pure che un figliolo
even a child! that's all we need!
e non mi bastano tutti i pensieri
like if it wasn't enough all the worries
che te le da- che me le dá il tu figlio giá da solo
that already your son alone gives me
e te lo dice qui sí la Tamberi
Tamberi is going to tell you right here
con questa cosa spero ti consolo
with this fact I hope to console you
su questa cosa no non l'avra vinta
on this thing you will not win
se speri di vedemmi presto incinta
if you hope to see me pregnant soon

(Octet 3) Elidio/Mother-in-law
E non voglio per forza da' una spinta
I do not want forcefully give a push
Dovesse fatto sí ben volentieri
it must be done indeed well willingly
E piano piano tu sarai convinta
and slowly you will be convinced

Lo sai nun siam que di ieri
you know we are no more those of yesterday[304]
Una famiglia l'abbiamo recinta
we have gathered together a family
Su il nostro avvenire se ci speri
if you have hope for our future
Non sará oggi ma se Dio vole
it won't be today, but if God wants
Ci dará alla luce un'antra bella prole
she will give birth to another beautiful progeny

(Octet 4) Liliana/Daughter-in-Law
Ma a capitti qui sí non si pole
but it is impossible to understand you
e ci s'ha in questa casa un gran da ffare
in this house we have a lot to do
ci mancherebbe pure della prole
that's all we need! children!
non basta giá il pulire e il cucinare
like if it was not enough the cleaning and cooking
Vorrei sape' esta socera il che vole
I would like to know what this mother-in-law wants
Che tutti i giorni gli fo da mangiare
every day I cook for her
    Liliana*: Nun só il che ditti*
     I do not know what to tell you
    Elidio*: fa come ti pare*
     do as you wish
    Liliana: ha ha
É sempre lí il nipote che l'attende
she is always there waiting for her grandchild
Io invece so qui a fare le merende
and instead I am here to prepare/eat the afternoon snacks

(Octet 5) Elidio/Mother-in-law
Noi altri il discorso un si sospende
we are not going to suspend this discourse

---

[304] Namely: things have changed, and families are different from the way they were before.

Lo sento un po' ki ti sei annoiata
I can see you have gotten a bit bored
Soddisfazione in qualche modo si rende
in some way we give back satisfaction[305]
Per poter tirá avanti la casata
to be able to pull forward the household
Un ca- un cambio ci sará o di vicende
there will be a change in the events
Pare che tu sia sagrificata
it seems like you feel victimized
Mia moglie lo sai quel figlioletto
my wife[306], you know, that little son
L'ha tenuto al petto tanto stretto
she kept him to her breast so tight

(Octet 6) Liliana/Daughter-in-Law
Ti dico questo sí con gran diletto
I tell you this, yes, with great delight
Mi voglio riferire al tu figliolo
I am referring to your son
Ti dico che nun é tanto bravo a letto
I tell you that he is not very good in bed
Mi sa che presto dormirá da solo
I have a feeling that soon he will sleep alone
          Ha ha ha ha
Nun va, la sera lui nun va diretto
he does not go, the night he does not go direct[307]
Lo vedi che col vino mi honsolo
you see that I am consoling myself with wine
          Ha ha ha ha
Lui dorme sempre da sera a mattina
he is always sleeping from the evening to the morning
Se aspetti un nipote sí tu sta harina
if you are waiting for a grandchild, yes, will you wait for long![308]

---

[305] The meaning of this verse is unclear to me.

[306] The poet seems confused about his own personage here. His words seem to be coming from the father-in-law rather than the mother-in-law. He probably meant to say: "herself as a wife."

[307] An allusion to sexual intercourse.

(Octet 7) Elidio/Mother-in-law
Una nora cosí un po' genuina
a daughter in law like this, a bit ingenous
Credevo non dovesse capitare
I didn' t believed it could happen to me
Ma ha nervi dalla sera alla mattina
she feels nervous from the evening to the morning
Mio figlio nun la viene a soddisfare
my son cannot satisfy her
Lei gli piace di andare in cantina
she likes to go in the cellar
Il vino spesso spesso tracannare
to gulp down wine all too often
E qualche volta con qualche riposatella
and sometines when she tapes a nap
E si bagna ancora la gonnella
she still wets her gown

(Octet 8) Liliana/Daughter-in-Law
    Liliana: *Ella?* [309]

      Realdo: *padella vai*
         pan, go on[310]

O socera io ti racconto una novella
o mother-in-law I am going to tell you a story
    Hum hum
Lo sai che nu lo bevo piú quel vino
you know I am not drinking that wine anymore
E sono poverina e mendichella
I am a poor little beggar
La notte poi nun dormo e fó mattino
I do not sleep at night, I wake until morning
Adesso ui la dio proprio bella
now I am going to tell a real good one

---

[308] Literally, "you stay pretty."
[309] Liliana interrupts herself because she cannot think of a rhyme in "ella."
[310] Suggestion from other poet in the audience.

E chiudo osí interviene Davide Riondino
so after Riondino can have his turn[311]
    Liliana : *pausa*
        [I need a] pause

    Elidio: *vai!*
        go!

Lo so che a te ti metto ne tormenti
I know I make you suffer
Peró dammi un po di suggerimenti
but give me some suggestions[312]

(Octet 9) Alternated[313]
Elidio/Mother-in-law
Ma uno solo mi ce ne vole venti
Only one? I need to give you twenty

Liliana/Daughter-in-Law
Ti prego socerina facciam pace
please little mother-in-law, let's make peace

Elidio/Mother-in-law
Quanto fai a me non mi spaventi
what you do does not scare me[314]

Liliana/Daughter-in-Law
Lo sai quello che ho in cuore non si tace
you know what is in the heart cannot be silenced

---

[311] Liliana is referring to the poet Davide Riondino who will sing next.

[312] Here the novice poet, who seems to be at a loss, asks for suggestions from her mentor, Elidio. In doing so, she is momentarily out of the narrative frame of the *Contrasto*. Notice that she first excuses herself for making him "suffer" by having to see his disciple failing in the performance.

[313] This octet is interesting because there are two dialogues going on at the same time, one between the personages, and another one between the elder poet and his disciple. Many sentences have double meaning according to which of these two dialogue we are looking at.

[314] As a mother-in-law: I do not fear your actions. As a poet: even if you produce difficult rhymes or strange verses I can deal with them.

Elidio/Mother-in-law
I movimenti non li fai lenti
you do not make the movements slow[315]

Liliana/Daughter-in-Law
Lo sai vado veloce a me mi piace
you know, I go fast, that's how I like it

Elidio/Mother-in-law
E gireresti dall'uno all'altro polo
you would travel from one pole to another
Lo sento un ti contenta il mi figliolo
I hear that my son cannot satisfy you.

III Housewife Vs. Employed Woman.

This *Contrasto* was sung as part of a performance of several poets at the sixth meeting of the *Poeti Bernescanti* in Ribolla (Grosseto), on April 19, 1998. The audience chose the theme. The poets and the personages were chosen and assigned randomly.

(Octet 1) Poet 2 - Housewife
Ci hanno dato un bellissimo argomento
they gave us a beautiful argument
che danno la memoria e un si ristringa
they gave us, may memory not shrink
e che marchi e la virgola e l'accento
and that may mark the comma and the accent
che ben si svolga e meglio si dipinga
that we may develop it good and paint it better
il mio stato che vivo nel momento
my state, that I am living in this moment
sara' quello di fa la casalinga
will be to do the housewife
questa e' la parte e che me l'hanno data
this is the part that they gave me
e il mio collega fara' l'impiegata
and my colleague will do the employee

---

[315] As a mother-in-law: you want to change too many things quickly. As a poet: you should slow down your singing, so to have more time to think the verse.

(Octet 2) Realdo Tonti - Employed Woman
Vedi come distinta sono nata
see how distinct I was born
o forse questo gl' era il mio destino
or maybe this was my destiny
e te che alla famiglia sei piu' legata
and you, who are more bound to the family
o lo vo dir con questo fa il tuo cammino
I want to say with this you do your path[316]
ad altri spazzi sono relagata
to other spaces I am bound
nu rigoverno i piatto i tegamino
I do not wash the dish or the little pan
forse a fa l'impiegata e mi conviene
maybe it is convenient for me to be employed
a me mi pa di sta dimorto bene.
it seems to me that I am very well off

(Octet 3) Poet 2 - Housewife
Intanto il tuo stipendio si mantiene
While your salary is maintained
tu ti senti contenta e decorosa
you feel content and decourous
in casa mia altra cosa avviene
in my house another thing happens
per la famiglia io vivo che e' preziosa
I live for my family, which is precious
guardero' sempre che ognuno stia bene
I will always take care that everybody is fine
per vive per mangia' in frettolosa
You are in a haste: living, eating
tu che vai null' ufficio e la (ser ede)
you go in the office and (come out in the evening)
a volte di un mangiar ti po succede
and sometimes you do not even eat

---

[316] The meaning of this verse is unclear.

(Octet 4) Realdo Tonti - Employed Woman
Succede sempre quello che non si crede
what we do not believe always happens
ma questa nun succede alle impiegate
but this does not happens to the employees
quello che fanno la massaia un vede
the housewife does not see what they do
perche' in famiglia sono relegate
because she is relegated in the family
sai l'impiegata a te nulla ti chiede
you know, the employed asks you nothing
che piu' splendenti son le sue giornate
since her days are more spendid
le parte la mattina presto cosi alla svelta
she leaves in the early morning. so quickly
un po n'uffico un po all'aria aperta.
a bit in the office and a bit in open air

(Octet 5) Poet 2 - Housewife
Io chedo che di tanto un ti diverta
I believe that you are not really having that much fun
alzarsi tanto presto la mattina
to wake up so early in the morning
sai bell' onesta nella coperta
you know, beautifully honest in the covers
or che il maggio a noi ci si avvicina
now that May is getting closer
io sai che sono una cuoca esperta
you know that I am an expert cook
e per il pranzo e la mia meddicina
and for lunch (which is) my medicine
il pronto sempre all'ora e' lo facevo
I would make [it] ready always at the right time
e a mezzogiorno sempre mangio e bevo
and at noon I always eat and drink [well]

(Octet 6) Realdo Tonti - Employed Woman
O quello che facevi lo vedevo
What you would do I did see
indaffarata da mattina a sera
always busy from morning to evening

ma anche io credi e mangio e bevo
but I too, believe me, eat and drink [well]
e po n' ufficio tasto la tastiera
then in the office I write on the typewriter
su una bella poltrona mi sedevo
I seat on a beautiful chair
tanto sia d' inverno o primavera
in winter like in spring
e poi quando comincia la giornata
and then when the day starts
sempre prima di me ti trovo alzata
I always find you awoken before me

(Octet 7) Poet 2 - Housewife
La nostra l'e' una vita combinata
Our is a combined[317] life
pero' non c'e' riguardi o sospensioni
thought there are no regards or suspensions
ma la tua l'e' una vita delicata
but yours is a delicate life
se tu fai sbaglio la trovi i padroni
if you make a mistake the boss is right there
io invece in casa mia so abbituata
instead in my home I am used [to the fact that]
ognuno accettera' le mie opinioni
everybody accepts my opinions
ma se tu scrivi a volte e scrivi male
but if you write sometimes, if you write something wrong
i conti poi te(i) fai col principale
then you have to deal with the boss

(Octet 8) Realdo Tonti - Employed Woman
Questo lo so lo vedi e' naturale
This I know, you see, it is natural
ma guarda casalinga cosa fai
but look, housewife, what you do
se fo un'errore io un sara' tanto male
if I do a mistake is not a bit deal

---

[317] The meaning of this verse is unclear.

ma dimmi te d'erori quanti ne fai
but tell me how many mistakes do you do
lo so che i ttuo lavor e' piu' naturale
I know that your work is more natural
e alla famiglia che accuderai
and the family that you take care of
gli e' vero e' bello il tuo lavor di gusto invito
it's true, your work is good of taste I invite[318]
accudir la famiglia di' mmarito.
to take care of the family of your husband.[319]

(Octet 9) Poet 2 - Housewife
Se tu l'accetti ti vo fa un invito
If you accept I am going to invite you
se tu venissi a cena a casa mia
if you would come for dinner in my home
lo troverai un pranzo gradito
you would find a good meal
che tu l'accetterai con energia
and you would accept it in earnest
vedrai che il mio racconto e un e' fallito
you will see that my story is not false
sono certa un andereste via
I am sure you would not leave anymore
anzi te lo ripeto e se tu vieni
in fact I repeat it to you and if you come
e l'e' una mia tradizione che mantieni
you will want to keep my tradition

(Octet 10) Realdo Tonti - Employed Woman
Certo vo dir che a dirgli le convieni
of course, I mean to say, it must be said
lo so prepari bona sciccheria
I know you prepare good rich food
sempre a lavare ti si rompe i reni
always washing until your kidneys are broken

---

[318] The meaning of these last two words is unclear.
[319] I think the last two verses should be taken in an ironic sense, namely, referring to the fact that the housewife has to take care of the in-laws.

ma tu lo fai si con bramosia
but you do it indeed with desire
se nel mio mondo poi tu ci vieni
then, if you come in my world
e tu vivrai con piu' allegria
you will live with more joy
l'impiegata no resta a bocca amara
the employed does not remain with a bitter mouth
c'e' sempre la massaia e gli prepara.
there is always an housewife to prepare for her

(Octet 11) Poet 2 - Housewife
La nostra vita ormai non e'(fara)
our life now it is not (hard) anymore
anche da noi il progresso e l'e' arrivato
the progress has arrived for us as well
c'e' chi li lava i panni e li rischiara
there is something that washes the clothes and makes them tidy
che l'ingegnere tutto ha inventato
that the engineer has invented everything
quindi la nostra sorte non e' amara
thus our sort is not bitter
quando che nei fornelli ho cucinato
when I have cooked on the stove
anch'io cio' quei bottoni co i riscatti
I too have those buttons to push
che stanno pronti per lavarmi i piatti
that are there, ready to wash my plates

(Octet 12) Realdo Tonti - Employed Woman
Invero sulle modernita' tu mi ribatti
Indeed on modernity you want to answer me back
allor vor dire che ho ragione io
then it means that I am right
se alla lavastoviglie (l)i do bicchieri e piatti
if I give the glasses and the plates to the dishwasher
e stanne p- certo nun ci penso io
and you can be certain I do not have to think about it
i panni piu' sulla pietra tu non gli batti
if you do not beat the chothes on the stone anymore

e ritorna con me cco ol viver mio
and return to me, to my life style
io io si fo piu' presto e tiro via
indeed I do everything fast
i panni li porto alla lavanderia
and I can bring the chothes to the dry-cleaner

(Octet 13) Poet 2 - Housewife
Questa l'e' verita non e' bugia
this is the truth, it is no lie
ma quella poi tu la dovrai pagare
but then you have to pay her
io vedi faccio tutto in casa mia
you see, I do everything in my home
e cosi avanti si potra' andare
in this way we can go on
ognun percorrera' per la sua via
each one of us will go her way
qualcuno anche in ufficio deve stare
someone has to be in the office
per far la vita piu' vivace e cara
to make life more lively and dear
ognuno e' un sentimento che s'impara.
each is a feeling to be learned

(Octet 14) Alternati
Realdo Tonti - Employed Woman
Se questa vita e' dolce e un poco amara
if this life is sweet and a bit bitter

Poet 2 - Housewife
Si tratta sempre ognun di lavorare
after all each of us has to work

Realdo Tonti - Employed Woman
gli e' vero un uomo all'altro e che gl' impara
a true human is the one that learns from others

Poet 2 - Housewife
ma l'importante avanti di tirare
but the important thing is to go on

Realdo Tonti - Employed Woman
si tira avanti anche dopo la bara
we keep going even after being in a coffin

Poet 2 - Housewife
se anche la' abbiamo poco da sperare
if even there we have little to hope

Realdo Tonti - Employed Woman
se vo dir se la vita sia bella e gaia
I want to say if life has to be beautiful and joyful
ci vole l'impiegata e la massaia
both the housewife and the employed one are needed

IV. The Boy Vs. the Girl.

This *Contrasto* was sung during a performance in Malmantile (Firenze) on July 5, 1997. The audience requested the theme. In the first two octets the poets discussed who is taking each personage. Then at the third octet, Altamante started the duel.

(Octet 3) Altamante/Boy
Ti si vede a viaggiare sopra lla piazza
We see, when you walk around in the plaza
Che te nun sei un mastio sviluppato
that you are not a developed male
Te t'apparteni alla femminile razza
you belong to the female race
Perché te un omo puro non se nato
because you were not born a pure man[320]
Ma io non m'ammollo alla prima guazza
but I do not get wet at the first dew
Le trovo e- alla fiera e a il mercano
I find [women] at the fair and in the market
Lo sai che in questa tera ho piú di un covo
you know that in this land I have more than one lair

---

[320] Before this *Contrasto*, the poets had been doing an "open theme" insulting each other. Part of the insults involved each other's masculinity. After Realdo chose to impersonate the girl, Altamante, in the first part of this octet, is launching a final attack to the other poet's masculinity, before entering in his new personage, namely the boy.

Ma me le prendo ndoe le trovo le trovo
but I take [women] for myself wherever I find them

(Octet 4) Realdo/Girl
O nun confonde la gallina e l'ovo
Do not confuse the hen with the egg
O dimmi te che maschio che tu sei
tell me what kind of male are you
Non só dice la ragazza indoe la trovo
I don't know, he says, where I find a girlfriend
Guarda non é come mangiare e bei
look, it's not like eating and drinking
Il tuo pensiero io e null'approvo
I do not approve your way of thinking
Che tu fosssi osí non lo credei
I wouldn't have believed that you were like this
Io so' ragazza di bona famiglia
I am a girl from a good family
Mi par che questo maschio m'assomiglia
it seems to me that this male looks like me

(Octet 5) Altamante/Boy
A me tu m'ha a dire- a me tu mi devi dire chi ti piglia
you have got to tell me- you should tell me who is going to take you
o ragazzina se' troppo pendente
o little girl you are pending too much
l'omo gli é un cavallo a sciolte briglia
man is a horse galloping with loose reins
e gira da i ssud e da i pponente
he goes around to the south and to the occident
vá dalla madre, la socera e la figlia
he goes to the mother, the mother-in-law and the daughter
e dappertutto ce l'arota i ddente
and everywhere he sharpens his tooth
e te tu se una ragazza abbandonata
and you are an abandoned girl
da tanti giovanotti rigirata
turned around by so many young men

(Octet 6) Realdo/Girl
Fó come te nun vivo alla giornata
I do not live day by day like you
sono ragazza il mio lavor me lo guadagno
I am a girl that earns her work
quando gli arriva poi la mia serata
then, when my evening comes
io esco fori con il mio compagno
I go out with my partner
te una vedi un te n'é capitata
you, see, you haven't gotten one
e io lo capisco il tuo lagno
and I do understand why you are grumbling/whining
ragazze nun ne trovi dappertutto
you will not find girls everywhere
mi pare a me tu sia troppo brutto
it seems to me that you are too ugly

(Octet 7) Altamante/Boy
A vení con te si vestirebbano a lutto
if they came with you they would wear mourning
I giovanotti son trevilisati
the young men are *trevilisati*[321]
Te agli omini non gli dai quel frutto
you don't give to the men that fruit
Prima di tutto t'hai tanti peccati
first of all you have too many sins
Con le donne come te nun mi ci butto
I do not waste myself with women like you
Tante giovanotti e t'hanno lasciati
so many young men have left you
Tu sse' bella come un raggio di sole
you are beutiful like a ray of the sun
Tutti ti guardano ma nessun ti vole
everybody looks at you but nobody wants you

---

[321] This word does not exist in Italian or Tuscan.

(Octet 8) Realdo/Girl
La mosca tira il carcio che le pole
the fly will kick as she can[322]
Lui una sera mi venne a corteggiare
he came to court me one evening
S'era tra i giardini e le viole
we were among the gardens and the violets
E io e cche lo venni a invitare
and I even came to the point of inviting him
O porammé quel dente che mi dole
poor me! that tooth is painful[323]
O perché gnente che mi venne a fare
because he did not do anything with me
Si stette insieme dalle sei fino alle nove
we were there from six till nine
Ma un c'era un punto da una parte he gli si move
but there was not un point in any part of him that would move

(Octet 9) Altamante/Boy
Lo só con me tu un le fai mai le prove
I know with me you will never practice
Te tu sei una donna poverina
you are a poor woman
Nemmen t'andessi su Marte e giu- su Giove
not even if you would go on Mars or on Jupiter
Ti ci vorrebbe un po' di medicina
you rather need some medicine
Sarei all'otto sarei alle nove
I would be at eight I would be at nine
O se sia di sera o di mattina
equally in the evening or in the morning
Nemmen se mi chiedessi i pportafoglio
not even if you would ask me for my wallet[324]
Sgangherate come te io non le voglio
I do not want any [woman] rickety like you are

---

[322] This expression often used by the poets, means "a person will do what s/he can."

[323] Idiomatic expression meeting that something is giving pain to somebody.

[324] Namely, not even if you were a prostitute, asking for my money.

(Octet 10) Realdo/Girl
Ecco l'omo indoe casca nell'imbroglio
there it is, where the man falls into a mess
Ed ecco quello che non ha calore
and here is the one who has no warmt
E alla donna dice io non ti voglio
and to the woman he says, I do not want you
Non conosce i segreti dell'amore
he does not know the secrets of love
é di quegli ricore al portafoglio
he is one of those who resort to the wallet
Le trova sulle strade a tutte l'ore
he finds [women] on the streets at every hour
Ma di quel sentimento gerin- gentile e caliente
but of that feeling gentle and warm
Questo gli é un omo che nun sente niente
this is a man that does not feel anything

(Octet 11) Altamante/Boy
Vedi tu se' una carta un po penden- perdente
you see, you are a card a bit pend- loosing
é inutile tu parli le tue parole
it is useless that you say so many words
un maschio come te- con te un ci sente
a male does not feel [right] like you- with you
perché di torno gli ha tante figliole
because around he has so many girls
e te ni mmondo sai nun vali niente
and you, you know, you count for nothing in the world
tu se' cialtrona e nun ha piú parole
you are a good-for-nothing and you have no more words
qualunque mastio grullo ti rifiuta
any male, even an idiot, would refuse you
un ti tocca che fa la prostituta
you have nothing left but being a prostitute

(Octet 12) Realdo/Girl
Della vita non conosci quella cosa arguta
you do not know what is smart in life
anche la prostituta viene a condannare
you want to condemn even the prostitute

e da tutte le cose e l'ha per muta
and, of all things, he has her for mute
é qu- é lui che che non viene ad amare
is it- it is him that cannot love
ti ci vorrebbe a te una donna muta
you would need a mute woman
che da nessuna parte puó cominciare
that could not start from any side
tu fai discorsi che son troppo mosci
your discourses are too sluggish
vol di' che te le donne un le conosci[325]
it means that you do not know women

(Octet 13) Altamante/Boy
Te tu sta bene a mangia le briosci
you are good for eating briosches[326]
senti che rime esto poeta mi lascia
listen what kind of rhymes this poet is leaving to me[327]
ma io l'ho visto la pancia con le cosci
but i have seen him the belly with the thighs
ma la persona mia nun si sfascia
but my person does not fall apart[328]
(son-) tu dovresti viaggiá colle calosci
(i am-) you should travel with the galoshes
tu se detti da- da tiratti sai coll'scia
you would be to- to throw an axe against you
e portatti dentro una bottega
and to carry you inside a shop

---

[325] Realdo here is leaving a closed rhyme to Altamante: *-osci*.

[326] Altamante has to make an effort to find a rhyme, so the discourse looses meaning. Still, Altamante is able to obtain a comic effect. Notice also that he has to use "poetic license," namely, he transforms the word "briosce" into "briosci." In addition, in the following verses, he transforms "cosce" into "cosci" and "calosce" into "calosci.

[327] Here Altamante is addressing the audience and recalling their attention on the difficulty of the closed rhyme. He is thus inviting from them a negative judgement of the other poet, since an expert poet should avoid leaving closed rhymes. He is at the same time justifying the fact that his discourse is less meaningful.

[328] Here Altamante claims that he can deal with the difficult rhyme fine.

e tu un se bona per fare una sega
you are not good enough to jack me off

(Octet 14) Alternated
Realdo/Girl
Via (...) delle donne un e ne frega
come on (....) you do not care about women

Altamante/Boy
Voglio sapere te il che tu dici
I wish I knew what you are saying

Realdo/Girl
Guarda ti batte il tasto come la strega
look, he harps on the same thing[329] like a witch

Altamante/Boy
Ma marce tu ce l'hai te le radici
but your roots are rotten

Realdo/Girl
É proprio lui ell'uomo che fa la sega
and indeed he is the man that jacks off

Altamante/Boy
T'hanno visto a Firenze lá nelle pendici
they have seen you in Florence there on the hillsides

Realdo/Girl
Per questo ritornó a casa a Scandicci
that's why he went to live in Scandicci[330]
Perché pe' il mondo si trovó un pien di pasticci
because in the world he found himself in the middle of troubles

Although the Alternated octet is supposed to close a *Contrasto,* in this case the poets when on producing several other Alternated octets, leaving the theme of "Boy vs. Girl" and reverting to free insults.

---

[329] Literally: he beats the key like a witch.
[330] The town where Altamante lives.

V. The Nun Vs. The Prostitute.

This *Contrasto* was sung during a performance in Migliana (Prato) on August 2, 1997. The audience requested the theme and the poets chose their personage before starting to sing. I present here four octets from that *Contrasto*.

(Octet 3) Altamante - Prostitute
(Belle-) vederle la sua posizione non mi dole
(beautiful-) it is not painful for me to see your position
il tuo avvenire credi é bell'e spento
your future, believe me, it's already doused
non hai ne un marito e ne una prole
you do not have an husband nor children
te schiava tu rimani in un convento
you, like a slave, remain in the convent
e sono io ai raggi del sole
I am instead under the rays of the sun
della mia vita sai ((lights goes momentarily off))
of my life you know
della mia vita sai non me ne pento
of my life, you know, I do not repent
io vivo gli ontento i cittadini
I live, make the citizens happy
io mi diverto e guadagno i quattrini
I have fun and earn lots of money

Altamante: *sono io la prostituta é? riordatelo, un tu se te*
 I am the prostitute, ok? remember, not you

Davide: *ma qui ci sarebbero delle rime che nun faccio*
 but here there are rhymes that I cannot do[331]

Altamante: *vai vai vai (casini)*
 go go go (brothels)[332]

Davide: ((sound with mouth))

---

[331] Riondino is not an expert poet, and here he is doubting that he may not be able to answer to the rhyme in *-ini*.

[332] Altamante suggests a rhyme to Riondino. Later, he suggests other rhymes as well.

Altamante: *la legge Merlini, vai nei casini vai vai lí un c'é mia nulladi (.......)*
the Merlini law, go, in the brothels, go go, there is not really nothing of
(....)

    Davide: *e:::: lí, com'é finito? I cittadini n:::: li faccio i quattrini*
       and there, how did it end? the citizens, n:::: I make the money

(Octet 4) Davide - Nun
All'inferno piuttosto ti avvicini
you rather draw near the hell

      Altamante: *ecco bravo bravo bravo bravo bravo*
        there, bravo bravo bravo bra vo bravo

con questa maledetta scostumanza
with this cursed dissolutedness
tu dai scandalo ai vecchi ed ai bambini
you are a scandal for the elders and for the children
possibile non n' abbia abbastanza
is it possible that you haven't enough?
ci si impaurisce se tu ti avvicini
we get scared if you come near

    Davide: ((sounds withth mouth))
basta vederti ((sounds with mouth)) gli anelli nella panza
it's enough to look at ((sound with mouth)) the rings in your belly
    Davide: m:: m::
smettila Altamante cambia vita
stop it Altamante, change life

    Altamante: *falla finita*
      stop it for good

guarda perlomeno come sei vestita.
look at least at the way you are dressed

(Octet 5) Altamante - Prostitute
Vedi la natura la razza ha stabilita
you see, nature, race, has established
ci dev'esse un legame coniugale
there has to be a conjugal link

pe poté risorve la partita
to be able to solve the game
ma anche te sorella tu sta male
but even you, sister, you are feeling bad
sé come l'erba quando l'é appassita
you are like the grass when it is withered
ma la tua gioventú cosa la vale
what does your young age count for?
troppo schiava tu sei te del cielo
too much a slave you are of the sky
resti un fiore appassito sullo stelo
you remain a flower withered on the stem

(Octet 6) Davide - Nun
Te sempre in giro con i ssacco a pelo
you, always traveling around with the sleeping bag
    Altamante: (......)
    Davide: *ecco ha*
       there ha

lungo la via ti stanchi inutilmente
along the road you get tired uselessly
ma invece io alla Madonna del Carmelo
but I, instead, to the Madonna of Carmelo
vivo tranquilla me non mi importa niente
I live peacefully, I do not care at all
tutta la gente per un po' di pelo
all the people for a bit of body hair
si muove intorno vorticosamente
moves around in a whirl
io resto ferma e prego delle ore
I remain still and I pray for hours
perché il mio sposo sai é lui il Signore.
because my spouse, you know, is him, the Lord

    Davide: *E? La- la so é?*
      Right? I- I know it right?

    Altamante: *Bella be- bravo gli ha fatto una bella poesia*
      beautiful, bea- bravo he has done a beautiful poetry

APPENDIX G

I have included here the original excerpts from the interviews to Altamante Logli and Realdo Tonti, which were analyzed in chapter 7.

I. On Art and Its Origins.
1) Code: 5/23/99, tape 1, side A, 096 and fol.

Realdo: Ma é una voce che ho sentito sempre io questa qui fin da ragazzo, quella del cantare. (Sono stato) sempre attratto da questi canti storici appunto. Prima come Cantastorie, poi al tempo mio qui in questo paese, o ne paesi vicini o nella provincia c'erano parecchi poeti improvvisatori molto bravi, molto piu' bravi di me, assai. E:: e rimanevo molto attratto da loro io, fino a i ppunto spesse volte di- di lasciare i giochi da ragazzo e andalli a sentire nella piazza, il mercato, perche' cantavano, la domenica veniva fatto il mercato nelle piazze. Allora c'erano questi poeti a Braccio, tra i quali ci si puo' menzionare l'Andreini, il Piccardi, il Ceccherini, e::: (Pescini). E io naturalmente ero:- ero preso ero: prorpio- un resistevo ecco a::: a nun andarli a sentire e spesse volte mi sarebbe venuto anche l'idea di- di di qualcosa. Pero' lo sai il timor panico no? di fronte a certi poeti.

Realdo: It is a voice that I always heard, this one, since I was a boy, this thing of singing. (I have been) always attracted by these historical songs, that's it. First as a Storysinger. When I was young, in this town, or in the nearby towns in the province, there were many very good improvising poets, much better than I was, much more. And I would feel very attracted by them, to the point oftentimes of leaving my games as a boy, and going to listen to them in the plaza, in the market. They would sing on Sunday. They would be in the market, in the plaza. At that time, there were many *poeti a Braccio*. Among them, we can mention Andreini, Piccardi, Ceccherini, and (Pescini). ... And I naturally was- I was taken. I was really- I could not resist, that's it, I had to go listen to them and oftentimes the idea would come to me, to say something. But, you know, [I had] a panicky fear, right? In front of such poets.

2) Code: 9/11/97, tape 1, side A, 120 and fol.

Altamante: Partivo col gregge la mattina, tornavo la sera. Fu proprio a contatto con la natura che- sa principiai a improvvisare qualche verso rimato. Ebbi il dono di poesia. Per la pastura, quando nu avevo tristezza, canticchiavo questi umili versi, cantavo. Mi ascolto' un giovane, faceva lo stradino, vale a di stava a Vaiano, gli e' morto sara' sette o otto anni. Gli era un mio amio, gli ero anche affezionato. Una quindicina d'anni- se io aveo, dodici anni avra' avuto ventitre', avea fatto il militare e gli era a fa lo stradino che da Vaiano va su monti della Calvana. E:: sicche', mi ascoltava esto stradino- in quella, in quelle mula- facea lo stradino in quelle mulattiere di montagna. Si chiamaa Paranti Nello ... era un poeta. Fatto questa conoscenza, quando ci si incontrava fu proprio con lui che i- che acquisii la conoscenza della poesia. Bisogna dire che fu il mio estro. La mia sortita fu in pratia, fu alla festa dell'uva a Vaiano inverso in trentaquattro mi pare, di una (festa) locale, cantavan di poesia. Il mio amico, questo Nello (gia' mi) par di li- di (.......) chiamo' (......) mi (fece)- mi dice- mi invito', Nello mi invito', c'erano altri poeti. Anche io presi parte a quella serata. Ma ero troppo- ero troppo piccolo nun mi potevano vedere "vieni poetino coraggio, aiutaci"- NO fa- a- a- "accetta" NO- dice- fatto che accettai, mi misero su un tavolino, altrimenti sarei rimasto chiuso tra la gente, che in piedi mi faceva- e- e- mi- che era in piedi. Mi feci coraggio, cantai qualche poesia, quello che dissi non ricordo. Per me, ragazzo, fu una bella soddisfazione, fui applaudito da tutti e abbracciato dai poeti.

"I would leave with the sheep in the morning, I would come back at night. It was exactly in contact with nature, you know, that I started to improvise a few rhymed verses. I received the gift of poetry. In the pasture, when I had no sadness, I would singsong these simple verses. As I sang, a young man heard me. He was a road maker from Vaiano. Now he has been dead maybe for seven or eight years. He was my friend, I was very affectionate to him. [He was] maybe fifteen years [older than me]. Well if I was, twelve years old, he must have been twenty-three. He had been in the draft already and he was working at making the road that from Vaiano goes up on the mountains of the Calvana. So, this road maker was listening to me- in that *mulattiera* [road used by mules]. He was making the road in the *mulattiere* of those mountains. His name was Nello Paranti. ... He was a poet. After getting acquainted with him, when we would meet it was with him indeed that I acquired the knowledge of poetry. We need to say that it was my *estro* [inspiration, gift]. My coming out was, practically, it was at the feast of grapes in Vaiano, around 1934 I believe, in a local (feast). They were singing poetry. My friend Nello invited me. There were other poets. I too took part to that evening. But I was too small, they could not see me: "come little poet, courage! Help us, do accept," one said. So it was that I accepted. They put me on the table, otherwise I would have remained hidden among the people, who were standing, and [the poets] were also standing. I took courage and I sung some poetry. What I said I cannot remember. For me, a boy, it was a great satisfaction. I was applauded by everybody and hugged by the poets.

3) Code: 9/11/97, tape 1, side B, 183 and fol.

Altamante: E che lo so? He he un lo so. Un me ne so rende conto, capito? Ho! Un me ne so rende mia onto- un me ne so rende conto. Mi venia esti versi osi, capito? E::: capito? In ve- mi venia sti versi ...

Altamante: Do you think I know it? He! he! I don't know it. I don't know how to account to myself for it, you see? Ho! I don't know how to account to myself for it indeed- I don't know how to account for it. These verses would come to me, like this, you see? These verses would come to me.

4) Code: 5/23/99, tape 1, side A, 096 and fol.

Realdo: E' non la compri e non la studi.

Anthropologist: ecco

Realdo: E'::: hh hh he he he se ce l'hai ce l'hai, senno', senno', e un la fai, ecco. Neanche se tu studi cinquantanni all'universitá. Tu poi pigliá la penna e scriverla, improvvisare (non lo poi fare). Ecco quindi perché (questa) é un arte naturale. Questa cosa, questo canto.

Translation:

Realdo: You cannot buy it and you cannot study it.

Anthropologist: I see

Realdo: It is hh hh he he he! If you have it you have it, otherwise, you are not going to make it, that's it. Not even if you study at the university for fifty years. You can take the pen and write it, but to improvise (you cannot). This is why this thing, this singing is a natural art.

5) Code: 5/23/99, tape 1, side A, 096 and fol.

Realdo: Naturalmente tu esprimi il che tu senti dentro e quindi, é quello che trasporta. Perché io mi son trovato a cantare spesse volte ... con dei professionisti, che (va bene) lo hanno fatto di mestiere, hanno studiato la musica tutta la vita sicché un canto e un orchestra, ha- bon- (...). Sembran gessi. Peró naturalmente se un ci hai dentro- ... E allora che cos'é? E' che- e che che quello che tu trasmetti piú che quello- piú che la quadratura. ... Io a volte mi domando, o come si fa a garballi un lo so, peró e::: sai, é una osa che entra perché- appunto é stata definita un arte naturale.

Realdo: Naturally you express what you feel inside and thus, that is what is carrying you. Because I found myself oftentimes singing ... with professionals, who do it as their job, right? They have studied music all of their life so they have a voice and an orchestra. But they look like plaster casts. But of course if you do not have it inside- ... But then what is it? It is what you transmit more than what- more than the framing. ... Sometimes I ask myself, why is it that they like us? I do not know. But, you know, it is something that enters [inside you] because- that's why it has been defined a natural art.

II. From: "The Ethos of the Poet."
1) Code: 9/11/97, tape 1, side B, 452 and fol.

Altamante: Io son senza confini. Perché e Iddio gli é uno solo, anche dal lato cristiano, un gli avrá mia creato l'Ameria e poi la Russia e poi- e po noi. ... Penso che un ci sia nemmeno stato (...). Ma in hh ogni modo, ((laughing)) ... L'amor di patria- vabbé, bisogna ave l'amore d' i mmondo. L'amor di patria, di- (....) sarei confini, creati, nun ci dovrebbe esse frontiere ni mondo. Ci dovrebbe essere un mondo universale, che ci si potesse viaggiare, (senza guardare) (e a razza) e compagnia bella. Perché la patria, gli é a vantaggio di certi signori che ci peculano sulla patria. Un ha bisogno ne di martiri ne d'eroi. Avrebbe bisogno di gente onesta. Che sapessen fare il su dovere e desseno a mangiare a tutti. Questo avrebbe bisogno la patria. No degli eroi e dei martiri e da pen- (......) e come di essa un gli é morto uno. Poverino, io, lo posso patí bene, sí , ma d'altra parte, quando ni- nillo stesso tempo gli ammazzonno anche dugentocinquanta persone laggiue in Algeria. Gli hanno ammazzati. Gli hanno tagliato i- la gola a ottanta bambini. Quante se n'é parlato? Un giorno solo. Di lei se ne parla ancora su tutti i giornali d' mmondo. Si fa la storia sempre a quelli piú ricchi. E questo uí a me nun mi va bene.

Altamante: I have no borders. Because – even from a Christian point of view – God is one. You wouldn't think that he created first America and then Russia and then us. ... I believe [Jesus] did not even exist. But anyway, ((laughing)). ... The love for the country- ok! But we need to have love for the world. The love for the country! (There shouldn't) be borders created. There should not be any frontiers in the world. There should be a universal world, where you could travel, (without considering) (race) and similar things. Because the country is to the advantage of certain gentlemen that capitalize on it. It does not need martyrs or heroes. It would need honest people, people that would know how to do their duty and would give to everybody something to eat. This is what the country needs, not heroes and not martyrs and to think- So if someone is dead – poor one – I can feel sorry indeed. Yes, but on the other side, when at the same time they killed two hundred and fifty people there in Algeria. They killed them. They cut the throats of eighty children. How long have we talked about it? One day only. Of [Princess Diana], all the newspapers of the world are still talking. We always make the history of the rich. And this I do not accept.

2) Code: 5/23/99, tape 1, side A, 096 and fol.

Realdo: La poesia a braccio un po'- tu hai:- tu lo sai tu l'ha capita un po' com'é. E' nata nell'aia dei contadini di (....) capito. Siccome un si potevano esprimere tanto, allora parlavano sempre di sottinteso. Forse noi Toscani, il buttare le cose di sottinteso nel nostro linguaggio s'é preso proprio da- da quelle tradizioni lí. Perché noi Toscani nun s'ha un linguaggio schietto.

Realdo: The poetry *a braccio* you know- you understood a bit of the way it is. It was born in the threshing-floor of the peasants, you know. Because they could not really express themselves, then they would always talk implicitly. Maybe us Tuscans, this [usage of] throwing things out through allusion in our language, we took it from those traditions indeed. Because us Tuscans, we do not have a straight talk.

3) Code: 8/24/98, tape 1, side A, 000 and fol

Altamante: Perché te tu devi batte sempre: se no siamo nati uguali, ma se il mondo gli é di Dio, l'ha creato Iddio, perché uno deve avere 30,000 ettari di tereno, e uno un avere una baracca ndove sta dentro? Il problema sociale l'é questo. Ti danno un tema, tra il capitale e il lavoro. Te tu se un lavoratore o un capitalista. Peró bisogna domandagli- s- per arrivare a far questo, ... uno pole avanzá con la propria intelligenza. Ma chi accaparra tutto, vale a dire, e sfrutta sempre sempre- una classe di sfruttatori. E allora va buttato lí: perché si fa queste ose ui? Se mar- (si va) l'ingiustizia sociale, e gli esiste, e si lotta, anche senza esse ne Comunista e ne niente, si lotta per la guistizia sociale e l'uguaglianza, per sistemare un mondo. Nel mondo ci dovrebbe essere il pane per tutti no? Uno gli ha pane da buttarsi via, capito, e uno un ha (nulla). (La giustizia) sociale gli é questa.

Altamante: You have to hammer home always this [idea]: if we are born equal, and if the world belongs to God, it was created by God, then why should one have 30,000 hectares of land, and another one have not even a hovel where to live? This is the social problem. They give you a theme, let's say between the capital and the labor. You are going to be a worker or a capitalist. You must ask [the capitalist]: to arrive where you are- ... some may advance with their own intelligence. But those who hoard everything, I mean, and exploit always and always, they are a class of exploiters. Then you must throw [this question] there: why are we doing these things? The social injustice exists, and we fight it, even without being a communist or anything. We fight for social justice and equality, and to create order in the world. In the world, there should be bread for everybody, right? Someone has bread to throw away, you see, and someone else does not have (anything). This is (about social justice).

III. Aesthetic System.
1) Code: 8/24/98, tape 1, side A, 386 and fol.

Altamante: Se ti lascio una rima chiusa ti butto a gambe ritte un tu ce la ripigli mia é?

Anthropologist: Una rima chiusa é una rima difficile?

Altamante: Una difficile che nun ce n'é altre capito? A me quande mi fecero un'ottava a Sant'Angelo (dalle Ore), ...:
        "Te tu se venuo a cantá a Sant'Angelo dalléore
        ti manderei a badá capre e pecore"
peore vero? Io dissi
        "esprodo come una meteore"
dice egli ha ha ha

Anthropologist: Con una rima sdrucciola é piú difficile?

Altamante: Sdrucciola é come "cavolo" "diavolo" "trogolo"

Anthropologist: Sí sí

Altamante: "Nuvolo" hh sa ma questo un é per ripiglialla, son (sdrucciole), vedi. ... Come una meteore (feci) tecore e mecore. ... Insomma la riabbordai. Peró c'é delle rime che un ci si piglia anche al- un c'é (modo).

Translation:

Altamante: If I leave you a closed rhyme I throw you head over heals, you are not going to pick it up again, you know?

Anthropologist: A closed rhyme is a difficult rhyme?

Altamante: A difficult one because there isn't another one, you understand? Once at Sant'Angelo dalle Ore, they gave me this octet ...:
        'You have come to sing at Sant'Angelo *dallé Ore* [of Ore]
        I would send you to look after goats and *péore* [sheep]'

péore [sheep] right? I said:
    'I explode like *una metéore* [a meteor<u>s</u>]'
ha! ha! ha!

Anthropologist: Is it more difficult with a proparoxytone[333] rhyme?

Altamante: A proparoxytone is like '*cávolo*' [cabbage], '*diávolo*' [devil], '*trógolo*' [trough].

Anthropologist: Yes, yes

Altamante: '*núvolo*' [cloudy], hh you know, these are impossible to pick up again, they are (proparoxytone) words, you see. ... After *metéore* [meteor] I (said) *técore* [with you] and *mécore* [with me]. ... In the end, I was able to broach it again. But there are certain rhymes that you cannot pick up, no (way)!

  2) Code: 8/24/98, tape 1, side B, 027 and fol.

Altamante: A un poeta si vol fa fa bella figura, un si mette in imbarazzo con delle rime difficile.

Altamante: You want to make a poet look good, you should not embarrass him with difficult rhymes.

  3) Code: 8/24/98, tape1, side A, 494 and fol.

Altamante: E allora, noi si s- un si sorte di i ccerchio li' perche' nun s'allarga, a bene? Nun s'allarga apito, il coso.

Altamante: There, we do not get out of the circle anymore. Because we do not enlarge, right? We do not get larger, you understand?

  4) Code: 8/24/98, tape 1, side A, 386 and fol.

Altamante: La si pole riusare, magari se ce n'é una sola. Anche Dante in un punto mi par che ripete la stessa parola. Dante Alighieri. In un certo punto mi par che-

---

[333] Accent on the third from the last syllable.

Anthropologist: Ha sí?

Altamante: E::::: ripete perch´un c'é altre rime, che gli ha a fare, viene messo quella.

Anthropologist: Alle volte ecco lo vedo

Altamante: Perché se io dio- lo stantuffo della pompa, un voglio e a stantufare ti si rompa. Come tu fai a ripete tre rime sull'ottava con rompa?

Translation:

Altamante: We can use [a rhyme] again, maybe if there is only one of them. Even Dante in one place, I believe he repeats the same word. Dante Alighieri. In a certain point, I believe that-

Anthropologist: Is that so?

Altamante: Hu:::::m he repeats because there is no other rhyme. What can we do? We put that one.

Anthropologist: Sometime, that's it, I see.

Altamante: Because if I say "the piston of the *pompa* [pump], I do not want that by chugging it *rompa* [may break down]. How would you do to repeat three rhymes in an octet with *rompa* [may break down]?

5) Code: 8/24/98, tape 1, side A, 386 and fol.

Altamante: Ma se tu dici rime che un hanno ne significato, come tu fai? Ti pare? Colla rima ci sia anche un significato del discorso.

Altamante: If you say rhymes that have no meaning, how are you going to do? With the rhyme there has to be also a meaning for the discourse.

6) Code: 8/24/98, tape 1, side A, 386 and fol.

Altamante: Ci son le rime. Peró il discorso un vien bello. Le rime son belle su::- 'andare' ce n'é troppe: 'andare,' 'arare.' Sennó come 'agli,' 'a seminagli,' a levagli,' 'a zappagli,' 'a rincalzagli,' sennó son tutte rime, he! he!

bá! Allora torna bene il discorso. Vedi il discorso su un 'cuore,' 'amore,' 'splendore.' O 'sole,' 'parole,' 'scuole,' (   ), 'viole,' ha capito? 'Crea,' 'orchidea,' 'assemblea,' 'idea,' 'giudea,' 'dea.'

Altamante: [In some cases] there are the [correct] rhymes. But the discourse won't come out beautiful. The rhymes are beautiful on- (*'andare'* [to go] there are too many: *'andare,' 'arare'* [to go, to sow]. Or also like *'agli'* [to him], *'a seminagli'* [to sow to him], *'a zappagli'* [to hoe to him], *'a rincalzagli'* [to tuck in to him]. That way anything can rhyme. He! He! Indeed! Then the discourse turns out fine.) You see, the discourse [should be] on a *'cuore'* [heart], *'amore'* [love], *'splendore'* [splendor]. Or *'sole'* [sun] *'parole'* [words] *'scuole'* [schools], (.........), *'viole'* [violets], you see? *'Crea'* [s/he creates], *'orchidea'* [orchid], *'assemblea'* [assembly], *'idea'* [idea], *'Giudea'* [Judaea/Judaean], *'dea'* [goddess].

7) Code: 8/24/98, tape 1, side B, 027 and fol.

Anthropologist: Quando te tu senti una rima, che é il finale, tu ci hai pochissimo tempo, no? Per pensá il prossimo verso. ... E te, la prima cosa che tu pensi é il verso? ... O pensi prima alla rima?

Altamante: No bisogna pensi a quello che dice lui! Come, se lui mi dice mettiamo il che- un so ... che io sono, un son bono a niente, ... bisogna e gli risponda a quello e ma detto pe difesa é?

Anthropologist: When you hear a rhyme, which is the final one, you have very little time, right? To think the next verse. ... Is the verse the first thing that you think? ... Or do you think about the rhyme first?

Altamante: No, I need to think about what he is saying! Like, if he tells me let's say ... that I am good for nothing, ... I need to answer to what he told me to defend [myself], right?

BIBILIOGRAPHY

1988. *The Random House College Dictionary. Revised Edition.* New York: Random House.

Abu-Lughod, L. 1986. *Veiled Sentiments: Honor and Poetry in a Bedouin Society.* Berkeley: University of California Press.

Adachi, N. 2000. " 'Oh No! But I'm Married to Your Company!': The Linguistic Influence of 'Aristocratic' Housewives' Speech on Everyday Japanese Women's Discourse." Unpublished Presentation. Stanford: International Gender and Language Association Conference.

Agamennone, M. 1988. "I Tratti Melodici dell'Ottava Cantata. L'Ottava Popolare Moderna." In G. Kezich and L. Sarego (eds.), *L'Ottava Popolare Moderna.* Siena: Nuova Immagine Editrice.

Agostiniani, L. 1989. "Fenomenologia dell'Elisione nel Parlato in Toscana." *Rivista Italiana di Dialettologia. Scuola, Società, Territorio,* a. XIII (1989). Bologna: CLEUB.

Agostiniani, L. and L. Giannelli 1990. "Considerazioni per un' Analisi del Parlato

Toscano." In M. A. Cortellazzo and A. M. Mioni (eds.), *L' Italiano Regionale.* Roma: Bulzoni.

Alleyne, M. 1988. *The Roots of Jamaican Culture.* London: Pluto Press.

Anderson, B. R. O'G. 1983. *Imagined Communities. Reflections on the Origins and Spread of Nationalism.* London and New York: Verso.

_____. 1990. *Language and Power: Exploring Political Cultures in Indonesia.* Ithaca and London: Cornell University Press.

Anzaldua, G. 1987. *Borderlands/La Frontera: The New Mestiza*. San Francisco: Aunt Lute.

Bakhtin, M. M. 1981. *The Dialogic Imagination*. Austin: University of Texas Press.

_____. 1984. *Problems of Dostoevsky's Poetics*. Manchester: Manchester University Press.

Balikci, A. 1970. *The Netsilik Eskimo*. Garden City: Natural History Press.

Barba, E. 1995. *The Paper Canoe: A Guide to Theatre Anthropology*. London and New York: Routledge.

Barth, F. 1969. *Ethnic Groups and Boundaries. The Social Organization of Culture Difference*. Boston: Little, Brown & Co.

Basso, K. H. 1988. "Speaking with Names: Language and Landscape among the Western Apache." *Cultural Anthropology* 3:99-130.

_____. 1990. *Western Apache Language and Culture*. Tucson and London: University of Arizona Press.

_____. 1996. "Wisdom Sits in Places: Notes on Western Apache Landscape." In S. Feld and K. H. Basso (eds.), *Senses of Place*. Santa Fe: School of American Research Press.

Bauman, R. 1977. *Verbal Art as Performance*. Prospect Heights: Waveland Press.

_____. 1986. *Story, performance and event: Contextual Studies of Oral Narrative*. Cambridge: Cambridge University Press.

_____. 1992a. *Folklore, Cultural Performances, and Popular Entertainments*. New York and Oxford: Oxford University Press.

_____. 1992b. "Contextualization, Tradition, and the Dialogue of Genres: Icelandic Legends of the *Kraftaskald*." In A. Duranti and C. Goodwin (eds.), *Rethinking Context: Language as an Interactive Phenomenon*. Cambridge: Cambridge University Press.

_____. 1993. "The Nationalization and Internationalization of Folklore: The Case of Schoolcraft's *Gitshee Gauzinee*." *Western Folklore*, 52(2,3,4): 247-269.

Bauman, R. and C. L. Briggs 1990. "Poetics and Performance as Critical Perspectives on Language and Social Life." *Annual Review of Anthropology*, 19: 59-88.

_____. 2000. "Language Philosophy as Language Ideology: John Locke and Johann Gottfried Herder." In P. V. Kroskrity (ed.), *Regimes of Language: Ideologies, Polities and Identities*. Santa Fe: School of American Research Press.

Becker, A. L. 1979. "Text Building, Epistemology, and Aesthetics in Javanese Shadow Theatre." In A. Yengoyan and A. L. Becker (eds.), *The Imagination of Reality*. Norwood: Ablex.

Becker, C. 1994. "Introduction: Presenting the Problem." In C. Becker (ed.) *The Subversive Imagination: Artists, Society and Social Responsibility*. London and New York: Routledge.

Bencistá, A. 1990. *I Poeti del Mercato: Raccolta di Contrasti in Ottava Rima dei Poeti Estemporanei Gino Ceccherini e Elio Piccardi*. Radda in Chianti: Studium Editrice.

_____. 1994. *I Bernescanti: Il Contrasto in Ottava Rima e le Tematiche Attuali*. Firenze: Edizioni Polistampa.

Berger, P. L. and T. Luckmann 1966. *The Social Construction of Reality: A Treatise in the Sociology of Knowledge*. Garden City: Anchor Books.

Bini, M. P. 1974. *Parole che Scompaiono*. Firenze: Libreria Editrice Fiorentina.

Bloch, M. 1975. *Political Language and Oratory in Traditional Society*. London: Academic Press.

Blommaert, J. and J. Verschueren 1998. "The Role of Language in European Nationalist Ideologies." In B.B. Schieffelin, K. A. Woolard and P. V. Kroskrity (eds.) *Language Ideologies: Practice and Theory*. New York and Oxford: Oxford University Press.

Blu, K. I. 1996. "*Where Do You stay At?*: Homeplace and Community among the Lumbee." In S. Feld and K. H. Basso (eds.), *Senses of Place*. Santa Fe: School of American Research Press.

Bobbio, A. Accame 1951. "Carlo Gozzi e la Polemica sulla Lingua Italiana." *Convivio*, 31-58.

Bodnar, J. 1985. *The Transplanted. A History of Immigrants in Urban America*. Bloomington: Indiana University Press.

Bourdieu, P. 1977. *Outline of a Theory of Practice*. Trans. by Richard Nice. Cambridge: Cambridge University Press.

_____. 1990. *The Logic of Practice*. Trans. by Richard Nice. Stanford: Stanford University Press.

Briggs, C. L. 1988. *Competence in Performance: The Creativity of Tradition in Mexicano Verbal Art*. Philadelphia: Philadelphia University Press.

_____. 1992. "Linguistic Ideologies and the Naturalization of Power in Warao Discourse." *Pragmatics* 2:387-404.

_____. 1996. "Introduction." In C. L. Briggs (ed.) *Disorderly Discourse: Narrative, Conflict and Inequality*. New York and Oxford: Oxford University Press.

_____. 1998. "'You Are a Liar – You're Just Like a Woman!': Constructing Dominant Ideologies of language in Warao Men's Gossip." In B. Schieffelin, K. A. Woolard and P. V. Kroskrity (eds.) *Language Ideologies: Practice and Theory*. New York and Oxford: Oxford University Press.

Brodin, G. 1970. *Termini Dimostrativi Toscani. Studio Storico di Morfologia, Sintassi e Semantica*. Lund: Ètudes Romanes de Lund.

Butler, J. 1997. "Gender is Burning: Questions of Appropriation and Subversion." In A.

McClintock, A. Mufti and E Shohat (eds.), *Dangerous Liaisons: Gender, Nation, & Postcolonial Perspectives*. Minneapolis and London: University of Minnesota Press.

Cammarano, F. 1995. "La Costruzione dello Stato e la Classe Dirigente." In G. Sabbatucci and V. Vidotto (eds.) *Storia d'Italia: 2. Il Nuovo Stato e la Societá Civile 1861-1887*. Roma and Bari: Editori Laterza.

Canepari, L. 1979. *Introduzione alla Fonetica*. Torino: Einaudi.

_____. 1985. *L'Intonazione Linguistica e Paralinguistica*. Napoli: Liguori Editore.

Capps, L. and E. Ochs 1995. *Constructing Panic: The Discourse of Agoraphobia*. Cambridge: Harvard University Press.

Caraveli, A. 1986. "The Bitter Wounding: The Lament as Social Protest in Rural Greece." In J. Dubisch (ed.), *Gender and Power in Rural Greece*. Princeton: Princeton University Press.

Carby, H. V. 1997. "*On the Threshold of Woman's Era*: Lynching, Empire, and Sexuality in Black Feminist Theory." In A. McClintock, A. Mufti and E. Shohat (eds.), *Dangerous Liaisons: Gender, Nation, & Postcolonial Perspectives*. Minneapolis and London: University of Minnesota Press.

Casey, E. S. 1996. "How to Get from Space to Place in a Fairly Short Stretch of Time: Phenomenological Prolegomena." In S. Feld and K. H. Basso (eds.), *Senses of Place*. Santa Fe: School of American Research Press.

Caton, S. C. 1990. *"Peaks of Yemen I Summon:" Poetry as Cultural Practice in a North Yemeni Tribe*. Berkeley: California University Press.

Chatterjee, P. 1993. *The Nation and Its Fragments: Colonial and Postcolonial Histories*. Princeton: Princeton University Press.

Chaudhuri, N., and M. Strobel, (eds.) 1992. *Western Women and Imperialism. Complicity and Resistance*. Bloomington and Indianapolis: Indiana University Press.

Chechi, M. 1997. *Come si Improvvisa Cantando (Storia e Tecnica sull'Uso di Versi e Rime)*. Grosseto: Laboratorio di Cartotecnica e Stampa, Archivio di Stato di Grosseto.

Cirese, A. M. 1969. *La Poesia Popolare*. Palermo: Sellerio Editore.

_____. 1973. *Cultura Egemonica e Culture Subalterne: Rassegna degli Studi sul Mondo Popolare Tradizionale*. Palermo: Palumbo Editore.

_____. 1988. *Ragioni Metriche: Versificazione e Tradizioni Orali*. Palermo: Sellerio Editore.

Clemente, P. 1988. "Aria d'Ottave." In G. Kezich and L. Sarego (eds.), *L'Ottava Popolare Moderna*. Siena: Nuova Immagine Editrice.

Clemente, P., M. Fresta and L. Giannelli 1982. "Scritti di Contadini Senesi: Note sul Teatro Popolare e Altri Usi della Scrittura." In G. Cerina, C. Lavinio and L. Mulas (eds.), *Oralitá e Scrittura nel Sistema Letterario: Atti del Convegno, Cagliari, 14-16 Aprile 1980*. Roma: Bulzoni Editore.

Clough, S. B. and S. Saladino 1968. *A History of Modern Italy; Documents, Readings, & Commentary*. New York: Columbia University Press.

Cohen, R. 1978. "Ethnicity: Problem and Focus in Anthropology." *Annual Review of Anthropology*, 7:379-403.

Comaroff, J. L. and S. Roberts 1981. *Rules and Processes: The Cultural Logic of Dispute in African Context*. Chicago: University of Chicago Press.

Connerton, P. 1989. *How Societies Remember*. New York: Cambridge University Press.

Cortellazzo, M. 1984. *Curiositá Linguistica nella Cultura Popolare*. Lecce: Milella.

Collier, J. F. 1974. "Women in Politics." In M. Z. Rosaldo and L. Lamphere (eds.), *Women, Culture and Society*. Stanford: Stanford University Press.

D'Argemir, D. C. 1994. "Gender Relations and Social Change in Europe: On Support and Care." In V. A. Goddard, J. R. Llobera and C. Shore (eds.) *The Anthropology of Europe. Identities and Boundaries in Conflict*. Oxford and Providence: Berg.

Davis, J. A. 1996. "Changing Perspectives on Italy's 'Southern Problem.' " In C. Levy (ed.) *Italian Regionalism: History, Identity and Politics*. Oxford and Washington D.C: Berg.

De Martino, E. 1986. *Ernesto de Martino: Scritti Inediti sulla Ricerca in Lucania*. Ed. by C. Gallini. La Ricerca Folklorica, 13.

De Mauro, T. 1970. *Storia Linguistica dell'Italia Unita*. Bari: Laterza.

De Simonis, P. 1984/85. "*Noi* e *Loro*. Note su Identità e Confini Linguistici e Culturali in Toscana." *Quaderni Dell'Atlante Lessicale Toscano*, 2/3 - 1984/85. Firenze: L. S. Olschki Editore.

Del Giudice, L. 1995. *Italian Traditional Songs*. Los Angeles: Istituto Italiano di Cultura.

Dentith, S. 1995. *Bakhtinian Thought: An Introductory Reader.* London and New York: Routledge.

Di Leonardo, M. (ed.) 1991. *Gender at the Crossroads of Knowledge: Feminist Anthropology in the Postmodern Era.* Berkeley and Los Angeles: University of California Press.

Dubisch, J. (ed.) 1986. *Gender and Power in Rural Greece.* Princeton: Princeton University Press.

_____. 1995. *In a Different Place: Pilgrimage, Gender and Politics at a Greek Island Shrine.* Princeton: Princeton University Press.

Dundes, A., J. W. Leach, et al. 1970. "The Strategy of Turkish Boys' Verbal Dueling Rhymes." *Journal of American Folklore* 78: 337-344.

Duranti, A. 1992a. *Etnografia del Parlare Quotidiano.* Roma: La Nuova Italia Scientifica.

_____. 1992b. "Language and Bodies in Social Space: Samoan Ceremonial Greetings." *American Anthropologist,* 94:657-91.

_____. 1992c. "Language in Context and Language as Context: The Samoan Respect Vocabulary." In A. Duranti and C. Goodwin (eds.) *Rethinking Context: Language as an Interactive Phenomenon.* Cambridge: Cambridge University Press.

_____. 1994. *From Grammar to Politics: Linguistic Anthropology in a Western Samoan Village.* Berkeley, Los Angeles and London: University of California Press.

_____. 1997. *Linguistic Anthropology.* Cambridge: Cambridge University Press.

Duranti, A., E. Ochs, and E. K. Ta'ase 1995. "Change and Tradition in Literacy Instruction in a Samoan American Community." *Educational Foundations,* 9(4), 57-74.

Ehrenberg, F. 1994. "East and West – The Twain Do Meet: A Tale of More than Two Worlds." In C. Becker (ed.) *The Subversive Imagination: Artists, Society and Social Responsibility.* London and New York: Routledge.

Errington, J. 2000. "Indonesian ('s) Authority." In P. V. Kroskrity (ed.), *Regimes of Language: Ideologies, Polities and Identities.* Santa Fe: School of American Research Press.

Farb, P. 1974. *Word Play: What Happens When people Talk.* New York: Knopf inc.

Feld, S. 1996. "Waterfalls of Song: An Acustemology of Place Resounding in Bosavi, Papua New Guinea." In S. Feld and K. H. Basso (eds.), *Senses of Place.* Santa Fe: School of American Research Press.

Fernandez, J. W. 1993. "Ceferino Suarez: A Village Versifier." In S. Lavie, K. Narayan and R. Rosaldo (eds.), *Creativity/Anthropology*. Ithaca and London: Cornell University Press.

Fichera, S. 1981. *The Meaning of Community: A History of the Italians in San Francisco*. Ph. D. Dissertation. University of California Los Angeles.

Fichte, J. Gottlieb 1845-46. "Reden an die Deutsche Nation." In H. Fichte (ed.), *Sämtliche Werke*, vol. 7. Pp. 264-499. Berlin: Veit.

Flax, J. 1987. "Postmodernism and Gender Relations in Feminist Theory." *Signs*, 12(4): 621-643.

Foucault, M. 1978. *The History of Sexuality. Volume I: An Introduction*. New York: Random House.

_____. 1980. *Power/Knowledge: Selected Interviews and Other Writings, 1972-1977*. C. Gordon (ed.). New York: Pantheon.

Frake, C. O. 1996. "Pleasant Places, Past Times, and Shared Identity in Rural East Anglia." In S. Feld and K. H. Basso (eds.), *Senses of Place*. Santa Fe: School of American Research Press.

Franceschini, F. 1983. *I Contrasti in Ottava Rima e l'Opera di Vasco Cai da Bientina*. Pisa: Pacini Editore.

_____. 1988. "Geografia, Storia, Societá nella Tradizione dell'Ottava Rima." In G. Kezich and L. Sarego (eds.), *L'Ottava Popolare Moderna*. Siena: Nuova Immagine Editrice.

_____. 1989. *Cultura Popolare e Intellettuali: Appunti su Carducci, Gramsci, De Martino*. Pisa: Giardini Editori.

Fretz, R. L. 1987. *In Performance: Narrating Skills and Listener Responses*. Unpublished Ph.D. Dissertation.

_____. 1995. "Answering in Song: Listener Responses in *Yishima* Performances." *Western Folklore*, 54(2) :95-112.

Friedl, E. 1986. "The Position of Women: Appearance and Reality." In J. Dubisch (ed.) *Gender and Power in Rural Greece*. Princeton: Princeton University Press.

Gainor, E. (ed.) 1995. *Imperialism and Theatre: Essays on World Theatre, Drama and Performance*. London and New York: Routledge.

Gal, S. 1989. "Language and Political Economy." *Annual Review of Anthropology*, 18:345-367.

Garfinkel, H. 1967. *Studies in Ethnomethodology*. Cambridge: Polity Press.

Georges, R. A. 1981. "Do Narrators Really Digress? A Reconsideration of 'Audience Asides' in Narrating." *Western Folklore*, 15(3): 245-252.

Giacomelli, G. 1975. "Aree Lessicali Toscane." In M. Cortellazzo (ed.), *La Ricerca Dialettale, No. 7.* Firenze: Pacini Editore.

_____. 1984/85. "Parole Toscane." *Quaderni Dell'Atlante Lessicale Toscano,* 2/3 - 1984/85. Firenze: L. S. Olschki Editore.

Giacomelli, G., L. Gori and S. Lucarelli 1984. *Vocabolario Pistoiese.* Pistoia: Societá Pistoiese di Storia Patria.

Giannelli, L. 1988. "Repertorio e Selettivitá nell'Ottava del Contrasto." In G. Kezich and L. Sarego (eds.), *L'Ottava Popolare Moderna.* Siena: Nuova Immagine Editrice.

_____. 1989. "Toscana: Nuovi *Continua* e Prospettive di Ricerca." In G. Holtus, M. Metzeltin and M. Pfister (eds.) *La Dialettologia Italiana Oggi.* Tubingen: Gunter Narr Verlag.

Goddard, V. A. 1994. "From the Mediterranean to Europe: Honor, Kinship and Gender." In V. A. Goddard, J. R. Llobera and C. Shore (eds.) *The Anthropology of Europe. Identities and Boundaries in Conflict.* Oxford and Providence: Berg.

Goodwin, C. 1986. "Audience Diversity, Participation and Interpretation." *Text,* 6(3): 283-316.

Goodwin, C. and A. Duranti 1992. "Rethinking Context: An Introduction." In A. Duranti and C. Goodwin (eds.), *Rethinking Context. Language as an Interactive Phenomenon.* Cambridge: Cambridge University Press.

Goodwin, M. H. 1990. *He-Said-She-Said: Talk as Social Organization among Black Children.* Bloomington and Indianapolis: Indiana University Press.

Gorni, G. 1978. "Un' Ipotesi sull' Origine dell' Ottava Rima." *Metrica,* I:79-94.

Gossen, G. 1976. "Verbal Dueling in Chamula." In B. Kirshenblatt-Gimblett (ed.) *Speech Play: Research and Resources for the Study of Linguistic Creativity.* Philadelphia, University of Pennsylvania Press.

Gramsci, A. 1975. *Quaderni del Carcere.* Ed. by V. Gerratana. Torino: Einaudi.

_____. 1993. *Grammatica e Linguistica.* Roma: Editori Riuniti.

Grassi, C., A. A. Sobrero and T. Telmon 1997. *Fondamenti di Dialettologia Italiana.* Bari: Editori Laterza.

Grimes, B. F. (ed.) 1988 "Ethnologue. Languages of the World." Dallas: Summer Institute of Linguistics, INC.

Gumperz, J. J. 1992. "Contextualization and Understanding." In A. Duranti and C. Goodwin (eds.), *Rethinking Context: Language as an Interactive Phenomenon.* Cambridge: Cambridge University Press.

Hall, K., M. Bucholtz, and B. Moonwomon (eds.) 1992. *Locating Power.* Proceedings of the Second Berkeley Women and Language Conference. Vol. 1-2. Berkeley: Berkeley Women and Language Group.

Halliday, M. A. K. 1978. *Language as a Social Semiotic: The Social Interpretation of Language and Meaning.* Baltimore: University Park Press.

Hearder, H. 1983. *Italy in the Age of the Risorgimento, 1790-1870.* London and New York: Longman.

Herder, J. Gottfried 1967 [1877-1913]. *Sämtliche Werke.* Bernhard Suphan (ed.), 33 vols. Hildesheim: Georg Olms Verlagsbuchhandlung.

Heritage, J. 1984. *Garfinkel and Ethnomethodology.* Cambridge: Polity Press.

Herzfeld, M. 1985. *The Poetics of Manhood: Context and Identity in a Cretan Mountain Village.* Princeton: Princeton University Press.

_____. 1996. "Embarrassment as Pride: Narrative Resourcefulness and Strategies of Normativity among Cretan Animal-Thieves." In C. L. Briggs (ed.) *Disorderly Discourse: Narrative, Conflict and Inequality.* New York and Oxford: Oxford University Press.

Hine, D. 1996. "Federalism, Regionalism and the Unitary State: Contemporary Regional Pressures in Historical Perspective." In C. Levy (ed.) *Italian Regionalism: History, Identity and Politics.* Oxford and Washington D.C: Berg.

Hymes, D. 1974. *Foundations in Sociolinguistics: An Ethnographic Perspective.* Philadelphia: University of Pennsylvania Press.

_____. 1981. *"In vain I tried to tell you": Essays in Native American Ethnopoetics.* Philadelphia: University of Pennsylvania Press.

Irvine, J. T. 1979. "Formality and Informality in Communicative Events." *American Anthropologist,* 81: 773-790.

_____. 1989. "When Talk Isn't Cheap: Language and Political Economy." *American Ethnologist,* 16(2): 248-267.

Irvine, J. T. and S. Gal 2000. "Language Ideology and Linguistic Differentiation." In P. V. Kroskrity (ed.), *Regimes of Language: Ideologies, Polities and Identities.* Santa Fe: School of American Research Press.

Kahn, M. 1996. "Your Place and Mine: Sharing Emotional Landscapes in Wamira, Papua New Guinea." In S. Feld and K. H. Basso (eds.), *Senses of Place.* Santa Fe: School of American Research Press.

Kapchan, D. A. 1995. "Performance." *Journal of American Folklore*, 108(430): 479-508.

Kertzer, D. I. & Saller, R. P. 1991. *The Family in Italy*. London and New Haven: Yale University Press.

King, B. 1967. *A History of Italian Unity*. New York: Russel & Russel.

Kondo, D. 1990. *Crafting Selves: Power, Gender, and Discourses of Identity in a Japanese Workplace*. Chicago: University of Chicago Press.

_____. 1997. *About Face: Performing Race in Fashion and Theater*. New York and London: Routledge.

Kristeva, J. 1980. "Woman Can Never Be Defined." In E. Marks and I. De Courtivon (eds.) *New French Feminism*. Amherst: University of Massachusetts Press.

Kroskrity, P. V. 1992. "Arizona Tewa Kiwa Speech as a Manifestation of Linguistic Ideology." *Pragmatics*, 2(3): 297-309.

_____. 1993. *Language, History, and Identity: Ethnolinguistic Studies of the Arizona Tewa*. Tucson: University of Arizona Press.

_____. 1998. "Arizona Tewa Speech as a Manifestation of a Dominant Language Ideology." In B. Schieffelin, K. A. Woolard and P. V. Kroskrity (eds.) *Language Ideologies: Practice and Theory*. New York and Oxford: Oxford University Press.

_____. 2000. "Regimenting Languages: Language Ideological Perspectives." In P. V. Kroskrity (ed.), *Regimes of Language: Ideologies, Polities and Identities*. Santa Fe: School of American Research Press.

Kuipers, J. C. 1990. *Power in Performance: The Creation of Textual Authority in Weyewa Ritual Speech*. Philadelphia: University of Pennsylvania Press.

Labov, W. 1972. *Language in the Inner City: Studies in Black English Vernacular*. Philadelphia: University of Pennsylvania Press.

Lapucci, C. 1984. *Fiabe Toscane*. Milano: Mondadori.

Lavie, S., K. Narayan and R. Rosaldo (eds.) 1993. *Creativity/Anthropology*. Ithaca and London: Cornell University Press.

Lepre, A. 1978. *Il Risorgimento*. Torino: Loescher Editore.

Lepschy, A. L., G. Lepschy and M. Voghera 1996. "Linguistic Variety in Italy." In C. Levy (ed.) *Italian Regionalism: History, Identity and Politics*. Oxford and Washington D.C: Berg.

Levy, C. 1996. "Introduction: Italian Regionalism in Context." In C. Levy (ed.) *Italian Regionalism: History, Identity and Politics*. Oxford and Washington D.C: Berg.

Leydi, R., S. Mantovani and C. Pederiva 1973. *I Canti Popolari Italiani*.

Milano: Mondadori.

Lindstrom, L. 1992. "Context Contests: Debatable Truth Statements on Tanna (Vanuatu)." In A. Duranti and C. Goodwin (eds.), *Rethinking Context: Language as an Interactive Phenomenon.* Cambridge: Cambridge University Press.

Lippi-Green, R. 1997. *English with an Accent: Language Ideology and Discrimination in the United States.* New York: Routledge.

Livingston, R. E. 1995. "Decolonizing the Theater: Césaire, Serreau and the Drama of Negritude." In E. Gainor (ed.), *Imperialism and Theatre: Essays on World Theatre, Drama and Performance.* London and New York: Routledge.

Londi, F., R. Tonti and N. Landi 1997. "Contrasto Poetico fra Toscana, Emilia-Romagna e Lega Lombarda." *Toscana Folk,* Anno2 n. 2 Maggio 1997:30-33.

Lyttelton, A. 1996. "Shifting Identities: Nation, Region and City." In C. Levy (ed.) *Italian Regionalism: History, Identity and Politics.* Oxford and Washington D.C: Berg.

Marcuse, H. 1978. *The Aesthetic Dimension: Toward a Critique of Marxist Aesthetics.* Boston: Beacon Press.

Marriott, Sir J. A. R. 1931. *The Makers of Modern Italy: Napoleon - Mussolini.* Oxford: Oxford University Press.

Mascia-Lees, F. E., P. Sharpe and C. Ballerino Cohen 1989. "The Postmodernist Turn in Anthropology: Cautions from a Feminist Perspective." *Signs,* 15(1).

Masters, E. L. 1992. *Spoon River Anthology.* New York: Dover Publications Inc.

McClintock, A. 1995. *Imperial Leather: Race, Gender, and Sexuality in the Colonial Contest.* New York: Routledge.

Migliorini, B. 1975. *Cronologia della Lingua Italiana.* Firenze: Le Monnier.

Milroy, J. and L. Milroy 1991. *Authority in Language: Investigating Language Prescription and Standardization.* London and New York: Routledge.

Mohanty, C. T. 1997. "Under Western Eyes: Feminist Scholarship and Colonial Discourses." In A. McClintock, A. Mufti and E Shohat (eds.), *Dangerous Liaisons: Gender, Nation, & Postcolonial Perspectives.* Minneapolis and London: University of Minnesota Press.

Moerman, M. 1965. "Ethnic Identification in a Complex Civilization: Who are the Lue?" *American Anthropologist,* 67:1215-30.

Montroni, G. 1995. "Le Strutture Sociali e le Condizioni di Vita." In G. Sabbatucci and V. Vidotto (eds.) *Storia d'Italia: 2. Il Nuovo*

Stato e la Societá Civile 1861-1887. Roma and Bari: Editori Laterza.

Morgan, M. (ed.) 1994. *Language and the Social Construction of Identity*. Los Angeles: Center for Afro-American Studies, University of California Los Angeles.

Naroll, R. 1964. "On Ethnic Unit Classification." *Current Anthropology*, 5:283-91, 306-12.

Nerucci, R. 1901. *Racconti Popolari Pistoiesi in Vernacolo Pistoiese*. Pistoia: Premiata Tipografia Niccolai.

Ochs, E. 1979. "Transcription as Theory." In E. Ochs and B. Schieffelin (eds.), *Developmental Pragmatics*. New York: Academic Press.

_____. 1992. "Indexing Gender." In A. Duranti and C. Goodwin (eds.), *Rethinking Context. Language as an Interactive Phenomenon*. Cambridge: Cambridge University Press.

Ong, A. 1988. "Colonialism and Modernity: Feminist Representations of Women in Non-Western Societies." *Inscriptions*, 79-93.

Oommen, T. K. 1997. "Introduction: Conceptualizing the Linkage between Citizenshipand National Identity." In T. K. Oommen (ed.), *Citizenship and National Identity: From Colonialism to Globalism*. New Delhi, Thousand Oaks and London: Sage Publications.

Ortner, S. B. 1989-90. "Gender Hegemonies." *Cultural Critique*, (14): 35-80.

Pagliai, V. 1995a. *The Italian Americans in Los Angeles: Representations of Identity and Community*. Unpublished Master Thesis, Department of Anthropology, University of California Los Angeles.

_____. 1995b. "The Italian Americans in Los Angeles: Representations of Identity and Community." Unpublished presentation. Washington D.C.: American Anthropological Association National Meeting.

_____. 1996. "Code-Switching and the Communicative Construction of the Italian American Identity." Unpublished presentation. California State University Fullerton Conference on Theory and Research on Communication and Culture.

_____. 1997. "Narrando L' Identitá Etnica: Gli Italoamericani a Los Angeles." *Etnosistemi*, Anno IV, N°4 - Gennaio: 61-82.

_____. 1999. "Like Romeo and Juliet Upside Down: Gender and Power in Tuscan Community Theater." Unpublished presentation. Chicago: American Anthropological Association national meeting.

Peacock, J. L. 1968. *Rites of Modernization. Symbolic and Social Aspects of Indonesian Proletarian Drama.* Chicago & London: Chicago University Press.

Pecori, G. 1975. *Blasoni Popolari Toscani e Modi Proverbiali.* Firenze: Libreria Editrice Fiorentina.

Pellegrini, G. B. 1977. *Carta dei Dialetti d'Italia.* Pisa: Pacini.

Pollner, M. 1974. "Mundane Reasoning." *Philosophy of the Social Sciences*, 4:35-54.

Pratt, J. 1994. *The Rationality of Rural Life. Economic and Cultural Change in Tuscany.* Switzerland: Harwood Academic Publishers.

Rampton, B. 1998. "Language Crossing and the Redefinition of Minority." *Working Papers in Applied Linguistics*, 5/December: 15-30.

Revelli, N. 1977. *Il Mondo dei Vinti: Testimonianze di Vita Contadina.* Torino: Einaudi.

Riley, D. 1988. *'Am I That Name?' Feminism and the Category of 'Women' in History.* Minneapolis: University of Minnesota Press.

Rohlfs, G. 1966. *Grammatica Storica della Lingua Italiana e dei suoi Dialetti.* Vol. 1-2. Torino: Einaudi.

Roncaglia, A. 1952. "Il Mito delle 'Origini Popolari' e la Scoperta di Tradizioni Medievali Popolaresche." *Il Tesauro*, Anno IV, Numero 1-3, Gennaio, Giugno 1952.

Rosaldo, R. 1986. "Ilongot Hunting as Story and Experience." In V. W. Turner and E. M. Bruner (eds.), *The Anthropology of Experience.* Urbana and Chicago: University of Illinois Press.

Rosler, M. 1994. "Place, Position, Power, Politics." In C. Becker (ed.) *The Subversive Imagination: Artists, Society and Social Responsibility.* London and New York: Routledge.

Rotelli, E. 1980. *La Ricostruzione in Toscana dal CLN ai Partiti.* Vol. 1-2. Bologna: Il Mulino.

Royce, A. Peterson 1982. *Ethnic Identity. Strategies of Diversity.* Bloomington: Indiana University Press.

Rubin, G. 1975. "The Traffic in Women: Notes on the 'Political Economy' of Sex." In R. R. Reiter (ed.) *Toward an Anthropology of Women.* New York: Monthly Review Press.

Schechner, R. 1992. "Drama Performance." In R. Bauman (ed.), *Folklore, Cultural Performances, and Popular Entertainments.* New York and Oxford: Oxford University Press.

Scott, J. 1992. "Multiculturalism and the Politics of Identity." In

October, 61:12-19.

Showstack Sassoon, A. 1987. *Gramsci's Politics*. Minneapolis: University of Minnesota Press.

Silverstein, M. 1979. "Language Structure and Linguistic Ideology." In R. Clyne, W. Hanks and C. Hofbauer (eds.), *The Elements: A Parasession on Linguistic Units and Levels*. Chicago: Chicago Linguistics Society.

_____. 2000. "Whorfianism and the Linguistic Imagination of Nationality." In P. V. Kroskrity (ed.), *Regimes of Language: Ideologies, Polities and Identities*. Santa Fe: School of American Research Press.

Smith, D. M. 1969. *Italy, A Modern History*. Ann Arbor: University of Michigan Press.

Smith, J. and A. Kornberg 1969. "Some Considerations Bearing upon Comparative Research in Canada and the United States." *Sociology*, 3:341-57.

Spivak, G. C. 1987. *In Other Worlds: Essays in Cultural Politics*. New York and London: Routledge.

Tamanoi, M. Asano 1998. *Under the Shadow of Nationalism: Politics and Poetics of Rural Japanese Women*. Honolulu: University of Hawai'i Press.

Taussig, M. 1987. *Shamanism, Colonialism, and the Wild Man. A Study in Terror and Healing*. Chicago: University of Chicago Press.

Tedlock, D. 1983. *The Spoken Word and the Work of Interpretation*. Philadelphia: University of Pennsylvania Press.

Tobia, B. 1995. "Una Cultura per la Nuova Italia." In G. Sabbatucci and V. Vidotto (eds.) *Storia d'Italia: 2. Il Nuovo Stato e la Società Civile 1861-1887*. Roma and Bari: Editori Laterza.

Tolomei, C. 1992. *Del Raddoppiamento da Parola a Parola*. Exeter: University of Exeter Press.

Vincent, J. 1974. "The Structuring of Ethnicity." *Human Organization*, 33:375-79.

Visweswaran, K. 1994. *Fictions of Feminist Ethnography*. Minneapolis and London: University of Minnesota Press.

Vizenor, G. R. 1994. *Manifest Manners: Postindian Warriors of Survivance*. Hanover: Wesleyan University Press.

White, A. J. 1944. *The Evolution of Modern Italy*. Oxford: Basil Blackwell.

Woolard, K. A. and B. B. Schieffelin 1994. "Language Ideology." *Annual Review of Anthropology*, 23:55-82.

Yanagisako, S. J. 1991. "Capital and Gendered Interest in Italian Family Firms." In D. I. Kertzer and R. P. Saller (eds.), *The*

Family in Italy from Antiquity to the Present. London and New Haven: Yale University Press.

Yeats, W. B. 1961. *Essays and Introductions.* New York: Macmillan Co.

Zentella, A. C. 1990. "Returned Migration, Language and Identity: Puerto Rican Bilinguals in Dos Worlds/Two Mundos." *International Journal of the Sociology of Language*, Special Issue, 84.

_____. 1997. *Growing up Bilingual.* Oxford: Blackwell Publishers.

www.ingramcontent.com/pod-product-compliance
Lightning Source LLC
Chambersburg PA
CBHW060836280326
41934CB00007B/804